Intelligent Organizations
Powerful Models for Systemic Management

Markus Schwaninger

Intelligent Organizations

Powerful Models
for Systemic Management

With 38 Figures and 6 Tables

 Springer

Prof. Dr. Markus Schwaninger
University of St. Gallen
Institute of Management
Dufourstrasse 40A
CH-9000 St. Gallen
Switzerland
markus.schwaninger@unisg.ch

ISBN-10   3-540-29876-2 Springer Berlin Heidelberg New York
ISBN-13   978-3-540-29876-2 Springer Berlin Heidelberg New York

Cataloging-in-Publication Data
Library of Congress Control Number: 2006929201

Springer is a part of Springer Science+Business Media

springeronline.com

© Springer Berlin · Heidelberg 2006
Printed in Germany

SPIN 11578345   Printed on acid-free paper – 42/3100 – 5 4 3 2 1 0

Preface

This is not a book about how to run a company. It is about how to look at the world differently. Ultimately, this will help the reader to deal with complexity more effectively.

The market today is flooded with books which claim to show paths to higher organizational effectiveness. Most of these recommendations are given as "recipes for success" and on pragmatic grounds.

This book, however, is targeted at all those who want access to the powerful models of systemic management in order to improve their skills in coping with complexity. The contents are of interest to people who deal with organizations – as leaders and managers or specialists, or as advanced students. The purpose is to give them conceptual and methodological guidelines by means of which they can

- Increase the "intelligence" of existing organizations by introducing or substituting a better design;
- Shape new organizations so that they are "intelligent" from the very start.

What are the distinctive features of this book?

The book is the result of a long-term research effort into the deep-seated, invariant features of organizations, based on the Systems Approach, namely Organizational Cybernetics and System Dynamics. These sciences have specialized in uncovering such basic properties. They convey a fresh, sophisticated and unorthodox perspective. It is therefore worthwhile acquiring the capability of looking at the social world in this different way. The effort pays off because the new understanding based on systems sciences is more enduring than much of what is currently offered under fashionable labels. I claim that the Framework for the Design of Intelligent Organizations developed here and in particular the methodological components which are at its core, have a long half-life. They are robust and durable, because they are theoretically well-founded.

This is not a quick fix; for there are no quick fixes to cope with complex situations adequately. It is a heuristic framework, no more and no less. As this book documents, there is evidence that it works, provided that it is put into practice properly. Here is one challenge: What does "proper application" mean? In this book, I reveal the respective principles which comprise not only lessons for applications but also warnings against traps. These should become clear to those who read the whole book. Given space restrictions, however, not everything can be explained from scratch. Therefore, readers for whom the subject is new are well advised to consult as possibilities for further reading the sources I have given. Managers plagued with complexity on the one hand and little time to cope with it on the other require clearly defined and theoretically well-grounded models. The results an organization can achieve are ultimately dependent on the quality of the models on which its management is based. The consequence is that the firms with the better models prevail. The models presented in this book are intended for the design of adaptive organizations, the steering and the development of organizations for enduring prosperity. They can be applied to any kind of organization – private firms, public institutions, non-governmental organizations and social initiatives.

To date, the literature has addressed organizational issues either by way of qualitative concepts, models and methods, or by quantitative techniques. Both approaches have their pros and cons, but neither is sufficient in itself. Despite the urgent necessity to do so, little effort has been made to combine them synergetically. For a long time my conviction has been that actors in organizations and organizations as actors can cope with the complexities of our time only, if they exploit the complementarities of both quantitative and qualitative methods. This book is the outcome of a sustained effort in this direction, on the transdisciplinary grounds of systems science. It is not the panacea for all corporate ills, but represents the starting-point of a path that may most profitably be followed up.

The work expounded here is conceptual-theoretical as well as empirically based. Whatever is proposed has emerged from a struggle with real-life issues, in a dialogue of practical „problem-solving" and theoretical reflection. However, the work has been underpinned with several empirical studies, to which I shall refer. Some of them were published in my earlier writings, others realized in conjunction with the work invested in this book. Given the broad scope of the subject of "organizational intelligence", not every single aspect has been as tested or even testable as might have been desired. This is work in progress, not its "definitive result". So I am taking the courage of my convictions in presenting these propositions despite the lack of some empirical tests which are still pending, or which will, perforce, have to be carried out by others.

These are the lessons I hope the readers of this book will derive from it:

• Designing and developing intelligent organizations is the new key to effective management.

- In the face of complexity, this can no longer be achieved by merely pragmatic means, or as prompted by fleeting fads and fashions.
- The lasting success of management will be determined by the quality of its models. Inadequate management models will lead to inadequate results, except in cases of exceptional good fortune, i.e., unless chance intervenes.
- The Systems Approach, namely Organizational Cybernetics and System Dynamics, provides exceedingly powerful models (as well as principles and methodologies) for the improvement of management and organizations.
- These are no longer esoteric concoctions, focused on technicalities and difficult to understand. They are mature and robust devices specifically designed to help managers cope with their practical challenges, namely real-life complexity.
- The prospective reader can use the instructions in this primer to start improving his or her conceptual capabilities with no further ado.

Structure of the Book

This book is made up of eleven chapters. The first introduces the reader to the purpose of the book and the innovative, systemic approach to coping with complexity which it offers. In the next three chapters, crucial concepts of systemic management are laid out: Chapter 2 relates to the environment or situation faced in terms of the complexity issue, while Chapter 3 discusses forms of distributed organization as a managerial response to that complexity. In Chapter 4, a framework for the design of Intelligent Organizations is presented. This framework is made up of five dimensions, which clearly define the logic of the following part of the book, in which a Methodology for the Design and Development of Intelligent Organizations is propounded. Each of the ensuing chapters is dedicated to one of these dimensions:

- Activities, or "What the Organization Does" (Chapter 5)
- Structure, or "Preconditions for Effective Action" (Chapter 6)
- Behavior, or "The Control of Cognition (and Emotion)" (Chapter 7)
- Ethos and Identity, or "Basic Parameters of Organizations" (Chapter 8)
- Time and Organizational Dynamics (Chapter 9)

Chapter 10 presents an integrative perspective by reviewing the framework presented at the outset, and closing loops related to the interrelationships elaborated thereafter. The book closes with a very brief synopsis and an outlook into the future (Chapter 11).

Acknowledgements

I am very grateful to Professor Roberto Moreno-Díaz for inviting me to stay, as a Visiting Professor, at the Instituto Universitario de Ciencias y Tecnologías Cibernéticas, Universidad de Las Palmas de Gran Canaria, Spain. Professor Moreno-Díaz and the Institute kindly provided me with an ideal environment for the writing of a large part of this book during my sabbatical there. The building-blocks for this work originated in a long-term research effort, going back to the Eighties, and enduring throughout the Nineties all the way into the new Millennium.

My special very thanks go to Professors Stafford Beer, Aloys Gaelweiler and Anatol Rapoport – mentors and friends – for conveying to me insights and encouragement which have been crucial throughout my work. Furthermore, I am indebted to several other persons for reading earlier drafts of the different papers on which this book is built up, and for giving me valuable comments. Especially to be mentioned in this respect are Dr. Allenna Leonard, The Complementary Set and TSI, Toronto, Canada; Dr. Amy A. Shuen, The Silicon Valley Strategy Group, Berkeley, California; Prof. Dr. Raúl Espejo, University of Humberside and Lincolnshire, U.K.; Prof. Dr. Werner Schuhmann, University of Mannheim, Germany; as well as my former doctoral students, Dr. Stefan Buettner, Dr. Heiko Eckert, and Dott. Andrea-Leopoldo Sablone (who also helped with the graphics); Dr. oec. Dr.sc.nat. Dipl. Math. Olaf Scherf and Dr. Peter Vrhovec. To the latter two I am also grateful for valuable support concerning epistemological and methological issues. Special thanks go to my assistants Camilo Olaya and Kristjan Ambroz, who read the manuscripts and made important suggestions for improvements. I am particularly indebted to Dr. John Peck and Prof. Colin Miskin for their wonderful, intelligent support in matters of language.

Finally, I thank my dear wife Katharina for reading every single word of the drafts for these chapters and giving me other support of every conceivable kind.

St. Gallen, April 2006
Markus Schwaninger

Table of Contents

Chapter 1 Organizational Intelligence in Systemic Terms

„Das Wissen gehe dem Handeln voraus!"[1]
Charlemagne, King of the Franks, first sovereign of the Christian Empire
of the West (742-814)

The first chapter will introduce the reader to the new approach offered by this book, and to its scientific basis. It is intended to help readers cope with the complexities faced in our turbulent age.

1.1 The Need for Organizational Innovation

In view of its ubiquitous complexity, speed of change and uncertainty, our time has been called „turbulent" (Drucker 1980), labeled the "age of chaos" (Abraham 1994), in which the unpredictability of "nonlinear, multiple-feedback loop dynamic systems" reigns (Senge 2000: 62). In this context, organizations of all kinds – private, public, and non-profit – face enormous challenges.

We live in a world of organizations, and all of us depend to a large extent on their smooth functioning and well-being. Therefore, organizational issues are of high priority and should therefore be of general interest.. Yet, in general public consciousness of organizations is still rather vague.. This is a problem, because without realizing the fact we both shape our organizations and are shaped by them. "Tell me what your organizations are like, and I shall tell you who you are..."

If our world is in crisis, this is to a large extent a function of regulatory problems – problems of auto-control, self-steering and self-reference. Much of this crisis can be traced back to organizational pathologies and ultimately to deficiencies in our thinking about what organizations should be, and about how to conceive of them.

But thinkers and actors seem to be caught in a double-bind. Trying to solve a complex organizational issue on the basis of a single discipline –

---

[1]   In English: "Let knowledge precede action!"

microeconomics, sociology, psychology, technology, etc.–.is an elegant way to optimize in a single dimension, but the path to unstable or even chaotic behavior of the system in question is thereby paved. Conversely, using a multidisciplinary approach is cumbersome and usually results in the erection of a Tower of Babel".

All kinds of efforts have been made to solve this "double-bind"[2] problem – from calls for "mixing and matching" different methodologies (cf. Mingers/Gill 1997) to a variety of pragmatic (and sometimes even esoteric) recipes. Practitioners and researchers of management have produced new concepts, recipes, models and methods at an accelerating rate. Organizational learning and knowledge creation are only two key terms to subsume much of this effort. No wonder the management books and consultancy markets have thriven on buzzwords, fads and sometimes outright charlatanism.

The following may seem paradoxical, but it holds nevertheless: The faster the change they confront, the more managers need durable concepts to contend with that change; the more variable the phenomena faced, the more vital knowledge about the invariants underlying the apparent chaos becomes.

This is the essence of staying abreast or even ahead of events, which, according to Peter Drucker, the Nestor among the management thinkers, is the only way of coping with change effectively (Drucker 1999: 73).

1.2 An Innovative View of Organizations

In the midst of all this turbulence a slow but steady rise in the relevance and acceptance of a scientific program has been evident: the sustained effort to build up theories and models which take into account the invariant features of complex systems. What we call „the systems approach", is a framework based on systems theory and cybernetics. This scientific endeavor – refraining from riding the fad and fashion waves swamping management literature today – provides a formal apparatus for dealing with complex systems of all kinds and is therefore increasingly being adopted in many fields of inquiry. Systems theory and cybernetics are also recognized as a new "language," which allows synergetic interaction between different

---

[2]   This term designates a situation in which an actor is simultaneously submitted to two contradictory messages or injunctions, in such a way that complying with one entails a transgression of the other. It was introduced by the eminent cybernetician Gregory Bateson (for practical examples, see especially Bateson 1973).

disciplines, thus increasing the possibility of innovative, transdisciplinary solutions to complex issues. It must be added that the term 'solution' as used here does not necessarily denote a definite or one-shot elimination of the problem , as is the case with first-order solutions (e.g., finding an optimal sequence for a product distribution process). Complex issues mostly require higher-order "solutions", which are often strategies to cope with rather than to eliminate the problems faced. This might be, for example:

- The design of a system which is better suited to deal with the issue, i.e., an organizational solution involving structures and management systems
- A strategy for merely "living with" a dilemma, so that it becomes bearable, i.e., obnoxious consequences are minimized, trade-offs made transparent, sacrifice-benefit-ratios minimized, and the like
- The problem is reframed in such a way that it becomes soluble or even resolves itself (cf. Ackoff 1999).

General Systems Theory is a science of the structure and behavior of organized wholes, which goes back to its founders' idea that systems of any kind can be described by means of one and the same formal apparatus (Bertalanffy 1968, Miller 1978, Rapoport 1986). The pertinent terms used are – among others – system & environment, relationships, elements, purpose, structure, function and evolution. Cybernetics is the branch of Systems Theory, which is most relevant to the issues addressed in this book. Cybernetics is the science of control and communication in complex, dynamical systems, as defined by its pioneer Norbert Wiener (1948). The title of Wiener's landmark book is "Cybernetics. Control and Communication in the Animal and in the Machine." The subtitle adverts to the fact that certain patterns of control and communication are inherent in different kinds of systems – natural and artificial. A practice-oriented definition conceives of Cybernetics broadly as the science of the emergence and design of order (after Malik 2001).

The systemic view focuses on organized wholes, taking into account the multidimensional and multilevel nature of complex systems. The benefits for organizations and management are huge. Therefore, it is no surprise that the Systems Approach has become the scientific basis for a new management science which generates an integrative, holistic effort to enable the design, the control (involving both steering and regulation) and the development of organizations and social systems in general (Ulrich 1984, 2001). It has provided the conceptual basis for research and education in general management at the University of St. Gallen, Switzerland (the author's academic base), for more than 30 years. This has proved to be a very fertile approach (for details, see Schwaninger 2001a).

The models of Organizational Cybernetics and the methodology of System Dynamics, both of which are basic to this book, focus on the dynamic features of complex systems. The cybernetic strain of systems research has developed powerful theories and models to enable effective design, control and transformation of organizations of all kinds. As a complement, the servomechanic strain has bred System Dynamics, a potent methodology to trace and understand the dynamic patterns of behavior of complex systems, and the structures underlying them (cf. Richardson 1999).

Given these features, the Systems Approach has met with increasing acclaim in managerial and organizational science in general and in practice (cf. Jackson 2000, Schwaninger 2001a). Its potential contribution to management science both in theory and practice will undoubtedly turn out to be enormous; though this is not yet widely realized or understood (cf. Beer 1988, Espejo/ Schuhmann/ Schwaninger 1996). There are many examples of new conceptualizations triggered by the Systems Approach, only two of which are going to be given here, namely adaptation and learning.

Systems theories and Cybernetics have inquired into the adaptation and learning of organisms and social systems for several decades (for an overview, see François 1999). Adaptation has hitherto usually been regarded as passive, e.g., as "the process of accommodating to change" (cf.: UNESCO-UNEP 1983:5). Systems thinkers, however, have introduced a concept of reciprocity, which implies that a system and its environment affect and change each other (e.g., Ashby 1965:58, Ackoff/Emery 1972:123f.)[3]

Similarly, the concept of learning derives from a notion focused on the acquisition of knowledge and skills (UNESCO-UNEP 1983), rooted in pedagogy and developmental psychology (e.g., Piaget 1967)[4]. Later, in the context of systems research the aspect of knowledge acquisition was extended to that of knowledge creation (Nonaka/Takeuchi 1995, von Krogh et al 2000), and linked to action: Learning was now conceived of as a system's enhancement of its potential for effective action (in extension of: Senge 1992).

Grounded in this tradition, a concept of the intelligent organization has emerged, which a) proceeds from the idea of organizations as complex adaptive systems and b) integrates the aspects of adaptation and learning with those of self-reference, (self-)transformation, (self-)renewal and ultimately (self-)transcendence. If our theoretical view of adaptation and learning is combined with a perspective on self-reference – in the sense of

---

[3] This is also the crucial principle underlying the more recent concept of co-evolution.

[4] For Piaget, a biologist by training, learning is essentially a (biological process of adaptation.

auto-observation and -reflection, the focus shifts from first-order observation to that of second order. In other words, we are dealing with phenomena such as

- higher-order adaptation, i.e., second-order adaptation or adaptiveness,
- higher-order learning, i.e., second-order learning, meta-learning or the ability to learn,
- higher-order control, i.e., second-order control, or the control of control.
- higher-order solutions, i.e., second-order solutions, or solutions for better solutions (cf. above).
  This differentiation is neither trivial nor sterile quibbling:
- As desirable as *adaptation at the object-level* ("first-order-adaptation") is, it may not be sufficient in itself. As Karl Weick, a master of organization theory, shrewdly observed, adaptation often precludes adaptiveness. For example, some firms are so good at adapting to their customers' needs (or the needs of another group of stakeholders), that they forget the even greater necessity of maintaining the adaptiveness of the firm as a whole, i.e., that of *long-term, higher-order adaptation*.
- If *first-order learning* – learning by correcting errors – is to be efficient, it must be complemented by higher forms of learning: second-order learning, a kind of learning which includes the revision of goals, principles or values, and finally, meta-learning (or, as Bateson called it, "deutero"-learning), which entails getting better at learning over time.
- Similarly, *first-order change* must be complemented by second-order change. The former is about doing things differently within a given framework, while the latter involves changing the framework or the mode of doing things, i.e., inventing different approaches or doing new things. Innovation can take place at both levels: in the first case as a continuous improvement, in the second as comprehensive change.
- *First-order control* is about regulating and steering the course of events. Second-order control is about reflecting upon and, if needed, changing the mode of control, – e.g., by designing management processes to allow of more participation with the stakeholders.
- Finally, the differentiation between first-order and second-order solutions has already been introduced. There, second-order solutions were defined as being essentially strategies for reconciling oneself to a problem or a dilemma. We also included the reframing of problems in such a way that they solve themselves, i.e., disappear altogether, or at least become soluble.

The second-order approaches are not offered as substitutes for the first-order approaches. They should rather be conceived in such a way that they integrate them on a higher level. Often, an organization finds itself in a situation in which two or more mutually exclusive "solutions" or "strategies" are proposed by different people. Rather than choosing one and completely rejecting the others, one can make a small-scale experiment, limited in time and space. This is a second-order solution, which creates an opportunity for the organization to learn. It enables a better decision to be made at the next stage, with wider implications.

1.3 Related Streams of Inquiry

As outlined, this book is located in the tradition of the System Approach, – Organizational Cybernetics and System Dynamics in particular. System theories have for decades focused on invariant features of systems of different kinds. For example, Miller (1978) developed a model to describe different systems at all levels – cell, organism, group, organization, community, society, supranational systems – by means of a set of 20 basic subsystems and their interrelationships. He considered all these kinds of systems to be "Living Systems" (Miller 1978).

It is remarkable to observe that the biological analogy has of late become pre-eminent, not only in the sciences but also in the domain of management[5]. The dictum that "biology is the new physics" reflects this new situation. Simon London, columnist of the Financial Times observed: "The matter of the moment is a company-as-organism, an entity that needs to be encouraged to adapt, learn and, of course, grow" (London 2003).

This is not only reflected in the language of top managers, who no longer talk about their companies as "machines", in which they manipulate the "levers of power". They rather revert to the organismic metaphor, conceiving of their companies as "complex adaptive systems", as is the case with Lord John Brown of BP or Rich Fairbank of Capital One. Also, a new generation of books on business and economics has arisen which bear names such as *Adaptive Enterprise* (Haeckel 1999), *Complexity and Management* (Stacey/Griffin/Shaw 2000), *It's Alive, The Coming Convergence of Information, Biology and Business* (Meyer/Davies 2003), *Conquering Complexity* (George & Wilson 2004), *Social Emergence: Societies As Complex Systems* (Sawyer 2005).

Earlier works in this tradition are *Out of Control* (Kelly 1994) and the *Science of Complexity* (Waldrop 1992). This literature is emerging from a

---

[5]   Also, the Population Ecology school of organizational science is rooted in an organismic perspective on populations of organizations and organizational forms (see, e.g., Hannan/Freemann 1989, Aldrich/Ruef 2006).

stream of inquiry which started with catastrophe theory (Thom), continued with chaos theory (Abraham), the theory of dissipative systems (Prigogine), and finally what today is called the science of complexity (Kaufmann 1995). The science of complexity is closely linked to the development of genetic and agent-based algorithms (Holland, Wolfram). These represent conceptual techniques for modelling and simulating a complex adaptive system in bottom-up mode, which is complementary to the traditional top-down approach to modelling and simulation.

A more comprehensive view on the Systems Movement and its different streams of inquiry is provided by Jackson (2000, 2003) and by Schwarz (forthcoming).

1.4 What Makes an Organization Intelligent?

Recently, a famous company presented itself with the battle-cry "We are fast, lean and strong". My immediate reaction was "... and dumb?" "Fast, lean and strong" is not enough! Every day, corporations suffering from "organizational dementia" inflict disastrous blows upon their economic, social and ecological environments, despite the fact that their members are, on average, intelligent and capable of learning. This means that organizational intelligence cannot simply be equated with human intelligence.

Therefore, it is not a trivial question to ask: How should organizations be conceived so as to be capable of behaving in an intelligent and sensitive way?

From a cybernetic point of view, , the basic faculties that distinguish intelligent organizations are the abilities[6]

1. *to adapt to changing situations*, i.e., to change as a function of external stimuli;
2. *to influence and shape their environment*;
3. if necessary, *to find a new milieu* („playing field") or *to reconfigure themselves anew within their environment*, and finally
4. *to make a positive net contribution to the viability and development*[7] *of the larger wholes* in which they are embedded.

Potential to develop these faculties can, as will be shown, be created purposefully. As social, and especially socio-technical, systems are at stake, the set of capabilities enumerated here goes far beyond the criteria of intelligence as established by diverse disciplines such as psychology or infor-

---

[6]   Schwaninger 1998; in extension of: Sternberg 1987.
[7]   One could also use the term *sustainability* here.

mation technology, wherein "business intelligence" has been defined as a set of technological instruments which support decision-making[8]. It also transcends those theories of management in which organizational performance is conceived of and measured in terms of criteria such as profit, efficiency or shareholder-value only.

Such a broader view promises to lead to better models and ultimately to better management. The foundation for this bold assumption lies in the Conant-Ashby-Theorem, which will be expounded in the next chapter.

1.5 Purpose and Scope of this Book

The purpose of this book is *to make managers and advanced students of management capable of coping with organizational complexity effectively.* The guiding question is: *"How can organizational intelligence be enhanced?"* The book is conceived as a *primer*, which gives readers concrete help and advice, by enabling them:

- to design their organization in such a way that it behaves intelligently, and
- to enhance their ability to cope with the complexities they face.

The innovative content is a source for the improvement of any kind of organization, private or public, non-profit, large or small, and is applicable to parts of organizations as well (e.g., divisions, business units, etc.).

These promises can be met thanks to a solid conceptual-theoretical foundation grounded in a long and sustained research effort. ranging over years in which I have often pioneered the scientific endeavours towards an *Integrative, Systemic Approach to Organization.* As I am a long-standing member of the international Systems Research community, much of my research has been carried out in appropriately collaborative forms. This has taken place on one hand with the "old masters" who pioneered the Systems Approach: Anatol Rapoport (one of the founders of General Systems Theory), Stafford Beer (the father of Managerial Cybernetics), and the school around Jay Forrester he inventor of System Dynamics), and on the other hand with young, interdisciplinary teams.

This work has led to the establishment of a *Framework for the Design and Development of Intelligent Organizations* founded on mature models and methodologies for the management of complexity, as presented in this

---

[8]   Source: eCompany Magazin – Das Intelligente Unternehmen, Nr. 5/2002, Verlagsgruppe Handelsblatt, H&T Verlag, Munich, Germany, editorial and diverse contributions.

book. These originate mainly in *Organizational Cybernetics and System Dynamics*, the most fertile streams of research for the purpose of improving organizations. So much for the theoretical sources.

As to the empirical or "practical" sources, the theoretical work briefly outlined above has by now been tested in a process of reflected applied research entailing a legion of applications in all kinds of organizations and throughout the world. Accounts of multiple practical examples and case studies drawn from this wide experience are to be found throughout the text.

The admittedly high density of the theoretical substance of the book should nevertheless prove to be digestible, thanks to its appealing mode of presentation and readability. For example, technical terms are clarified early on in each chapter. It is hoped that the examples and case studies will provide insights as well as meaningful and often gripping illustrations. The models are presented in graphical form, with hardly any mathematics. Finally, carefully thought-out sequencing should enhance understanding.

The book before you will enable its readers to improve their organizations. They will recognize timeless principles and long term referents, and weigh them up against their need for short-term efficiency. It will help managers align their efforts towards managing the dynamics of their organizations: by orchestrating interventions and synchronizing them over time.

The content revolves around the issue of introducing a systemic management to deal with complexity more effectively. The book's framework itself illustrates the importance of integration by linking the models introduced from the start, but this theme is explicitly taken up and emphasized towards the end.

In sum, this book should give readers an exceptionally powerful and fully integrated set of conceptual instruments grounded in a new, *systemic management science*. I trust that it will be a resource for coping with complexity.

Chapter 2 Complexity and Understanding

"Me gusta la complejidad."

Juan José Falcón Sanabria, Spanish composer[1]

"La uniformidad limita, la variedad dilata; y tanto es más sublime, cuanto más nobles perfecciones multiplica."

Balthasar Gracián, Spanish philosopher, 17th century[2]

"Variety is the spice of life."

English proverb

In this chapter a first set of crucial concepts of systemic management relating to the environment or situation faced by an organization is laid out – complexity and variety. In addition, the implications of complexity and variety are examined in the light of two fundamental theorems of organizational cybernetics – *Ashby's Law of Requisite Variety and the Conant-Ashby-Theorem.*

2.1 Two Crucial Concepts: Complexity and Variety

When do we call a matter complex? Complexity is linked to a lack of understanding; it has to do with the multifariousness and uncertainty of an object we have to deal with. A standard definition of complexity is "... the potentiality of a system to assume many different states". It thus becomes necessary to consider three aspects which are fundamental in the context of social systems and organizations, in particular:

1. As it is always observers or actors who are dealing with complexity, the attribute different here is always to be understood in terms of distinguishable.

---

[1] "I like complexity." Personal communication, Las Palmas de Gran Canaria, January 12, 2001.

[2] Uniformity restricts, variety broadens; the more it multiplies noble perfections, the more sublime it is." Gracián, 1993/II: Discurso III, Agudeza y Arte de Ingenio.

2. As social systems are dynamic systems, it is not so much discrete states which are of interest, but rather dynamic patterns or *modes of behavior.*

3. When dealing with social systems the potential as well as the current states and modes of behavior have to be considered and the difference between potentiality and actuality is of great importance.

We therefore have to specify that *complexity consists in a large number of distinct (potential or actual) states or modes of behavior.* In principle, the complexity of a system is proportionate to the quantity of (syntactical) information which is necessary a) to describe the system and b) to dispel the uncertainty associated with it (Klir 1991).

Organizational intelligence is intrinsically linked to the ability to deal with *dynamic complexity* effectively, and both these concepts are at the core of *organizational cybernetics.* From a cybernetic viewpoint, management is about ensuring that a system does not assume all potential states or behaviors but only desirable ones. Let us first analyze the role of complexity to get beyond the naive application of that overused catchword.

A technical term to express and measure complexity is *variety* – the number of potential states or behaviors of a system.

Mathematically there are two main formulas in use to calculate variety:

Relationship-oriented formula (1): $V = m \cdot \dfrac{n \cdot (n-1)}{2}$

Element-oriented formula (2): $V = z^n$
  Codes:
  V: Variety
  m: number of relationships between each pair of elements
  n: number of elements
  z: number of potential states for each element

Whichever formula is used, variety always follows a law of power:

It grows exponentially with the number of elements, and if equation (1) is applied, also with the number of relationships (which are not distinguished in equation (2)). These formulas are of little practical value except for the sake of visualizing the strength of the variety concept. Even though they are not adequate to calculate dynamic complexity, i.e., variety as the multiplicity of potential behaviors, they give a general idea of the fact that overwhelming complexity is a fundamental issue with which organizations and their managements are confronted.

We have seen that variety is a synonym for "multiplicity", which expresses the number of different states or modes of behavior a certain system – let us say a company or a market – can adopt. The scheme in Figure 2-1 makes it clear that an agent – no matter a company, an organizational unit or a manager – is embedded in a relevant environmental milieu, the variety of which by far exceeds the variety of the agent.

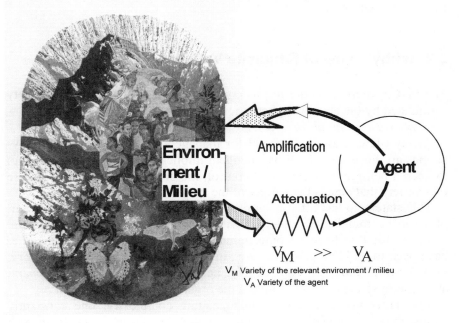

Fig. 2-1. Difference of varieties between an agent and its environment

Let us take a look at a practical example:

Anyone wishing to entrust a bank with their savings, while not being a capital markets expert, will find it almost impossible to orientate themselves in the bewildering "jungle" of offers. Back in the nineties I visited branches of various different banks to determine whether a different facility than an ordinary bank account would be more advantageous for depositing one's money. The following experience repeated itself: with a "take it or leave it" attitude the bank-clerk confronted me with two or three options a so-called high-interest bank account and perhaps one or two bonds. What I would have wished to see, however, was a simple graph with three dimensions – risk, yield, and social / ecological performance of the companies to be invested in which would have given me an immediate overview of the options available. Nobody was able to show me that. Cybernetically speaking: the variety, in other words the repertory of potential behaviors of these banks was insufficient to cope with the complexity of the situation at hand[3].

In the following two sections the implications of complexity and variety will be examined in the light of two fundamental theorems of organizationa lcybernetics.

2.2 Ashby's Law of Requisite Variety

The first theorem essential in this context is the Law of Requisite Variety formulated by the eminent cybernetician Ross Ashby:

"Only variety can absorb variety"[4]

Ashby's law is as fundamental for managers as the laws of thermodynamics are for engineers. It has a cogent implication of enormous bearing: to keep a complex system under control, the control-system must dispose of a variety that equals the variety of the system to be controlled.

This statement has often been grossly misunderstood. A host of examples can be found in those organizations which have built up structural complexities that have become unmanageable[5]. The quest should rather have been to build up *eigen-variety*[6], in other words, *behavioral repertory*, in order to attenuate *foreign* variety, i.e., *complexity of the environment*, and also to select or create a milieu the organization can cope with.

This latter aspect is crucial in managing complexity: one constantly comes across organizations which have defined their environments in such a way as to confront themselves with completely baffling complexities of their own making, which they are unable to deal with.

The challenge is to balance the *varieties of the interacting systems* through both *attenuation and amplification* (figure 2-1). The term variety engineering has been used in this context (Beer 1979).

One must add that the system at hand is not primarily subject to exogenous control but that it regulates and steers itself to a great extent. These

---

[3]   A recent survey of the financial-services sector, published in the Economist, suggests that the single incident reported here is an ideal-typical symptom of an industry in crisis, heading for a radical shake-up (Drucker 1999)

[4]   In the original: "Only variety can *destroy* variety" (Ashby 1956); the verb *absorb* was later introduced by Stafford Beer.

[5]   An impressive practical account of the dynamics of bureaucracy plus an ensuing corporate transformation in a leading company of the chemical industry is analyzed in a detailed case study by Rüegg-Stürm 2002, Chapter 4.

[6]   *"Eigen-"* stands for *own*. *"Eigen-variety"* denotes an agent's or system's own variety.

forces of self-organization must be purposefully leveraged. The management of a company need not be confronted with the totality of problems occurring inside the organization because most of them can be solved autonomously within the subsystems. Management is only supposed to face the residual variety, i.e., those issues which cannot be brought under control by these subsystems themselves (figure 2-2[7]). The same applies to the relationship between an organization and the environment. I instance the case of an insurance company that can shield itself against the bulk of the market's complexity thanks to a network of insurance agents which efficiently absorbs that variety. The company can then concentrate on designing products and on honing its informational and financial skills.

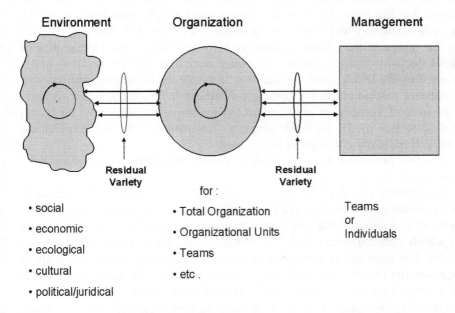

Fig. 2-2. How organizations and their managements cope with complexity

The design of organizations can essentially revert to three types of amplifiers and attenuators, cognitive, structural and interactive/ conversational ones:

- *Structural*: e.g., segmentation of the market and concentration of forces to build up behavioral repertory, differentiation, modularization, redundancy, decentralization and autonomy as well as all manner of constraints (norms, rules, conditions, values), which can absorb complexity.

---

[7]   The concept of Residual Variety goes back to: Espejo 1989a.

- *Conversational/interactive*: e.g., solving problems in teams, discursive approach to strategy formation etc.
- *Cognitive*: these are the sensory organs and the perception as well as the information system by means of which vital signs are perpetually filtered out from the flow of events.

The strongest cognitive attenuators of variety are prejudice and ignorance, but they are counterproductive in the longer run. In other words: functional and dysfunctional attenuators and amplifiers can be clearly distinguished. This applies also to the domain of knowledge. Even tacit knowledge, which bestsellers have offered as a panacea, can be right or it can be wrong. The decisive factor is the quality of the mental models, in other words that the right questions are posed at all levels. This leads us to the second theorem, which I have to introduce with a set of theses.

The image of the effective manager is by and large linked to the idea of rapid decision making. However, many decisions neither become better when they are taken faster nor can they improve the situation significantly.

Studies carried out at the Strategic Planning Institute show that the performance of companies only hinges on operative decisions by 20 %, on skilled tactics by 10 %, while strategy "determines" 70 % (Buzzell/Gale 1987). Here is my consequent first thesis:

It is less important to decide quickly than to recognize the need for decisions in good time.

The quality of a decision depends essentially on recognizing at an early stage which events and especially changes are relevant. The crucial aspect here is the aptness of the orientators to assess a state of affairs on the basis of which a management body decides and acts. For example only a more recent development in management theories has shown that profit, with its components of revenue and costs, is an inherently short-term indicator. It is inadequate to orientate the evaluation of strategically relevant matters. To do that it is necessary to look at those factors which *pre-control* profit. This is the reason why time management should primarily rely above all on starting earlier, and not on merely acting (or reacting) faster and therefore even hectically or prematurely.

This leads to my second thesis:

The quality of a decision depends less on the supply of data than on the demand for information.

The main problem is not the availability of data, but the model (or scheme) which directs an inquiry. Technology has eliminated space- and time-related restrictions to data procurement. The edge now is in recognizing the relevant orientators in time and in articulating the need for relevant information. Very often the adequate data are available within the company itself but remain unexplored because their relevance is not seen.

Therefore, my third thesis (following Russell Ackoff):

Managers suffer less from a lack of relevant data than from an excess of irrelevant data.

In this context it is necessary to draw an important distinction which has hitherto been widely unheeded: The concepts of "data" and "information" are often used synonymously. Distinct from the technical concept of information by Shannon and Weaver, cybernetics uses the following helpful grading (after Beer 1979):

1. *Facts:* Whatever is the case.
2. *Data:* Statements about facts.
3. *Information:* What changes us.

Between making data available and generating information lies a kind of quantum leap: making out the difference between what is irrelevant and what is relevant. Bateson (1973) defines information as "a difference which makes the difference".[8]

Hence information implies an insight which may trigger a change. Therefore, information always emerges within a recipient, as we know from communication theory. Naturally, relevance is often only discerned once an exchange with others has occurred; therefore: discourse between different perspectives is essential (this could be a thesis 4).

In this context, three further concepts are of importance (Schwaninger 1998a):

4. Knowledge: Generally speaking, "knowledge is whatever is known – the body of truth, information and principles acquired" (Longman 1985: 768) by some subject on some subject. Knowledge, therefore, is always embodied in somebody[9].

Knowledge implies insights, which enable orientation; in other words, knowledge can be conceived of as action potential. This is closely linked to learning – enhancing one's potential for effective action (Kim 1993). Learning, by this account, is the process of developing and grounding knowledge. When we are able to use information in an action domain, then

---

[8] These cybernetic definitions of "information" already imply the semantic dimension of meaning attached to a signal by the one who receives it.

[9] The corollary to calling some data or even rules stored in a medium "knowledge" is to confuse reading the recipe for a dish in a cookbook with eating that dish.

we start to know. When we can transform that knowledge into effective action, we have reached the point of understanding something.

5. Understanding: Understanding is in-depth knowledge, involving deep insights into patterns of relationships generating the behavior of a system. Understanding is often referred to as the "knowledge of masters". It implies the capability of conveying subject knowledge to others. However, we do not define understanding as knowing every detail about a complex system (this would be a faculty both impossible to acquire and useless to possess.).

6. Wisdom: By wisdom we mean a higher quality of knowledge and understanding, implying the ethical and aesthetic dimensions of knowledge. We can even go so far as to state that true wisdom is so constituted that it brings about the good, the true and the beautiful. Wisdom is accessible to those who struggle for it. Anyone can and should strive for it.

As we advance from data to wisdom our action potential increases. This is schematically represented in Figure 2-3.

Action potential

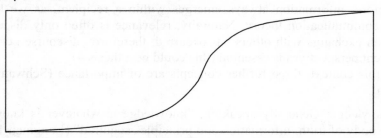

Data   Information   Knowledge Understanding Wisdom

Fig. 2-3. The growth in action potential from data to knowledge to wisdom

The traditional scientific mode of inquiry relies on *analysis* – taking a system apart and studying the components and their behavior. This produces knowledge but not in a such way that the behavior of a complex system could be explained or understood. For that purpose *synthesis* is required – putting the pieces together, looking at the whole and its function in the larger system (Ackoff 1999). Systemic thinking uses both, analysis and synthesis as complementary modes of the process of inquiry.

2.3 The Conant-Ashby-Theorem: Models are Crucial

Organizations continuously receive messages or signals about events for which they do not possess a schema enabling them to be informed of the relevant facts. Whatever the importance of such messages might be for their viability, they remain unheard and therefore dissipate.

This leads us to the vital importance of the models (or schemes) on which those responsible rely and so to our second law: the Conant-Ashby-Theorem (Conant/Ashby 1981). This derives directly from the Law of Requisite Variety and states:

"Every good regulator of a system must be a model of that system".

In other words: the result of an organizational process can not be better than the model on which the management of that process is based, except by chance.

This proposition contradicts commonplace "knowledge", which often claims that management models are a thing of the past, usually with the explanation "that today everything changes so fast". Arguments of this kind fail to consider that all managerial activity is based on models, whether the respective agents are aware of them or not. In the light of the Conant-Ashby-Theorem most of the more or less trivial recipes given by current bestsellers on management must be dismissed as insufficient and even dangerous.

The fact that many or even most organizations are still managed on the basis of inadequate models is a serious problem. The traditional models of management are dominantly oriented towards profitability. The ROI (Return-On-Investment) – based system of indicators[10] is well-proven but insufficient because in the context of rapid change profit rates are inadequate as a means of measuring the performance of an organization. Basically, they are not much more than short-term and partial indicators of the success of a business. "Shareholder value" is a term which, in principle, is supposed to reflect longer term aspects, too, namely the anticipated evolution of a business or firm. In practice, however, the shareholder value estimates are strongly determined by projections or extrapolations of sales, cost and profit figures.

These models lack the requisite variety. Relying on them is therefore likely to be misleading; they might point in precisely the wrong direction. The following analogy is useful: assessing the effectiveness of a business by the level of its profits is like measuring the temperature to decide the current season of the year. However, for this purpose, the calendar, not the thermometer would be the appropriate source of information. Long-term-

---

[10]   Originally this system of indicators became famous as the "Du Pont Scheme".

patterns originate from different causal mechanisms which double-entry bookkeeping is unable to ascertain. It is essential to make this point in the face of the current frenzy about "management by financial figures" whereby short-term-thinking tends to drive out long-term orientation.

These critical remarks are not meant to cast doubt upon the relevance of profits as such. In the long run no company can survive without being profitable. Profits are a prerequisite to realize investments and to maintain the substance of a firm. In Peter Drucker's precise though paradoxical words, profits are "the cost of staying in business" (Drucker 1980). But if profits are necessary for the survival of a company, profit-mindedness is not apt to ensure its viability and development. On the contrary, the oft referred to goal of profit-maximization is a hindrance rather than a help towards acquiring greater organizational intelligence.

It must be conceded, however, that a number of efforts during the nineties have bred new initiatives to overcome this narrowness of control models. Management accounting has generated multidimensional sets of indicators to measure and control organizational performance. A much discussed approach is the Balanced Scorecard, which is aimed at balancing different aspects of control, e.g., market, process, finance, development (see Kaplan/Norton 1996). It must be observed that this instrument is much less widespread than one might expect[11]. Other efforts try to include the social and ecological perspectives into all aspects of management, control and auditing in particular. However, much of this effort is still superficial (cf. Sharma/Henriques 2005) and lacking in solid theoretical foundations.

Another issue of concern is related to the models for organization design which are in use today. They are manifold and often contradictory. Much of what is advocated reflects the latest fashions, mostly developed on pragmatic grounds. But the theoretical basis of these models is in general weak thus limiting their practical effectiveness.

---

[11] "Research suggests that 60 percent of Fortune 1000 companies have experimented with the BSC and data from the Gartner Group suggest that over 50% of large US firms had adopted the BSC by the end of 2000." (Kaplan 2003). From a sample of the 200 largest German corporations, 46% of the responding 129 companies indicated that they made use of the Balanced Scorecard (Price Waterhouse 2001). In one non-representative sample, equally from Germany, 58% of the responding 33 firms used or planned to use the Balanced Scorecard (Abel 2001). According to a survey from Denmark, answered by 59 companies, the level of knowledge about the Balanced Scorecard appears to be high, about 80%, whereas less than 20% give a high priority to the BSC. Only 4% of the respondents claim full use, 28% partial use of the BSC (Nielsen/Sorensen 2004).

This has to do mainly with two developmental patterns widely in use. One is the inclination of consultants to propose a model which either reflects the insights from a limited number of experiences made, or is based on hypotheses which have not been extensively corroborated. To overcome this deficiency, academic researchers adopt the second mode, i.e., empirically based theory building. Their hypotheses are often thoroughly tested, but they are usually very limited in their relevance. Furthermore, the theoretical reasoning on which they are based necessarily tends to extrapolate conventional theories. A new strain of theorizing seldom emerges from the mainstream academic journals.

A final issue of concern is related to the fact that most of the models in use rely on discrete and rather static pictures of organizational reality, in spite of the necessity to understand the patterns of behavior generated by those organizations in the mid- and long-term.

In the following chapters of this book, newer and more powerful models will be expounded which promise a much higher potential for coping with dynamic complexity effectively than the established ones criticized here.

Even though the models that will be addressed in the different chapters (especially 5, 6 and 7) are specific as to their purpose and capabilities, in this book models are conceived in a broad sense. Discussion of models in general, as in this chapter, includes not only formal models and mental models; *frame(work)s, schemes, philosophies, mindsets* and *paradigms* may also be subsumed under this term.

Models confine and they enable. It is our models which "determine", to a large extent, what our future realities will be like. I write *determine* in italics because organizations are not deterministic, like commonplace, trivial machines (von Foerster 1984a). Social and human actors are non-trivial, i.e., they do not respond algorithmically to stimuli or conditions. They pursue ideals, ends, objectives, and have preferences and values, all of which may change. They make choices. They are able to invent new solutions and come up with different modes of behavior. That is why the management models to be presented here are of a *heuristic, not an algorithmic* kind[12].

---

[12] A heuristic (from the Greek word *heuriskein,*–to discover) is a set of methodological instructions for the solutin of problems or for an exploration to find new insighets. The goal may be unknown; progress is continually or repeatedly assessed according to known criteria (Cf. Beer 1981: 402). An algorithm (from *al-Khuwarizmi*, Arab mathematician) is a systematic procedure for the solution of a mathematical problem in a finite sequence of precisely defined steps.

Chapter 3 Management – A Distributed Function

„In a society of organizations, managing becomes a key social function and management the constitutive, the determining, the differential organ of society." [1]

"As more and more organizations become information-based, they are transforming themselves into soccer or tennis teams, that is, into responsibility-based organizations in which every member must act as a responsible decision maker. All members, in other words, have to see themselves as "executives". Even so, an organization must be managed." [2]

Peter F. Drucker, Austro-American management thinker

Chapter 3 is about crucial concepts related to the organizational and managerial *response to complexity*. These provide the key to an Intelligent Organization's ability to cope with complexity effectively.

3.1 On Leadership and Management

The concepts of leadership and management have often been separated (e.g., Kotter 1988, 1999). In these cases, the visionary and innovative functions, and people responsible for the fate of organizations, were subsumed under the terms leadership and leaders on one hand, whereas on the other, the routine aspects of administrative control and the people taking care of them were denominated as management and managers respectively.

A proper systemic view does not approve of this distinction. Especially Organizational Cybernetics has shown that the challenge of coping with complexity can be mastered only if many people at many levels take responsibility for the fate of their organization. From this perspective, leadership is a distributed function, and there is no class of managers which can be exempted from it. In the context of this book, it would be counterproductive to separate the leadership function from the other management functions. Therefore, whenever I talk about management, I subsume all

---

[1]   Drucker 1986: 173.
[2]   Drucker 1965: 91.

forms of leadership under this term. Whenever managers are mentioned, these are also to be understood as leaders, not only as administrators.

Management thinkers who have taken a systemic view have adopted a similar position. For instance, Peter Drucker, who is a systems thinker (even though he does not claim to be one), has for a long time advocated an understanding of management as a ubiquitous function, which is fundamental to the viability and self-renewal of organizations and society.

In principle, social and organizational innovation is needed – even more than technological innovation. In fact, to be a protagonist of social and organizational change is one of the fundamental roles in a manager's repertoire. This holds good despite the fact that many managers have not always regarded themselves as such agents. At this point, it is necessary to specify our concept of *management*.

Management, as defined in the tradition of systemic management, is the design, *control* and *development* of an organization, or – to use a broader term – of a complex, productive social system (after Hans Ulrich 2001).

Design denotes the function of conceiving and maintaining organization as an operational entity in such a way that it is able to fulfill its functions or tasks while remaining capable of (self-)control and development (after Krieg 1985). This book is very much about the design function, which, after all, is supposed to help actors conceive of organizations as intelligent social systems.

Control is the process by which a system achieves its purpose and attains its goals, by way of constant adaptation to the milieu in which it operates. In other words, control is the maintenance of a dynamic equilibrium, at a satisfactory level of performance, between the organization and its environment. Control has two complementary aspects, namely regulation and steering. Perceived in terms of different logical levels, control involves pre-controls, which are crucial to creating preconditions for success. These aspects will have to be specified in later sections (Chapter 5).

Finally, *development* can be defined as a system's growing ability and desire to fulfill its own and others' needs (after Ackoff 1994). In the context of organizations, development processes are not by any means the outcome of chance. They are organization-wide processes obeying an evolutionary logic of their own. As such, they can – within limits – be influenced in the sense of a "planned evolution". In this process, as our case study illustrates, the catalytic amplification of dynamic forces in the system plays a crucial part. On a higher level, however, the development process itself is the object of design and control measures (Krieg 1985).

3.2 On Control Loops

Control is a core term in this context. As the definitions of the three components of management just expounded show, in one way or another they all have to do with control. *Design is* about improving a system's capability of (self-)control. *Development* is about the control of development-processes. And control, in cybernetic terms, is about a kind of control which is more than merely direct interventions in operations. This is in contrast to its normal usage in everyday diction, which has influenced established control models counterproductively. Anyone will understand that *control by design*, i.e., by indirect intervention *(second-order intervention)*, is in general more effective than control by manipulations at the object level, i.e., by direct interventions.

Let us look at the concept of control more narrowly, starting from a classical representation of what has been called the *management cycle* (Figure 3-1).

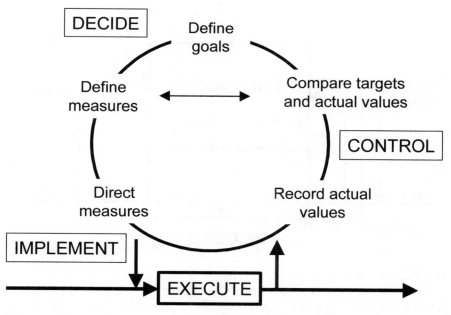

Fig. 3-1. The management process as a cycle (Ulrich/Krieg 1974)

The process passes through the phases of decision, implementation and control. Completion of the cycle leads back to the point – in a higher-level decision cycle – at which the decision was made. Each phase of the management process in Figure 3-1 may itself be considered a cyclic sub-process. Let us take a more sophisticated view of the process in terms of a control loop. The diagram in Figure 3-2 is more abstract and therefore probably less familiar to a managerial readership. However, abstractions of this type can be very useful conceptualizations which help to reflect (at a mental meta-level), what is taking place (at a real-life object level). Therefore they will be used in several instances throughout this book.

In the model shown in Figure 3-2, management appears first of all as the 'regulator' of a process by which actual data are verified, then fed into a control unit, where they are compared with goals. The comparison between actual and target values may then lead to corrective decisions. So far, this is a process controlled on the basis of outputs only. We have a self-correcting *feedback* mechanism based on historical values. In such a regulatory process, the possible effect of disturbances is not anticipated.

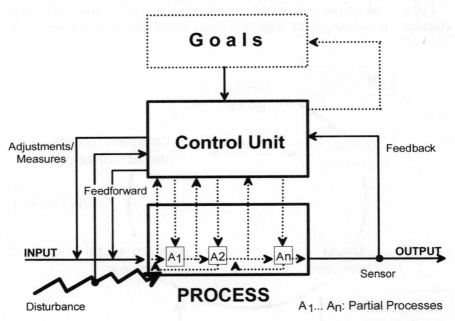

Fig. 3-2. A Control Loop

A complementary principle must therefore be put into effect – one that is proactive. This is the mechanism of *feedforward*, based upon the detection of possible future disturbances, against which prospective, precautionary measures can be taken. The creation of a desirable future is largely based on what we call steering; that is, on feedforward, and on the *pre-control-concepts*, further discussed below.

Regulation and steering are the complementary principles of control. As our diagram of the control loop shows, these principles rely on the processes of communication.

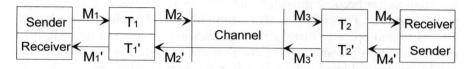

Code: M ... Message
        T ... Transducer

Ideal Case: $M_1 = M_2 = M_3 = M_4$

Real Case: $M_1 \approx M_2 \approx M_3 \approx M_4$

Fig. 3-3. General Model of a Communication Process

In its broadest sense, *communication* denotes all the processes by which one system may affect another (after Shannon/ Weaver 1949). A more detailed, "technical" diagram of communication processes is set out in Figure 3-3; which reveals that communication processes convey information; that they are subject to constraints; and that they can be described in terms of transformations. These transformations include:

- transduction, including encoding and decoding, and
- transmission, which involves
- distortions due to noise, i.e., errors of transmission.

The most important lessons following from this analysis: first, communication must always be designed and handled in such a way that loops are closed, i.e., that there is adequate confirmation that a signal has been received or acted on. Secondly, there must be sufficient *redundancy* for distortions to be compensated for; this means that the transducers and the channel must have a variety that exceeds the variety of the information to be transmitted. Non-abidance by these two principles can have disastrous consequences, and does! My favorite example to corroborate this is the famous story of Romeo and Juliet, in which the cost of not closing one loop was the lives of three people. A more mundane example of the second principle is the gross distortions of an initial message which regularly occur along a chain of interpersonal communications, both in experiments and in real life.

3.3 Control versus Pre-control

Under the evolutionary pressures of complexity and change, a logical differentiation has become important, namely the difference between *control* and *pre-control*. Pre-control is also a form of control but involves a longer time vista and operates thereby on a distinct logical level of its own. Pre-control concerns the anticipative creation of preconditions or prerequisites at a higher logical level, which largely predetermine what can be achieved in terms of control and performance at later stages and on the lower logical levels. These lower levels are orientated towards a shorter time horizon. It must be clear by now that this differentiation of the notion of pre-control from control is crucial for enhancing a firm's long-term orientation. This will be further elaborated on in Chapter 5.

3.4 Extrinsic versus Intrinsic Control

Cybernetics originates from the world of engineering[3]. The term derives from the Greek word *"kybernetes"*, which denoted the steersman, a classical version of a control agent. Early applications were centered on mechanical systems. With the study and use of Cybernetics in the context of social systems, some conceptual reframing took place. Social systems consist of individuals and groups, who have their own goals and adhere to their own values. They are self-conscious and introspective, i.e., they are capable of reflecting upon who they are and what they do.Social systems are therefore capable of self-control, self-organization, self-reference and self-transformation. What do these terms denote exactly?

- *Self-control:* A system's ability to control itself, which includes setting and adjusting its own goals, as well as autonomous adaptation;
- *Self-organization:* The autonomous, often spontaneous formation of relationships, activities and structural patterns;
- *Self-reference:* A system's capability to reflect upon itself, and therewith on aspects such as its identity, values, purpose, goals and tasks or activities;
- *Self-transformation:* The ability of a system to reorganize and restructure itself.

---

[3]   Norbert Wiener's seminal book "Cybernetics or Control and Communication in the Animal and in the Machine" (1948) was written at the Massachusetts Institute of Technology.

In ordinary language, we express these properties by using attributes such as "intrinsic" or "autonomous" and prefixes such as *self-, auto-, and eigen-* the latter coming from the German expression for "of its own". Pertinent terms such as autonomous action, eigenbehavior[4], self-organization, etc., are used to indicate the intrinsic value attributed to individuals in organizations and the concern for the autonomy of decentralized actors, whether they are individuals, teams or organizational units.

In the light of what has been said hitherto, a conceptual distinction between *first-order cybernetics and second-order cybernetics* can be seen to have emerged.

In *first-order cybernetics*, the controller is seen as separate from or outside of the system (Figure 3-4). The system is purposive, in the sense that goals are established from outside or "above". This view is applicable to mechanical systems, but inadequate to capture the *purposeful*, intentional and also largely voluntarist character of individuals and groups who constitute modern organizations.

In *second-order cybernetics* the controller is an integral part of the system itself. The system is purposeful, i.e., it develops its goals internally and is made up of subsystems, which in their turn pursue their own goals. In this conception, goal formation is a process of dialogue and reciprocal alignment between a system and the larger whole into which it is embedded. Heinz von Foerster, the eminent cybernetician, defines the difference as follows (von Foerster et al.1974):

- First-order cybernetics: "the cybernetics of observed systems";
- Second-order cybernetics: "the cybernetics of observing systems".

---

[4]   The scientific term eigenbehavior denotes the characteristic behavior mode of a certain system, which is an expression of its identity.

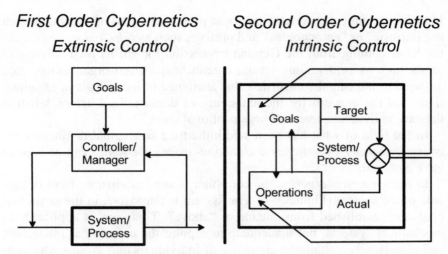

Fig. 3-4 Control according to first- and second-order cybernetics

Not only the human and social nature of organizations but also the complexity they face makes it necessary to emphasize *intrinsic control* as opposed to *extrinsic control*. If intrinsic control is to predominate, this must lead to a *recursive* process of intrinsic control in the case of organizations with several layers of basic units, i.e., units which create the value that is at the core of the organization's mission (e.g., divisions – business units – business segments). This will be a major subject of Chapter 6.

3.5 Hierarchy versus Heterarchy

A concept of organization that is closely linked to the concept of *intrinsic control* has emerged in recent years. This is the concept of heterarchy, which is considered an alternative to hierarchical organization. Specifically, heterarchical networks are increasingly being considered more suitable than one-dimensional "tree-like" hierarchical structures for handling issues in an environment characterized by uncertainty, complexity and dynamics[5]. Such organizations possess, in principle, a greater capacity for absorbing complexities. To express it in the language of cybernetics, heterarchical organizations are superior to hierarchical systems as far as their "redundancy of potential command" (McCulloch 1988) is concerned, i.e., in their excess capacity to control themselves. However, networks are not

---

[5]   Gomez/Zimmermann 1997; Hedlund 1986, 1993; Probst 1992; Schwaninger 1994b, 2000b; Weber 1994, and other literature cited therein.

necessarily heterarchies, although all heterarchies are structured in the same way as networks. For this reason, it is important to distinguish precisely between the concepts of *heterarchy* and *hierarchy*. Both of these concepts are derived from the Greek verb "archein", which means, "to reign". Hierarchy (derived from the word "hieros", meaning holy, belonging to the gods, priestly) stands for the command of the few, "initiated" ones. Heterarchy (derived from the word "heteros", meaning different, many) refers to the command vested in different and distributed instances.

The structure and culture of an organization are very closely interconnected. The ideal-types of two models of organization are presented below (Figure 3-5).

Each of them embraces both of the aspects mentioned, namely the cultural and the structural:

- HAT: the hierarchical-authoritarian type,
- HPT: the heterarchical-participative type.

Hierarchical structures are associated with autocratic patterns of behavior including monological commands emanating from one single center. As opposed to these, a heterarchical organization can have many centers of command and is characterized by a culture involving a high degree of participation and dialogue. In such a form of organization, participation and empowerment are so deeply entrenched that any unit whatsoever of the organization is, in principle, in a position to take command of the entire organization with reference to a specific aspect, while remaining at the same time in a subordinate role with reference to other aspects (Hedlund 1986, 1993).

The HAT is characterized by a high degree of control (extrinsic control) and very little autonomy in the workplace. The emphasis is on long-lasting structures and an extensive division of labor. The HPT, in contrast, endows units at all levels with considerable autonomy, which encourages high levels of self-determination and intrinsic control (Figure 3-5). Here, the emphasis is laid on temporary structures, on multiplication and recombination. While hierarchies are *ceteris paribus*[6] efficient at utilizing available resources, the power of heterarchies lies in their flexibility and capacity for innovation.

---

[6] *Ceteris paribus* is a scientific term which stands for *all other things being equal*, in comparisons like the one being made here.

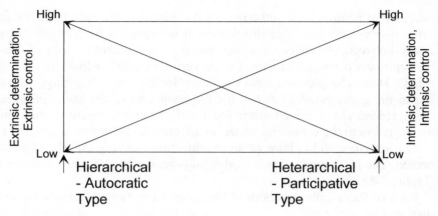

Fig. 3-5. Two ideal-types of organization

In reality, organizations do not conform rigorously to one or the other of these ideal-types. Hierarchical systems will always exhibit some elements of a dialogue, even if they operate in a placid environment. On the other hand, network-type heterarchical systems will never be completely free of some characteristics of hierarchies, since certain units within the organization will have to assume the global responsibility in some specific area in their relation to the superordinate systems.

At this point, it is important to emphasize that the framework presented here is fully compatible with the need for heterarchical control (see in particular chapters 6 and 7).

3.6 Distributed Management

There is a need for and a trend towards decentralizing the functions of management. It would nevertheless be naive to assume that in the new organizations, intrinsic control will replace all extrinsic control, or that dependence should or will be abolished, while autonomy becomes absolute. It would also be an error to believe that hierarchy will cease to exist, giving way completely to heterarchy. Similarly, it is not enough to pre-control with one's eye solely on the long run, while neglecting the supervision of ongoing processes. In all of these cases, the apparent opposites are in fact complementary, not mutually exclusive.

Indeed, a prime challenge to the design of organizations is to distribute the abilities which make up organizational intelligence, and therewith the management functions across the whole system.

To sum up, the historical separation between the functions of execution and control, a characteristic of the age of mass production, needs to be relaxed. Indeed, at the operative level many of these functions might well be re-united in the same hands, whereby certain functions of planning and decision as well as of quality control would be integrated and made the responsibility of workers. Essentially, this is meant to heal the unnatural cleft between thinking and acting which has afflicted so many organizations. But it also indicates that virtually every actor in an organization should as a matter of course be expected to fulfill certain managerial functions to some extent.[7]

Notwithstanding what has been said above, however, it still makes sense to hive off the management functions for the purpose of analysis (only), because they need to be designed appropriately. The analytical differentiation of the management function does not affect the principle that managers do and should consider themselves parts of the units for which they bear responsibility. Nor is the re-integration of thinking and doing intended as a proposal to detract from the fundamental purpose of management, but as a means of helping the organization to achieve its purpose, and to review or, if necessary, revise it.

All this progress can be attained only if management is a distributed function, just as an organization can be intelligent only if its intelligence is a distributed property.

---

[7]   This is actually what consultants like Cloke & Goldsmith (2002) mean when they use the trendy but misleading jargon about "The End of Management". Management as a function distributed across the whole organization is an idea that systems thinkers on management have advocated for decades: Peter Drucker (1974) pleaded for building as much discretion and responsibility as possible into every workplace. The cybernetician Heinz von Foerster (1984b) observed: "In a self-organizing managerial system each participant is also a manager of this system." (p. 8).

Chapter 4 Intelligent Organization – A Systemic Framework

"In principio erat verbum ..."[1]

John 1, The Holy Bible

In this chapter, a *Framework for the Design and Development of Intelligent* Organizations will be developed. This, then, will be a "dry" chapter. But defining concepts at the outset is crucial, if this book is to be more than mere entertainment for its readers. The citation above from the Fourth Gospel gives a notion of the power of concepts, and for me supplies the motivation to try to be as selective and precise as possible in the choice of concepts. This chapter is mainly dedicated to the definition of those ruling ideas which make up the *Framework for the Design and Development of Intelligent Organizations*. Being clear when introducing each concept has the additional advantage of helping one to avoid both misunderstandings and the abuse of terms as buzzwords, which are always reductive and often misleading.

4.1 Postulates

From the reflections and concepts set forth in Chapters 1, 2 and 3, a number of postulates can be derived as basic requirements for the framework:

- The framework should show managers the way to enhance their organizations' intelligence.
- It should be a conceptual tool to support integrative, systemic management for enduring prosperity, viability and development of their organizational units.

---

[1] In English: "In the beginning was the Word..."

In particular the framework is intended to furnish models and methods which enable

- The balancing of short- and long-term views, especially control and pre-control;
- The combination of autonomous adaptation by individual actors or units with the maintenance of coherence and cohesiveness in the whole organization;
- The pursuit of multidimensional and multilevel (self-)control for optimal performance;
- The provision of high value for all stakeholders;
- Maximal organizational learning, as well as the constructive realization of necessary changes and transformations.

If we talk about learning and change in this context, both of the following levels are implied (see for example Espejo/Schuhmann/Schwaninger 1996):

- *First-order learning and change*, i.e., learning through error correction and pertinent alterations;
- *Higher-order learning and change*, i.e., learning completely new abilities *(second-order learning)* as well as learning to learn better *(meta-learning[2])*, and fundamental change, which may include modifications of goals and values. That is to say, higher-order learning and change always require adjustments of the models on which action is based.

The postulates above are formulated very broadly on purpose. At an earlier stage a set of postulates was formulated, with a related aim and in more detail, with respect to a book on organizational transformation and learning (Espejo/Schuhmann/Schwaninger 1996). It must be added that the framework should also provide a link to the actors' personalities, i.e., give them a hint on how to achieve these organization-bound goals in accordance with their own goals, values and needs. Chapter 6 will provide a theory for the link between such humanistic values as autonomy, interesting work and self-fulfillment on one hand, and organizational identity and structure on the other.

---

[2]   The term *deutero-learning* is also often used, which was coined by Gregory Bateson (1973).

4.2 Introducing the Framework

In this next step, a framework will be laid out which accommodates the postulates carried forward above. In other words, this framework is a conceptual tool to help managers enhance their organizations' intelligence and to support an integrative, systemic management for enduring prosperity, viability and development of the organization. An overview is given in Figure 4-1.

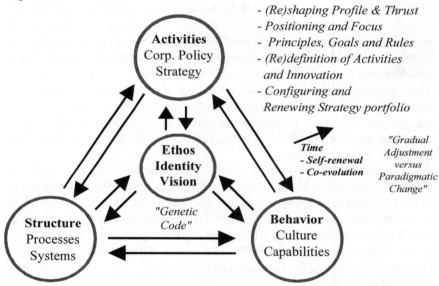

Fig. 4-1. Framework for the Design and Development of Intelligent Organizations
– Overview

This framework builds on a set of specific notions of systemic management:

1. The proposed framework is *integrative* – in what respect? In contrast
   with many frameworks that emphasize partial aspects of organizations –
   e.g., strategy, structure or organization culture – the emphasis in the one

proposed here is on bringing together the different components so as to provide a more complete picture. Integration – the making up or composition of wholes – is a natural capability of humans, largely based on unconscious inferences (Gregory 1987). In the face of the complexity of real-world phenomena, however, a proneness to reductionism and fragmentation of models has become widespread. The present framework is a device to overcome this limitation. It is made up of an integrated set of essential parameters and their identifiable interrelationships, which have to be developed in co-alignment, to enhance organizational intelligence. Thereby it does more than merely furnish a list of important aspects. It provides a frame of reference which is robust, broad enough and sufficiently structured to enable actors to initiate and catalyze organizational development and transformation more effectively.

2. The essential parameters which make up the framework can be *designed,* within limits. Certain aspects of design must take indirect paths; e.g., proper influence on behavior is taken via the design of rules for interaction, appropriate structures etc., rather than directly (see also Chapter 6.).

3. The framework is *multi-dimensional*. In the scheme, five crucial dimensions are combined. Three of them – activities, structure and behaviour – are the dimensions that constitute the pillars of the St. Gallen Management Framework, an architecture for structuring management issues developed at the University of St. Gallen (see especially: Bleicher 2004, Krieg 1985, Rüegg-Stürm 2002). The fourth dimension is made up of basic parameters, such as organizational identity, ethos and vision. The fifth dimension is time.

4. The components, which constitute the framework, are *dynamically interrelated*, as visualized in Figure 4-1. The terms in the diagram give an overview of the domains in which management/leadership can influence the essential parameters and thereby catalyze organizational transformation. The dynamic interrelationship between these components calls for balanced interventions but also for a thorough consideration of possible chain reactions and side effects.

After having introduced the models which are integrated by this framework, further systemic properties will have to be highlighted, when we revisit the framework in the 10th Chapter.

4.3 Dimensions of the Framework

It is worth introducing the dimensions of the framework one by one:

1. Activities
2. Structure
3. Behavior
4. Basic parameters
5. Time.

The first four dimensions represent areas which – to a certain extent – can be designed.

The first three dimensions are based on an original scheme by the biologist Ralph Gerard, one of the founders of the Systems Movement. Gerard proposed structure, function, and behavior as crucial characteristics, i.e., as basic dimensions of all kinds of living systems (Rapoport 1992a).

For our purpose, the following working definitions can be useful:

Activities: This dimension refers to the ensemble of intended operations of or actions taken by an organization. These are an embodiment of what Gerard called a system's *function*, which it fulfils in its environment. Stafford Beer at one point stated: "The purpose of the system is what it does" (Beer 1985).

Structure: This dimension refers to the actual or desired (relatively) stable arrangements or patterns of interrelations between the elements or components of an organization. Structures tend to be reproduced via operational closure, i.e., in self-referential processes.

Behavior: This dimension refers to the actual or desired qualitative features of conduct, which are characteristic of an organization or its subsystems. In other words, it is about the characteristic patterns of actions or operations, and the resulting states exhibited.

These three dimensions are interrelated.

- Structure→Activities: The carrying out of activities is facilitated by adequate structures or jeopardized by dysfunctional structures.
- *Activities→Behavior:* Sequences of activities generate patterns of behavior.
- *Structure→Behavior:* Behavior is enabled and constrained by structural properties.
- *Behavior→Activities:* Modes of behavior lead to the realization or lack of achievement of targeted activities, i.e., functions or tasks.
- *Structure→Activities:* Adequate structures are essential for the carrying out of activities.

- *Activities→Structure:* Putting targeted activities into operation may require adjustments of structure.

The fourth dimension, called basic parameters, is about those components of the framework which are linked to the specific nature of human and social systems, namely their self-consciousness and reflexivity. In Figure 4-1 these components have been labeled ethos, identity and vision. What do these denote?

- *Ethos:* The ideals, values, principles and norms, which provide normative guidance to an organization. Here, the metaphor of the genetic code or the architecture of life is a useful one.
- *Identity:* Any mark of an organization that can be consistently recognized or which persists over time (Leonard, forthcoming), therewith making it distinguishable or unique.
- *Vision:* A creative anticipation of, or a complex insight into, the possible or desired future of an organization.

These components are called fundamentals or basic *parameters,* because they often emanate from deep-seated values, and also because in relation to the organization in focus they represent ultimates, which can or need not be derived from higher-level parameters inside the firm. The important point here is that traditionally these fundamentals have hardly been addressed by management theory[3]. As practitioners have discovered the importance of these ultimates in recent years, intensive efforts to deal with them can be discerned – initiatives for ethical management, social responsibility and ecological sustainability have been thriving. Everyone talks about values, but in the context of the relativistic mainstream which currently dominates the epistemological landscape this has little or no significance in terms of orientation for practitioners (Bloom 1987). The problem is that the concepts of *relativity and relativism* are usually mixed up. On one hand, relativity, a major achievement of modern science, signifies that the models of systems differ between observers. This has been an important concept in constructivism, an epistemological strand spearheaded by Heinz von Foerster, an Austro-American pioneer of systems thinking. Constructivism deals with the construction of models and realities by observers and actors, which are shaped by their subjective stances and values. On the other hand relativism – in contrast to relativity – negates the possibility of objective knowledge. Moreover, relativists often tend to declare

---

[3]   One exception is the work of Hans Ulrich, the originator of the systems-oriented management framework of the University of St. Gallen, whose writings have been re-edited (Ulrich 2001).

the relative (namely their own position) as an absolute. This tendency has led to a situation where a substantive discussion of normative issues has been suppressed even further.

It is one of the merits of leading systems thinkers to have made substantive statements about values as orienting factors for management. Russell Ackoff, an authoritative voice on systemic management, has pleaded for putting values on the agenda of managers, which had already been advocated by Greek philosophers: The *good*, the *true* and the *beautiful*, besides the value of *plenty*, which has always been a goal in economics and managerial thinking and which has dominated or even usurped it (Ackoff 1981). De Raadt, a conceptual thinker from the University of Luleå, Sweden, has called attention to the religious heritage underlying culture and to its ethical potential for reinvigorating organizations and society (de Raadt 1997, 2000).

There is no doubt that organizations are complex and pluralistic systems, and sometimes coercive ones, as Flood and Jackson (1991) have noted. Therefore, it must be assumed that views of what is desirable can substantially diverge between the agents involved. But organizations can develop the necessary strength and momentum to weather the challenges they confront only if they unite the efforts of their members around a common purpose to be pursued through joint action. The social energy necessary for effective action derives to a large extent from the concepts of the good, true, beautiful, and plentiful, shared by those members. In organizations with several levels, what is said here about individuals is also applicable to organizational units, e.g., teams, divisions etc., all of which develop their own goals, values and preferences (Ackoff/Gharajedaghi 1984, Ackoff 1999).

Finally, the fifth dimension is time, along which the development and the evolutionary (or sometimes revolutionary) path of an organization can be traced. The dynamics of a system range from gradual adjustments to paradigmatic change – on a continuum rather than as a dichotomy of "either-or". They are linked to, even though not strictly determined by, the system's structure, and therefore can be anticipated to some degree. However, the challenge here lies less in attaining the traditional ideal of prediction – which is impossible[4] – than in exploring the potential consequences of decisions, in detecting sensitivities, e.g., those related to vulnerabilities and risks, and in assessing the robustness of strategies. Modeling and simulation techniques are essential for this purpose. In contrast to other living systems, the development of an organization can be conceived as a process of guided evolution (see especially Chapter 9). Finally, besides

---

[4]   Reliable prediction of detail is impossible, reliable prediction of principle is.

this firm-level aspect of adaptation through self-renewal, it is necessary to bring also the population-level aspect of selection into the picture, which triggers co-evolution (Volberda/Lewin 2003).

What is only implicit in this Framework for the Design and Development of Intelligent Organizations and will have to be made explicit in the next chapter is the multilevel character of control. This is to do with the differentiation between control at the object level (first-order control) and control at higher logical levels (higher-order control and mostly pre-control). It applies to all dimensions, one through four, over time (dimension five). Design and development are – in a precise sense – components of higher-order control, which is often called indirect control. Both design and development are also subject to controls themselves. The ultimate control of dimensions one to three emanates from the basic parameters (dimension four). These abstract notions will be operationalized in the following chapters.

4.4 Theoretical Models to Enhance Organizational Intelligence

The fundamental characteristic of complexity inherent in all kinds of social systems has triggered efforts to know more about a) the set of parameters which substantially impinge on a system's patterns of behavior, and b) the subset of design parameters and control variables, as well as their interrelationships, by which these patterns of behavior can be shaped[5]. In the domains of organization and society, these efforts have been focused on building better models that capture the structures or generative mechanisms underlying system behavior, and the evoked insights for better system design and (self-) control.

I shall draw on three theories from Organizational Cybernetics which have opened new dimensions in this endeavor:

1. The Model of Systemic Control (MSC)
2. The Viable System Model (VSM)
3. The Team Syntegrity model[6] (TSM).

---

[5]   See Ross Ashby's concept of "essential variables", which are meant to be indicators of viability, or at least of actual survival (Ashby 1965).

[6]   As the materials of TSI, Team Syntegrity Inc., Toronto, the firm which makes the Team Syntegrity protocols available to organizations, refer to Team Syntegrity as a methodology, the word "model", which I use in this context is not capitalized.

The construction of the *Framework for the Design and Development of Intelligent Organizations* started out with my proposal that integrating these theories can provide a systemic approach to development and learning, which enhances organizational intelligence (as defined in Chapter 1) more than do the isolated uses of one or more of these theories (Schwaninger 2001b).

In Chapters 5 to 7, the three theoretical models enumerated above will be outlined and discussed. All of them have been described and underpinned extensively elsewhere (see references below and in Chapters 5, 6 and 7). But not much had been done to combine them until a conceptual attempt of integration was made (documented in Schwaninger 2000, 2001b). That endeavor appears promising, because these theories are, in principle, complementary and potentially highly synergistic:

1. The *Model of Systemic Control* furnishes for a comprehensive (self-) control of the activities of an organization to enhance its fitness.
2. The *Viable System Model* addresses issues of diagnosing and designing the structures of an organization for viability and development.
3. The *Team Syntegrity model* provides a framework for developing interactive behavior in an organization so as to foster synergy, cohesion and knowledge-creation.

The beauty of all three theoretical models lies in a characteristic they share – all of them are based on insights about invariant features of organizations, which generate patterns of behavior that can be anticipated and therewith influenced proactively. In relation to the complexity of the events that continually occur in organizations, these features are relatively simple, i.e., they embody a degree of complexity which can be handled by the actors when designing those systems. In this sense, the present book addresses both

- the simplicity in complexity (i.e., the invariant characteristics of behavior patterns), and
- the simplicity underlying complexity (i.e., the comprehensibility of structural features which bring about complex events).

Substantial empirical evidence corroborates the effectiveness of each one of these models. The respective sources cannot be reviewed extensively here. However, I shall cite a subset of references which furnish empirical support and which are relatively easy to access:

- for the *MSC*: Schwaninger 1988, 1989, 2000, Gälweiler 2005;
- for the *VSM*: Espejo/Harnden 1989, Espejo/Schwaninger 1993, Espejo/Schuhmann/Schwaninger 1996;

- for the *TSm*: Beer 1994, Truss/Cullen/Leonard 2000, Schwaninger 2003a.

4.5 Relationships between the Models

The choice of these three models is not an arbitrary one, but it is cogent. The three models are linked by an inherent logic. It would not make much sense to try to prove this bold statement right now, and so I must ask my kind readers for their patience. The proof can be brought forward in a more efficient and profound way once all three models have been expounded. At that point, in Chapter 10, we shall revisit the framework under the aspect of integration, i.e., the logical links just mentioned.

Finally, it is recommended that one locate the three models in the context of the categories used at the outset of this book. The matrix in Table 4-1 is constituted by

- Three lines referring to activities, structure and behavior – the initial dimensions of our framework – and
- Three columns referring to design, control and development, the components of management, as specified in Chapter 3.

Table 4-1. Linking the Models to the Dimensions

	Design	Control	Development	
Activities	x	xx	x	MSC
Structure	xx	x	x	VSM
Behavior	x	x	xx	TSM

The scheme in Table 4-1 highlights two aspects: First, each one of the three dimensions of the framework makes a contribution to all of the aspects of management (denoted by x). Second, each one of the three models mentioned has a primordial link to one of the dimensions of the framework (denoted by xx):

- The Model of Systemic Control to the activities,
- The Viable System Model to structure,
- The Team Syntegrity model to behavior.

However, these links are not exclusive; this fact is indicated by the arrows on the right hand of the diagram. The three models are not only interlinked, as already emphasized, but also each of them can also contribute to any one of the dimensions of the framework – to activities, structure and behavior.

It must be added, however, that the models place different emphases on the three components of management (see Table 4-2), namely:

- The Viable System Model is a conceptual tool for organizational *design,*
- The Model of Systemic Control for organizational *control*, and
- The Team Syntegrity model for organization *development.*

If we close the loop now, we can recognize a correspondence between the abstract dimensions of management from which we started out and the dimensions of our framework:

Table 4-2. Correspondence between Dimensions and Linkages with Models

Design	<--->	Structure	<--->	VSM
Control	<--->	Activities	<--->	MSC
Development	<--->	Behavior	<--->	TSM

These conceptualizations are important insofar as they provide the building blocks of a "grammar" which allows the reader to grasp right from the start the different potentials of the models and their applicability. None of them alone can depict or solve any kind of complex managerial issues. But each one of them is very powerful within its specific domain.

Chapter 5 Activities: What the Organization Does

"It is much better to do the right thing wrong than the wrong thing right."
Russell L. Ackoff, American Systems Thinker[1]

"Though we cannot live one hundred years, we should be concerned about one thousand years hence."
Namikei Odaira, founder of Hitachi[2]

"Any system that makes one value absolute is wrong."
Peter F. Drucker, Austro-American management thinker[3]

As shown in Chapter 2, the Systems Approach (and Organizational Cybernetics in particular) conceives management in terms of coping with dynamic complexity. The Model of Systemic Control (MSC), to be outlined in this Chapter, specifies and interrelates the control variables which are necessary and sufficient to deal with that complexity in principle. This refers to the first dimension of our framework-*Activities*.

The cybernetic concept of control embraces the regulation and steering of a system in order to achieve its purpose or goals – i.e., to carry out its *tasks or activities* (what it has to do or what it does) – within the bandwidth defined by them. The cybernetics of social systems emphasizes intrinsic control[4] as opposed to extrinsic control. If Heinz von Foerster (1984) denominates social systems as *observing systems* in opposition to *observed systems*, he thereby addresses aspects such as self-control, self-reference, self-organization and self-transformation, which are among the main concerns of Organizational Cybernetics (See Chapter 3).

---

[1] Ackoff/Pourdehnad 2001: 200.
[2] These words of the man who founded Hitachi in 1919 are inscribed on the walls of Hitachi City. Concomitantly, Hitachi's stated research goal is to perform "long-term, continuous research to meet social needs and corporate policy in the next decades through development of original science and/or significant patents." (Source: www.wtec.org/Loyola/ep/c3s6.htm).
[3] Drucker 1986: 16.
[4] Geyer/van der Zouwen 1978 I, Schwaninger 2000b, Espejo et al. 1996. The terms *intrinsic control, eigen-control, auto-control* and *self-control* are used synonymously (Chapter 3)

Effective (self-) control implies a dynamic equilibrium at a satisfactory level of performance, between an organization (or an organizational unit) – e.g., a corporation, a company (or a division) – and the milieu in which it operates. But *which variables define adequate performance*?

5.1 The Model of Systemic Control (MSC)

Traditional corporate control models have largely or exclusively been oriented towards the goal of profit. It has been demonstrated that such models no longer meet today's requirements (Gälweiler 2005, Schwaninger 1989). This is not a dismissal of profit – there is no doubt that profit is a necessary prerequisite for a firm to stay in business. The claim here is a different one: Management models are insufficient if they leave out the *pre-controls*, which ultimately generate or obstruct profitability and finally liquidity. Under the evolutionary pressure of increasing complexity and turbulence a more sophisticated view of the criteria of competent management has emerged. This conceptual innovation has given rise to new management models, which show a much greater *variety*, i.e., potential for dealing with complexity, than do the traditional ones. In these new models, the criteria of competent management are instead defined in terms of a comprehensive *organizational fitness or organizational intelligence*. Profit, then – as an example – is an objective at the operative level, and an outcome of preconditions originating at higher logical levels.

In this context, a *Model of Systemic Control (MSC)* has been developed. It is presented in an abridged version for private firms (Figure 5-1)[5], and in a generalized version which is more comprehensive (Figure 5-2). In the latter especially, at the operative level value is conceived in a multidimensional mode, including aspects of customer, financial, social and ecological benefits. This generalized version is also applicable to public organizations and to social initiatives of all kinds.

---

[5] This diagram was inspired by Aloys Gälweiler (cf. Gälweiler 2005).

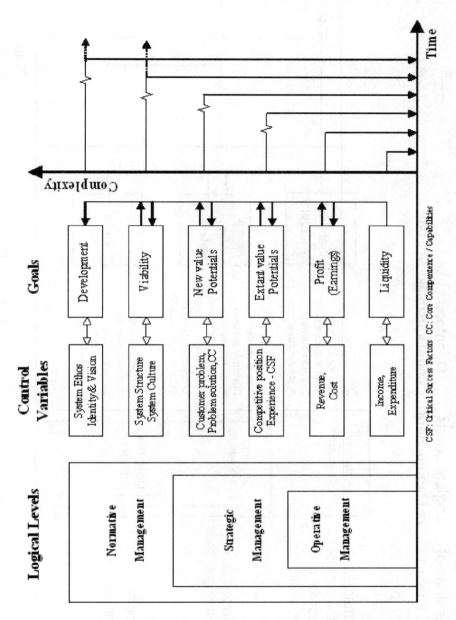

Fig. 5-1. Model of Systemic Control (version for private firms, abridged for didactical purposes).

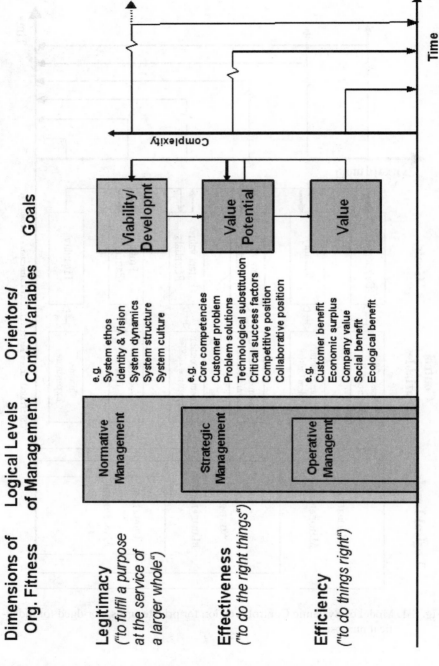

Fig. 5-2. Model of Systemic Control (generalized version)

The essence of the progress achieved with the MSC is based on a systemic insight – namely, that one and the same system must govern itself by means of a set of control variables which may (and often do) contradict each other, because they belong to different logical levels: the levels of operative, strategic and *normative management*. Balancing these out is a core task of leadership, a highly non-trivial one (Gälweiler 2005, Schwaninger 1989).

As shown in Figures 5-1 and 5-2, there are interrelationships between the three logical levels. In particular, the control variables of the higher logical levels exert a *pre-control* influence on those of the lower levels. This has been more thoroughly specified elsewhere for the case of business organizations (Schwaninger 1993, 2000a). Pre-control is about the creation of preconditions or prerequisites at earlier stages and at a higher logical level, which largely predetermine what can be achieved in terms of control and performance at later stages and by the lower logical levels of management (Gälweiler 2005, Schwaninger 2000a).

An important insertion is already necessary at this stage. If we talk about different logical levels of management, we are not necessarily talking about different people or different organizational units. This is going to be a major issue when we deal with the structural embodiments of the different logical levels of control (Chapter 6).

5.2 Operative Level

For a business, the control variables considered essential to the operative level are liquidity and profit. We know since Luca Pacioli introduced double-entry book-keeping more than 500 years ago (in 1494) that these are two distinct objects of thought and action. Note that until then this distinction had not been known! Ever since, the controls of liquidity on one hand and profit on the other have been handled distinctly (for example, by a controller and by a treasurer respectively).

Profit and Liquidity

For anyone who understands "modern" bookkeeping, the *pre-control effect*, which profit exerts on liquidity, should be clear. If profit is strong this will impinge positively on liquidity. This effect will usually occur with some time lag, because the time-related natures of profit and liquidity are distinct – *liquidity* materializes immediately as a consequence of income and expenditure, whereas profit has a longer time horizon (See horizontal axis in Figure 5-1) because its determinants – revenues and costs – span greater periods. There are costs which do not accrue in one event of consumption, but which accumulate over larger periods and are independent of the respective payments, e.g., interest and depreciation. Also, in most firms a large portion of the revenues is only paid with some delay, after the delivery of the merchandise. Consequently, the determinants of profit – revenue and cost – and those of liquidity – income and expenditure – are booked separately. The implication for control is that the level of profit is an early warning indicator in relation to liquidity. If profit is negative once, this can be compensated for with accumulated reserves or via credits. However, the longer such a situation persists, the more difficult it becomes for a firm to maintain liquidity. Once maintenance of liquidity turns out to be impossible, bankruptcy is the compelling consequence.

Management accounting came up a long time ago with sets of indicators which reflect the relationships of the components that determine liquidity and profit. A famous case in point is the classical Dupont scheme; versions of it have been taken on by virtually all firms. These are mature instruments. However, they are only necessary but not sufficient. Why are they insufficient? The answer is given by the Conant-Ashby-Theorem (Chapter 2): the reason is that these instruments convey models of corporate reality that lack variety.

First of all, they are merely financially oriented. But the general goal at the operative level is to create value, i.e., benefits not only for shareholders but also for the different stakeholder groups of an organization (particularly customers, personnel and owners).

Creating and Delivering Value

Value has several dimensions. Recently approaches to "sustainability management" have tried to establish criteria and define indicators which capture value in economic as well as social and ecological terms. Specialists also talk about the "triple bottom line" (Elkington 1998) in this context.

Specific control variables to achieve value creation are customer benefit[6], social and ecological benefits, and shareholder value, the latter being essentially determined by profits (more precisely: by the integral of discounted free cash flows). In all of this multidimensionality, one crucial fact is not to be forgotten: Ultimately, in the market place only those products and services of a firm will succeed which deliver the best perceived value to their customers (among all solutions available to them). This law is gen-

---

[6]   Depending on the organization in focus, "customer benefit" may be changed to a more specific term. For example, certain public institutions should rather speak of value for citizens (who are their *raison d'être*).

erally applicable, always with the *ceteris paribus* clausula – i.e., all other things being equal.

Second, profit behaves in an inherently short-term-mode and its level is largely predetermined by parameters of another nature (just as liquidity is largely predetermined by profits). Similarly, a customer benefit derived from a product or service hinges on prerequisites which must be fully available at – and therefore built up well ahead of – the "moments of truth" (Carlzon 1988) i.e., when production and delivery take place.

Good managers have always known that the attainment of operative goals is bound to preconditions that have to be created in advance. Practitioners and writers in many domains of management have become more and more aware of this. Attempts have been made to link the operative and the strategic logic, e.g., in production, logistics and marketing. Beyond that, however, a comprehensive theory has emerged which provides access to the relevant higher-order variables of control.

This theory makes the control variables and parameters of the higher logical levels accessible for analysis and understanding (Gälweiler 1986, 2005[7]; Schwaninger 1989, 2000a, 2001b). These are essential components of an advanced management model: They disclose the really powerful levers for influencing the destiny of an organization – i.e., the control parameters of the strategic and normative levels (Figure 5-1, 5-2).

5.3 Strategic Level

As has been said, pre-control is about the anticipative creation of prerequisites at a higher logical level for effective control at lower logical levels of management. In the context of strategy this can be shown by a descriptive and very common example – why do successful firms achieve sustained profitability? The answer is a very general one. Apart from steering events over the course of months to achieve a positive balance between revenue and costs in their profit and loss statement, at the end of the year such firms have an effective higher-level control mechanism in place. This one does not steer for profit itself but for achieving it in the future. It controls not only for the delivery of value but also for the preconditions of an ever better value creation and delivery. Therefore it is concerned with prerequisites such as innovation – which impinges on customer benefit, with competitive position and other factors that affect future financial performance, etc.

---

[7]   I am grateful to Aloys Gälweiler for having made me aware of the crucial aspect of pre-control.

The values a company can generate are largely predetermined by the value potentials created beforehand. What are these exactly? Value potentials are defined as the set of all applicable business-specific prerequisites (e.g., in the form of resources, capabilities, core competencies) that must be fulfilled when value is to be provided (in extension of: Gälweiler 2005). These require long-term efforts for building them up; think of the unique sound of a first rate orchestra or of the – often phantastic – products and services the best firms in a given industry create. Value potentials represent operational and calculable categories. Their patterns of behavior can be foreseen and influenced ("controlled"). One basic fact is that building value potentials requires a substantial, long-term effort. It creates future benefit and therefore demands sacrifices in the present.

Value potentials must be controlled separately from value, on the basis of independent criteria. Research on strategic management has clarified the nature of these criteria and shown, for instance, how to apprehend the *critical success factors* (such as market share[8], relative market share, experience[9], quality and customer benefit, speed, flexibility etc.) in a given business system. For example, with the help of the PIMS database and a statistical toolbox for quantitative analysis related to it, valuable conclusions about the strategic position of a business and the actions to be taken can be derived (for more details see section 5.6. and Buzzell/ Gale 1987). Getting clarity about the state of these orientators and their pre-control influences on the lower level "parameters" is essential for the leaders of any organization. Critical success factors vary according to the business. In the

---

[8]   Market share is not to be confounded with firm size. It is closely linked with the concept of experience: the larger a market share, the greater the possibility of accumulating experience and therewith cost advantages. Market share therefore is a success factor linked to organizational learning, which is captured by the experience curve (see next footnote):

[9]   The (relative) position on the experience curve is an important indicator of competitiveness. The experience curve reflects the following "law" which is valid for the production of homogenous units of a product or service: Each doubling of the experience (measured in cumulated units produced or cumulated expenses for that product) results in a cost reduction potential of 20 to 30%, at least on the value added (Henderson 1972). This is a benchmark, not a necessarily achieved result. Depending on the industry and on the stage the product is in, these percentages can be subject to an even stronger variation. The experience curve applies to both levels, business/firm and industry. A major implication of the experience curve is that, in principle, gains in efficiency are easy to achieve in early phases of the life cycle of a product or technology. The high returns realized apply until learning slows down and it becomes ever more difficult to improve performance.

beer industry, for example, the two main factors are strength of brand and distribution. Contrary to intuition, taste ranges only in third or fourth place. In much of the machine industry, technical performance and after-sales-service are critical. In airlines, three basic success factors are image, security, and capacity utilization. In addition there are critical success factors, which are different for business clients and mass tourists. While the former are sensitive to timeliness and service quality, the latter are primarily price-sensitive.

However, the analysis of these strategic orientators remains in the domain of *existing value potentials*; it needs to be complemented, if the environment is turbulent.

Existing versus new value potentials

The complexification and dynamization of strategy-relevant environments has made a logical differentiation necessary. This is reflected in the distinction between extant and *new value potentials*. The determinants of both are characterized by distinct time constants, and they may also reflect a different logic. For example, in many businesses large market shares and strong brands[10] may have been critical success factors and thereby reliable indicators of extant value potentials, i.e., a relative assurance for sustained profitability over a few years. But fundamental change may make formerly critical success factors obsolete at some point.

With regard to the longer time horizons of *new value potentials*, a very powerful orientator is *the solution-invariant definition of the customer problem[11]*. Customer problems can be manifest or latent. A powerful analysis is to pose them in relation to solutions which are:

1. Currently available,
2. Still in the development phase, and
3. Potentially available, i.e., still in the research process (Gälweiler 2005).

This is essentially related to the phenomenon of technological substitution. Here are some examples. BP, one of the traditional oil and gas companies, around the turn of the millennium revised its orientation, and redefined itself as "a leading energy business – delivering oil, gas and renewable en-

---

[10] Brands can have a very long life (even hundreds of years, as for example mentioned in the Nestlé case below), namely if they are linked to a strong corporate image.

[11] I prefer the term *customer problems* to *customer needs*, because, in principle, the value for a customer is more sustainable if a problem is solved superbly than if merely more or less ephemeral needs are covered.

ergy resources for a growing world". This led to massive efforts into the research for new energies. BP developed the most efficient solar cell in the world and opened the first hydrogen-tanking station, in Berlin, under the Aral brand.

To give another example, in certain markets, electronic channels of distribution and service replace (part of) the traditional ones. Only those firms survive which are prepared for these new modes of doing business, having built up *new value potentials* through persistent organizational and product / service innovation. If customers appear to desert to digital markets all of a sudden, this "suddenness" says more about the non-preparedness of the firms which lose the game than about the new phenomenon itself. They should (and most of them could) have prepared for this by anticipating this technological substitution and building up the necessary competencies in time. Starting earlier is more important than simply acting faster.

Similarly, breaking free from the trap of "competitive convergence" (Kim/Mauborgne 1999) requires questioning the conventional wisdom about how to compete, by reframing the problem, reinventing the game and avoiding head-on competition. The leapfrogging of competitors in turbulent markets is mostly founded on a redefinition of the relevant market or a new perspective on the customer problem and the superior benefit provided by new solutions.

Firms must ask the question what their business is over and over again. And they must ask if that will be the same within a few years, because not only ways of doing business change but certain markets may vanish altogether. For example, industrialized countries once had a large market for classical typewriters, which is now almost gone. Another case in point is electronic trade, which has absorbed a large share of business in many industries. However, some new electronic markets collapsed soon after they had been brought to life. On the other hand, new business models emerged which combine e-trade with bricks-and-mortar shops, as is the case in some of the media markets (e.g., Barnes & Noble books) and in the retail outlets for branded goods (e.g., high-profile watches)[12].

Leading producers of investment goods have increased the service component of their businesses dramatically (e.g., General Electric and IBM). Moreover many of them, e.g., in heavy machinery industries, computing and communications, and transportation equipment, have become involved in leasing, maintenance or other aspects of value enhancement.

Others have "created" new markets or more precisely uncovered latent market potentials. In the U.S., for instance, new services firms have

---

[12]   In the first case both channels are sales outlets. In the second case the websites rather fulfill the function of windows onto (chains of) sophisticated shops.

emerged in areas that used to belong to the domain of self-service. Examples: Online services for shopping, meals, personal-services companies who provide for housework, etc. In Europe, travel experts started to earn their fees from consulting for corporate customers as their income from airline commissions became threatened and then vanished, as commissions were totally abolished.

Some have shifted the dominant appeal in their industry from functional to emotional (e.g., Swatch, Starbucks) or the other way around (e.g., Body Shop). Several have defied established views of who their customers are. Bloomberg, for example, became one of the leading and most profitable information providers in the world, by shifting their focus from IT managers who had traditionally purchased their financial information systems to the traders using them. This changed the financial services industry (Kim/ Mauborgne 1999).

And finally, many firms have created new value through environment-friendlier or healthier products. For instance, Interface, the world's leading commercial carpet manufacturer, has even embedded its range of environmentally-friendly products in an innovative system of comprehensive flooring and facility solutions for commercial interiors, aligned with its comprehensive model for corporate sustainability (Anderson 1998).

The management of new value potentials includes changing established patterns, taking into account the dynamics of customer problems, problem solutions (i.e., products/services), technological substitution along the value chain or in the value-generating network, respectively. This involves a sustained long-term effort for innovation, and it often requires a redesign of the business system. As Hamel and Prahalad (1994) emphasize, too much strategic effort has rested on established modes. The essence of genuine innovation is reframing the reference system completely, which often leads to the emergence of new modes of doing business, creates new opportunities and may reshape entire industries.

IBM, for example, switched from providing hardware to supplying services to users of similar hardware. This shift of roles built a new business for IBM by offering its clients something new in which it was entitled to claim expertise. In the period from 1994 to 2003 the company's total revenues coming from services rose from 25% to almost 50%.[13] A similar case is Air Liquide, a French manufacturer of industrial gases that has innovated in an unconventional way and has grown dramatically as a consequence. The company responded to a situation of being in a mature market with little perspective for new products. Air Liquide transformed itself

---

[13] "The New Organisation, A Survey of the Company", in: The Economist, January 21st 2006.

from a simple maker of gas into a provider of energy services, and succeeded in persuading many of its corporate customers to outsource their energy management to it (Slywotzky/ Wise 2003).

25 years after the arrival of the personal computer, the scene was marked by mobile communication devices, which started to transform behaviors on a large scale and in many ways. Motorola, for example, a leader in this domain, proceeded to cooperate with car companies and credit-card firms, boosting R&D in order to come up with new technological solutions for what they called "seamless mobility" (Zander 2005).

Innovations of this kind can create uncontested market space, entailing a constellation in which a firm has no competitors at all. The market in that case, is placid, the situation peaceful (Kim/ Mauborgne 2005). The emphasis is not on fighting each other but on the creation of value (and value potential).

Strategic Business Unit versus Whole Firm

For strategic business units a mature strategy methodology has become accessible. This methodology has made more transparent and controllable the essential variables of the strategic level – just as bookkeeping did, a long time ago, for the operative domain. Gälweiler (2005) for the most part, but also Porter (1980, 1985), Schwaninger (1987, 1989), and other authors have elaborated on this methodological concept. A pertinent heuristic scheme can be found in Appendix A. It shows that the fields of strategic inquiry that one must deal with are today as well defined - with their interrelationships and therefore with respect to being usable – as only the components of the operative domain have been until quite recently.

A core issue of strategy at the business level is the design of the business system. This is one of the most challenging tasks of complexity engineering in management, where systemic thinking furnishes a most powerful heuristic device for coping with that challenge. I call this the *Generic Structure of the Business System* and recommend a methodology called *Configuration Analysis and Design* in this context. These shall be briefly outlined here.

For customer benefit as well as sustained competitive and collaborative advantage, positioning in the market and in the potential customer's mind is crucial. Uniqueness in this context is often the ideal approach, if that uniqueness is tied to an image of superiority and is viable in a market. Often, such superiority or uniqueness hinges on a redesign of the whole business system. One can proceed systematically to achieve that. The Generic Structure of Business Systems outlined in Figure 5-3 depicts a chain of relationships between the elements of a business system. An end-user or customer problem can be solved by different technologies, which produce products or services. These are delivered via distribution channels to users or customer groups, which aim at solving their customer problems, etc. Ultimately, these elements are also dimensions of design; the sequential diagram is a simplification. As the diagram shows, competitors and allies (cooperation partners, suppliers etc.) have to be included in the analysis as well, and often a differentiation under the regional aspect is necessary.

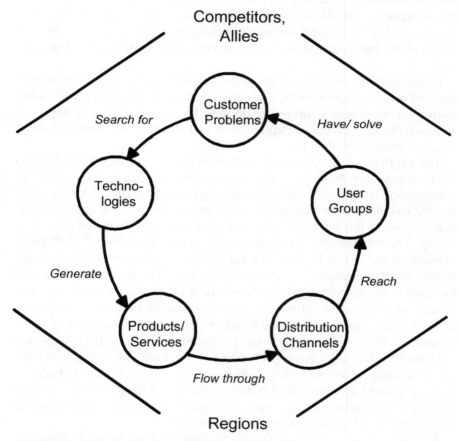

Fig. 5-3. The Generic Structure of Business Systems

In principle, this structure is applicable to any business system (generic or invariant), but the contents of each component (for example: the technology used) and the interplay among components (for example: the link between a technology and a distribution channel) are matters of design.

Applying a *systemic* approach here means optimizing the whole configuration, not individual components of it. This implies a reconsideration of the links and interactions between the elements and possibly a reframing of the whole. Such relationships can be relevant between any subset of the elements depicted in Figure 5-3, not only along the sequence highlighted. It is insightful to reflect on inventions and innovations. Take any example from the discovery and utilization of electricity to innovations which have induced substantial changes such as the personal computer, inline skates, online banking, mobile communication devices, etc. You will find that these were always based on substantial changes not only in one of the elements of the business system, but in several at the same time and in combination.

One direction in the design of business systems is the increasing importance of relationships with the customer. Customers are the most abundant source for innovations. Inventive designs for customer relationships can substantially change the perception, role and shape of the customer problem, technology, product etc.

The heuristic of the Generic Structure of Business Systems can be used for *Configuration Analysis*, comparing e.g., the configurations of different competitors. An example from the catering industry is shown in Appendix B. One can also explore scenarios and even anticipate future developments with the use of this heuristic scheme. For example, the future of the car industry: The technology is gradually moving in the direction of "distributed manufacturing" – that is, most of a car will be made in modules, which are simply snapped together in small assembly lines. The production units will be close to the consumer. Products will be built to order to a much larger extent, therewith solving the need for customized solutions and adaptation to local tastes. For some time the buyers of truck fleets have dictated to assemblers which engines, gearboxes or braking systems will go into their vehicles.[14] In this case, several elements of the business system and their interrelationships are changing, which indicates that the car industry is heading toward a fundamental transformation, including a fundamentally different distribution of roles between suppliers (who are becoming the producers), developers-marketers and distributors.

For the purpose of *Business Design* a related tool can be used (Appendix C). One proven way to proceed is to use the Generic Structure of the Business System, departing from the status quo, then developing an ideal or visionary design and finally a plan. This sequence is outlined by numbers in Appendix C. The approach used is a morphological one, related to Zwicky's Morphology, a structured creativity method used mostly in engi-

---

14   The Economist, February 23rd 2002, p. 77.

neering. It makes the space of design options palpable in a structured way; but it also helps to cope effectively with the huge complexity inherent in design problems. For example, in a design problem as outlined in Appendix B, the variety of options amounts to approximately

$$V = 4^{11} = 4'194'304$$

We have 11 dimensions (n) with roughly 4 options (z) in each. The formula used is $V = z^n$; see Chapter 2). An exact calculation which multiplies the numbers of options/modes for each dimension used in Appendix B (Product, Services/Presentation, etc.; competition is considered a given parameter, not a design variable) would result in a number of similar size, albeit larger:

$$V = 4 * 4 * 5 * 3 * 4 * 3 * 5 * 4 * 5 * 4 * 3 = 3'456'000$$

Anyway, given the size of these two numbers, applying the administrative principle that "all options must be examined as to their consequences" would be completely absurd. All the more, then, the usefulness of morphology lies in

- making visible those variants which deserve being pursued or studied further, and
- drawing attention to new possibilities.

The systematic component of the procedure is drawing the map of options – i.e., the matrix – while the more intuitive part is discovering interesting options. More detailed methods for shaping of the landscape ("landscaping") via reframing and reconfiguring value creating systems, have been proposed by Normann (2001). This concludes the part on strategy at the business level.

The support for strategy at the corporate level has grown into a relatively mature methodology as well (Pümpin 1991, Hamel/Prahalad 1994, Goold et al. 1994, Collis/Montgomery 1998, Johnson/Scholes 2002, Müller-Stewens/Lechner 2003), even though the heuristic devices available are more general and abstract in this domain. The main ideas are around building and strengthening core competencies to ensure new value potentials and on improving strategy making processes.

Long-term empirical evidence and solid conceptual reflection (Utterback 1994, Christensen 1997) cogently suggest that organizations must consistently embrace innovation even when this appears to undermine traditional strengths. The respective authors plead for continually renewing core capabilities, while abandoning the logic of past successes – innovating incrementally is not enough because in the long run the regeneration of a corporation's business relies on radical innovation. A "strategic architecture" is needed, "that is less concerned with ensuring a tight fit between goals and resources and ... more ... with creating 'stretch goals' that challenge employees to accomplish the seemingly impossible" (Hamel/ Prahalad 1994: 23). In the language used here, the requirements of building up new core competencies to ensure new value potentials may contradict those of extant value potentials, but in the long run it must be assigned priority.

Core Competencies

An organization needs many different competencies to operate efficiently and effectively. But what distinguishes a *core competency* from competencies in general? Core competencies are those few competencies on which the long-term success of an organization is founded. Barney (1991) delivers a powerful set of criteria, which allow for a precise discernment if a competency is really "core". The criteria are embedded in four questions:

1. Is the competency valuable?
2. Is it rare?
3. Is it non-substitutable?
4. Is it non-imitable?

For a competency to qualify as "core", all four criteria must be fulfilled. It is quite evident that knowledge is crucial in building core competencies. Namely the non-explicit forms of knowledge – tacit, implicit and silent knowledge are some of the synonyms used – have become prominent. James Brian Quinn, a management expert from Dartmouth College showed in his empirical studies that the intelligent enterprises are eminently characterized by their ability to combine soft factors (such as skills, knowledge and behavioral aspects in general) and hard factors (such as process organization, metrics, management systems) in unique ways (Quinn 1992, 1997). However, pulling all of these levers simultaneously tends to be just as counterproductive as a one-sided approach. The Global Organization of Business Enterprise (GLOBE) Initiative, a research project headed by Stanford's strategy professor Joel Podolny, has identified both "hard companies" (General Electric, Toyota) and "soft companies" (3M, Hewlett Packard) which have performed well. In the exploratory study, out of a set of 15, the only firm which scored high on all seven dimensions (hard: process, incentives, metrics; soft: strategy, structure, networks, culture), was Enron, the now defunct commodities trading company (London 2002).

The management of new value potentials reverts to different but also more powerful levers of control than the management of extant value potentials. This includes changing established patterns, rethinking, reframing and redesigning business systems. But it can also reside simply in the nurturing of a system of strong brands over many years, as is the case with Nestlé. This company is known for its food and drink brands – Nestlé, Buitoni, Nescafé, Maggi etc. – with worldwide activities and the rank of Switzerland's largest firm. Some of their brands are more than a hundred years old. The value of the six umbrella brands amounts to 80% of the total value of the corporation.

In the context of the knowledge economy and globalized markets, firms localized anywhere have access to resources from wherever they need them. Paradoxically, it is the local factors which are of increasing importance for competitive strength and prosperity, and even as components of core competencies. The crucial point here is how knowledge is leveraged, and this is a matter of culture: Critical components of knowledge and behavior are often embodied in old local traditions. It is quite illuminating, if Daniel Swarowski, the head of Swarowski Optics in Tyrol, Austria, a world leader in the production of high-end optical products for hunting and bird-watching, claims: "For us, the location of Tyrol was and is optimal. We cannot achieve that quality in any other country...."[15]

One faculty which has become a core competence for several international companies is the ability to build up virtuous co-operations, often with multiple allies, and in different segments of the value chain, or to form larger networks. Cooperative effectiveness is a measure of strategic fitness.

Making strategy is a process of both, *theorizing* (modeling, assessing, designing) and *practicing* (acting/ implementing). As was pointed out earlier, strategy development first and foremost is a *cognitive process* in an organization (Schwaninger 1989) – a *knowledge-gaining process* (Gälweiler 2005). No doubt, the implementation of strategies is about knowledge deployment. However, as strategies are realized, knowledge can also be developed substantially further in a continual process of organizational learning. And learning is something which is ever more a process between firms or in networks, by which allies hone their faculties and acquire new capabilities together.

The Linkage between Strategy and Profit Revisited

To sum up, in broad outline, profit is not a strategic control variable, and consequently not a strategic goal either. Rather, its appearance or absence is a consequence of good or bad strategies. This divergence from the traditional view, which regarded profit (or other monetary values statistically

---

[15] Der Kurier, August 10, 2003, p. 10.

related to it) as the fundamental corporate objective has also been expressed to a certain extent in attempts to integrate finance theory with strategic considerations. The methodologies developed for assessing shareholder value of companies calculate the economic value added or net present value – which is derived from discounted future free cash flows – which a corporation can potentially generate at a certain point in time, as a function of possible strategies (Rappaport 1998; Ehrbar 1998, Koller/ Goedhart/Wessels 2005). The crux in these assessments is not – as it may seem – the calculus, which relies on more sophisticated accounting techniques, but the proper knowledge of the *variables pre-controlling profits* and their interrelationships. Consequently, entrepreneurs and advanced top managers have established a clear priority: The precedence of the long-term over the short-term, i.e., a concentration on the basic, enduring values and the strategic focus, over short-term exigencies.

Practically speaking, strong firms assign precedence to the long-term over the short-term imperatives. For example, one of Nestlé's main strengths is its long-term perspective.[16] The best firms bet on long-term orientation and the stability of the firm, rather than focusing on shareholder value.[17]

5.4 The Normative Level

Meanwhile, insights into the referents of normative management also have improved. The research which has led to these insights is primarily based on systems theory and cybernetics. Once more, it has come up with independent criteria for the assessment of the viability and development of organizations. Note that this assessment is possible even if the specifics of the other two logical levels, operative and strategic, are not known! Viability, understood as the ability to maintain a separate existence (Beer 1979: 113), i.e., a distinct configuration which makes a system identifiable as such, can be assessed on the grounds of structural considerations which are not bound by the orientators of the strategic and operational levels.

Viability

To date, the most advanced theory for assessing the viability of an organization in functional terms is Stafford Beer's *Viable System Model* – to be

---

[16]   According to Peter Brabeck's analysis, Nestlé's CEO and later president (Financial Times, April 8, 2002: 7).
[17]   According to Michael Hilti, president of the Hilti Group (Hilti 2002a: 21).

outlined in the next chapter. This model is an excellent conceptual device for diagnosing and enhancing the viability of an organization, independent of the steering criteria of the lower logical levels (strategic and operative).

As far as the *soft factors* of an organization are concerned – referred to under the common denominator of *culture* – some models have been elaborated, which for the time being appear more appropriate for description, analysis and diagnosis than for design purposes (e.g., Deal/Kennedy 1982, Schein 1985, Hofstede 1991, Danesi & Perron 1999; see also: Frank/ Fahrbach 1999, Parkes/Bochner/Schneider 2001). Beyond that, the emerging paradigms of the learning organization (Argyris/Schön 1978; Senge 1992, Espejo et al. 1996) and of organizational knowledge (Nonaka/Takeuchi 1995, Von Krogh/ Ichijo/ Nonaka 2000) are about to outline a developmental and transformational orientation to structure, process and culture. The question about the varying degrees of viability of different cultures has hardly been asked. Therefore we shall get back to it shortly.

Beyond Viability

Is viability the ultimate goal of an organization? From a systemic point of view, a different stance is indicated. It suggests that an organization should aim at *viability beyond survival* – i.e., a viability which transcends mere maintenance of a given identity (Schwaninger 1993, 2001b). Systems thinkers have become rather prone to designing evolving structures in which an organization's identity may completely change, instead of sticking to viability in the narrow sense. That borné approach, after all, has often led to the self-maintenance or self-production of organizations which show a dysfunctional behavior vis-à-vis the larger wholes into which they are embedded. This negative effect on the larger whole has been referred to as *pathological autopoiesis* (Beer 1979), in other words ill-guided self-perpetuation[18]. Progressive managers are increasingly adopting a systemic viewpoint in which they enlarge their reference system, eliminating narrow boundaries. Development in the sense used by Russell Ackoff is a good term for the viability beyond survival advocated here. Therefore as seen in Figures 5-1 and 5-2, development has been distinguished as a higher goal in its own right.

At the level of development – defined as a system's growing ability and desire to fulfill its own and others' needs and legitimate desires (after

---

[18] Pathological autopoiesis, as used here, is the self-maintenance or self-production of a system despite (over the long term) a consequently negative balance of its effects on the larger whole.

Ackoff 1986, 1999) – the quest of an organization is indeed for viability beyond survival. If this is an organization's purpose, then a fundamental transformation of the organization becomes an imperative once this goal can no longer be achieved within the given identity or structure. In cybernetic terms, once it can no longer provide a net benefit to external stakeholders (customers, society) in its current configuration. The relevance of this conjecture is corroborated by the growing rate of structural, economic and legal transformations of companies which aim at creating new viable organizational entities. For example, the Preussag Corporation has transformed itself from a heavy industry concern into a services company called TUI and has already become the largest travel enterprise of Europe. WPP, which is the world's leading advertising firm, started as Wire and Plastics Products, a company making shopping baskets, with two people in a room[19]. Nokia, the communications giant and world leader in mobile phones, started as a sawmill and continued as a producer of rubber boots and tires, long before it entered electronics.

At the level of normative management, it can become difficult to operationalize substantive indicators for management. Yet social system theories provide important insights necessary to diagnose a system's propensity for development. This can be assessed as a function of its ethos (e.g., integrity, openness, loyalty[20]), its identity, the vision it follows. Much of this is linked to organizational culture (see above) and discernible if that culture is analyzed.

We are getting to a stage where diagnosis of the likelihood of a firm's ability to endure can be accomplished in the light of its genetic code – the constituent values and principles of its founders (Cf. Von Werder et al. 2001). For example, an innovative orientation paired with a long-term outlook and certain conservative principles such as self-determination and entrepreneurial autonomy have turned out to be a strong base for great firms such as Boeing, Siemens and Hilti, as well as a number of Swiss banks, e.g., Raiffeisen and Wegelin. Honda and Sony are two more examples, and Dassault as well, where the founder's principle was that the planes need to be beautiful, which has been followed ever since (for more details see Chapters 8 and 10).

---

[19]   This firm was founded by Sir Martin Sorrell, who continues as its chairman (The Economist, February 24th, 2001, p.77).

[20]   Firms which conceive their relationships with stakeholders as something intrinsically valuable make a difference as opposed to those which cultivate these linkages with a merely instrumental outlook (Peter Ulrich 1993, Greenhalgh 2001, Helgesen 1995, Lewis 2000).

In this context, not only the genetic code as such but also its endurance after the retirement or death of the founders can be crucial indicators of the likelihood that the firm will also prosper in the longer run. On the other hand, spectacular collapses or at least the declines of several firms (e.g., AEG, Marconi) can to a large extent be attributed to the fact that traditional values of solidity and deliberateness were given up in favor of fashionable modes such as excessive leverage via foreign capital, profit maximization and the like. In these cases, path dependence[21] imposed bounds on structures and decisions, a factor which gradually entailed inescapable trajectories of decay (cf. Arthur 1994).

As far as an organization's dynamics[22] is concerned, additional criteria such as catalytic reinforcement, instability, consensus, self-governance and organizational learning are helpful to judge whether a process of change qualifies as development or not (Etzioni 1968; Jantsch/ Waddington 1976).

In sum, the field of indicators at the normative level is multifaceted. Social, political, cultural and ecological aspects have to be taken into consideration. Adequate space must also be given to ethical and esthetical concerns for the pursuit of ideals such as beauty, truth, good and plenty (Ackoff 1981, 1999). Multiple constituents and viewpoints ascribe different purposes to a social system, which leads to varying preferences concerning the criteria of organizational fitness (Espejo/ Schwaninger 1993). For an organization to be viable in the long run, the legitimate claims of these different stakeholders must be matched[23] (Kotter / Heskett 1992). See also Chapter 8.

The pre-control aspect in this context is that an organization with a relatively high level of viability and development should in principle have a relatively high likelihood of creating value potentials over time, and ultimately of performing well.

The concept of control, which applies at the level of normative management, is in a certain sense incompatible with the understanding derived from traditional sciences – instability is no longer a feature to be eliminated completely. In a sense and to a certain extent it is a necessary and valuable precondition for development (Prigogine 1989); (self-) control

---

21 For a definition of *path dependence* see Section 5.5.

22 The label *system dynamics* in Figure 5-2 is used in a general way there. Its meaning is not confined to Forrester's methodology of System Dynamics, albeit the same can be most useful to model a multilevel control system along the lines of the MSC (CF.: Schwaninger/Ambroz/Olaya 2006).

23 The fact that conflicts between stakeholders' claims do arise and ways of dealing with them have been addressed elsewhere (e.g., in Freeman 1984, Meyer/Zucker 1989, Janisch 1992, Wheeler/Sillanpää 1997).

must nevertheless maintain instability within acceptable levels and frequencies. The coming turbulent decades will increasingly demand *control by development, control by learning or control by transformation*[24]. Experienced businessmen and academics who assert that learning is the top corporate asset (e.g., de Geus 1997) lend support to this assumption.

5.5 Relationships between the three Levels

This concludes our survey of the goals and control variables of organizational management. It must be noted that they cannot be compared in every respect, since they belong to three different logical levels; ultimate consistency can be achieved within but not between these levels[25]. The variables regulated at one level are the pre-control parameters for the next level down. One corollary of the pre-control relationship is path dependency – the binding effect of past decisions and structures: What can be achieved at the level of value creation over time hinges on – i.e., is enabled or restricted by the prerequisites built up (or not) at earlier stages.

The feedback loop from lower to higher referents (Figures 5-1, 5-2) signifies at least two aspects:

1. Lower-level outcomes (e.g., liquidity, profit) impinge on the higher-level referents insofar as they can further or restrain the respective goals.
2. Additionally changes in operations (e.g., subcontracting) and ecological or social stakes may lead to changes in inherent or control risk.

The two figures illustrate that operational, strategic and normative management are by no means three subsystems detached from each other; rather, each higher level envelops those below it. However, a rigid view of this embeddedness would be too static. If a normative framework expresses a certain identity, this encapsulates a huge set of possible strategies. Nevertheless, at a certain stage strategy making may find new ways of relating to the environment, which may reach out beyond the borders of the identity defined by the actual normative framework. In many companies, such attempts are a priori out of the question - a trait of narrowness, which sooner or later turns out to be pathological. Even the distinctive fea-

---

[24]   The terms in italics should be read with the prefix *self-*, i.e., as *self-control by (self-)development, self-control by learning, self-control by (self-) transformation,* to indicate the priority of intrinsic control (or eigen-control) over extrinsic control.

[25]   In logical terms, the strategic level offers a metalanguage to the operative level, and the normative offers one to the strategic and the operative levels.

tures of an identity and its normative implications must be reviewed over time. Most industries are subject to fundamental change; boundaries between industries collapse, so organizational intelligence demands reinventing the company, abolishing outdated recipes of success (called *"unlearning"* by Hedberg 1981) and building new competencies. Constant creative tension between normative management and strategy making are necessary for a company to evolve. The pertinent connection is not an algorithmic one, but must instead express itself in a strenuous process of organizational discourse. In a large study Collins and Porras have given an empirical account of this „dynamic interplay between core ideology and the drive for progress" (Collins/ Porras 1994: 85).

Figures 5-1 and 5-2 further demonstrate that the relevant time horizon increases from operational to normative management. At the same time, the factual horizon is also extended, as is the complexity which is to be coped with. The dotted arrow indicates that certain principles relevant to normative management or the values for which a firm stands (e.g., ethical and aesthetic ones) can be largely timeless. Take for example the values of trust, quality, security and discretion, which have been key to the success of Swiss banking.

The diagrams also show that the concerns of the higher levels are linked to those of the lower ones. A company can survive only if it is in possession of value potentials that are realized, that is, converted into value. An equilibrium between the sacrifices incurred in building up value potentials and the reaping of their fruits is a further necessary precondition of viability, which normative management has to ensure.

5.6 Criteria of Systemic Effectiveness

At the three levels of management different criteria of organizational fitness – or, to use a more general term, systemic effectiveness – apply:

1. At the operative level, the criterion is efficiency, mainly in terms such as quality, productivity and profitability.
2. At the strategic level, it is effectiveness in both the competitive and the co-operative sense[26].
3. At the normative level it is legitimacy, defined as the ability to fulfill the legitimate claims of all relevant stakeholders.

In other words, a different language is needed for dealing with the issues of each level; each one of them obeys a distinct logic.

---

[26]   The best is being unique, which also means having no competitors at all.

Efficiency is very much an inward-looking goal; it adjusts the functioning of the system to criteria established on higher logical levels. The degree of this adjustment can be measured consecutively in terms of benefits provided through ongoing activities or, as Jan Carlzon (1987) – former CEO of SAS[27] – put it, at the "moments of truth":

- With the customer via products and services ("customer value"),
- With the "owners" via financial value ("shareholder value", dividends etc.)
- With employees via monetary and non-monetary benefits (pay, a good workplace, qualification etc.)
- With society via social benefit (employment, taxes etc.)
- With society and future generations via ecological benefits (sustaining or even "restoring" the environment[28]).

The strategic referents as outlined in Figures 5-1 and 5-2 link the internal perspective with the needs of the external environment - the market in the first place. The shorthand distinction between efficiency as "doing things right" and effectiveness as "doing the right things"[29], while it is not perfect, does convey metaphors that trigger insight and is therefore used in Figure 5-2. *Effectiveness* is a measure of the longer-term adaptation to those needs, and can be measured by indicators which reflect such aspects as market position, critical success factors, core competencies and innovation. These are often fuzzier measures, but their assessment can be accomplished as systematically as that of operational variables, given the advanced state of the theory of strategic management. Based on the PIMS-studies mentioned earlier, and his own work, Malik (2001a), an experienced consultant and outstanding management thinker, has proposed a catalogue of crucial indicators for general managers which embrace both, the strategic effectiveness and operational efficiency of a business. According to him, a system of indicators should first and foremost inform about:

1. Competitive position
2. Innovative performance
3. Productivity
4. Attractiveness for human resources

---

[27] Scandinavian Airline System.

[28] The concept of *restorative ecological management* was coined by Ray Anderson, chairman of the Interface Group (Anderson 1998).

[29] These definitions go back to Peter F. Drucker, the eminent thinker on management (Drucker 1977).

5. Cash flow / liquidity
6. Profit / profitability.

Finally, the criterion of *legitimacy* used at the level of normative management relates the organization to its socio-cultural context and brings to the fore the role of multiple stakeholders. It is even compatible with those stakeholder-oriented frameworks that define an organization as a system of multiple constituents (e.g., Mitroff 1983). If stakeholders are considered the sources of wealth (Post/ Preston/ Sachs 2002), then priority is with customers, employees and financiers.

The ultimate "indicator" of systemic effectiveness is the quality of the management itself, which has to keep the control variables of all three logical levels under control simultaneously (See next Section). Traditionally, a broadly shared view held that a company's performance was largely dictated by "the fundamental economics" of the industry it was in. Recent research, however, has shown that good management can produce a star performance whatever the sector. A team at INSEAD, the French business school, concludes that industry factors are very powerful for the typical average performers, while for the stars and the dogs of the sector company-specific factors predominate (Hawawini/ Verdin/ Subramanian 2003). Outstanding companies are really different; the average ones find it much harder to escape the industry cage (Martin 2002).

5.7 Revisiting the Feedback Cycle

At this point some readers may ask where the management feedback cycle, outlined in Chapter 3, has gone. Therefore it makes sense to revisit it, particularly for those who are interested in the conceptual specifics of our subject.

As has been shown, the key duty of an integral or systemic management is to meet all three requirements – efficiency, effectiveness and legitimacy – in the long run. In order to achieve such a delicate task a corporation will require – as has been illustrated – considerably more developed mental models than established ones and more complex control systems than the simple feedback systems traditionally used.

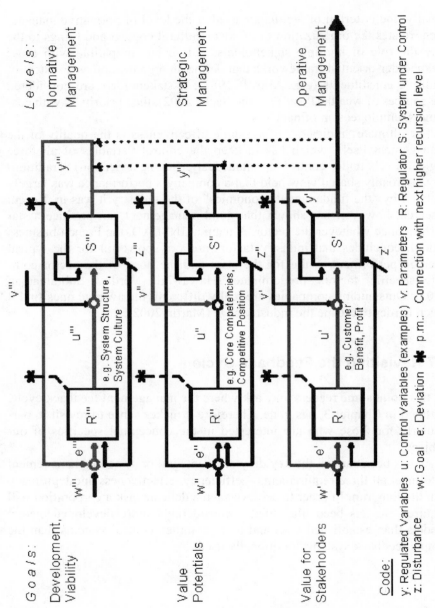

Fig. 5-4. Integral Management as a multilevel control cycle (abridged diagram for a recursion level y)

In terms of feedback loops the hierarchy of control variables delineated above results in a multilevel control structure (Figure 5-4). This clarifies the fact that one and the same state of affairs cannot be pre-controlled by means of the variables, by which it is controlled[30]. If, at the operative level of a firm, control is for example exercised in the interest of profit – by means of revenues and costs – then profit cannot be pre-controlled by means of these traditional accounting variables. For pre-control other kinds of referents are required – existing and new value potentials, which in turn are pre-controlled by viability and development. In Figure 5-4 this relationship is represented by the solid lines, which connect each cycle with the one immediately before it. A closure of the hierarchy of control variables is provided insofar as the outcomes at the operative level not only result from higher level pre-controls, but also pre-control higher level parameters in a specific sense[31]. For instance, not only the innovative capabilities but also the actually available liquid financial resources might play an important role in the building-up of value potentials – at least, the substantial funds directly on hand can add a degree of freedom to that process.[32]

5.8 An Application Perspective

The roots of the MSC date back to the early eighties[33], when its first versions were developed. Since then it has been expounded not only to generations of managers in the context of leadership seminars and consulting projects but also to future managers in my work as a university professor. A substantial number of students have made use of it in their master's and doctoral dissertations. In this way it has spread to many organizations. But all of this also has triggered a process of discourse in which the MSC has

---

[30] It has been argued (Jackson 1989: 428) that the use of *control models* prevents organizational learning, leading to "increasing dominance of history" (De Zeeuw 1986: 139). A concept of control that embraces development as a goal defies this argument in principle, although it cannot guarantee that there will be learning in every organization striving for development.

[31] This closure is a significant feature of models of social systems which adequately reproduce their dynamic patterns of behavior: They are made up of closed loops, as in the case for example in *System Dynamics* models (Forrester 1961, Richardson 1999, Sterman 2000).

[32] Anyhow, the availability of financial resources is on average only a "slightly significant" constraint to corporate development, as a survey of 1000 small- and medium-sized UK firms indicates (Cosh/Hughes 2000).

[33] The MSC was first published in Schwaninger 1984.

been improved, although the basic logic and the crucial categories have not changed. The schemes presented in this chapter are the most up to date version of this work in progress.

Intelligent organizations distinguish themselves from others by meeting all three criteria to a high degree – efficiency, effectiveness and legitimacy. They are led in a systemic way, i.e., so that the control variables of all three logical levels are *simultaneously kept under control* over time, despite the contradictions that may occur between them. Only a model of integral management can dissolve such conflicts. It is my consistent experience from many of these application situations that the conceptual schemes of the MSC are most helpful in:

1. Overcoming conflicts in matters of leadership and
2. Building better simulation and optimization models[34].

The important point here is not to recapitulate the details of these applications but to point out the strengths of the MSC. First, it is a framework which helps sort out the complexity of managerial situations in new ways. It enables the triage of relevant variables according to their role in the logical structure of control aspects. These aspects are to be considered along the sequence of pre-control relationships which make up the structure that underlies the patterns of behavior ultimately generated by a social system[35] Some of the applications have been documented in publications (e.g., Schwaninger 1988, 1989, 1993; Espejo/Schuhmann/Schwaninger 1996; Reyes 2000; Teuta Gómez/Espinosa 2000).

Second, the MSC serves as a precise instrument to orient the structuring of more detailed models. The advantage here is in overcoming the oft-lamented deficit of highly sophisticated simulation models, which lack theoretical grounding. Several applications in which I have been personally involved have been documented in publications. Four examples:

1. A microworld on the issue of *environmentally responsible management* was designed and implemented in a System Dynamics Model[36], for the

---

[34] Such a simulation model has been published in: Schwaninger/Ambroz/Olaya 2006.

[35] This is why the basic structure of the MSC has also been adopted in the St. Gallen Management Framework, which is the conceptual framework for management education and research at the University of St. Gallen. For details, Schwaninger 2001a.

[36] System Dynamics is a widely used methodology for the modeling and simulation of complex systems, developed by Prof. Jay Forrester at MIT– Massachusetts Institute of Technology (Forrester 1961). System Dynamics models are made up of closed feedback loops and the systems modeled are

purpose of training. This model showed that the dynamics of a firm can be modeled in a sophisticated way – capturing such diverse aspects as market, technology and production, human resources, ecology, and finance – in a small model with about 70 variables (Schwaninger 2003b).

2. A more complex model with about 200 variables was implemented for the purpose of giving the steering committee of the *Regional Innovation and Technology Transfer System* in Aachen, Germany, a decision support tool to understand and guide the development of the system at hand. This was part of a project called into being and financed by the EU (European Union). The results have been documented in Rios/Schwaninger 1996 and Schwaninger 1997.

3. A small model was used in the assessment of the *Impact of the Construction of a New Train Connection*, a high-duty and high-speed track leading through a tourist region, the Gasteinertal of Austria. The influence on the economic and social development of that valley and its resorts was captured in a much more sophisticated way than the alternative calculus by means of a spreadsheet. Both calculations were based on advanced techniques of economic modeling (hedonic price function, calculations of social costs etc.) but only the SD model enabled a cogent assessment of the dynamic implications of the different variants of the project envisaged. The calculations were part of the report submitted to the Ministry of Transportation of Austria, which ultimately led to the implementation of the ecologically least damaging option available. The full report (Schwaninger/Laesser 2000) has not been published, but accounts of the project and its outcomes are available to the public (Laesser et al. 2002; Schwaninger, forthcoming).

4. A relatively large model was elaborated in a famous pharmaceutical company, which is part of Johnson & Johnson. The model encapsulates the essential decision variables of the management. It was elaborated in a group model-building process, involving people from multiple sites of the company. The model-building exercise was accompanied by an introduction to System Dynamics and the elaboration of a number of

---

simulated as continuous processes, i.e., the mathematics of the models are based on differential equations. SD is particularly apt for the discernment of a system's dynamic patterns of behavior, which may be "counterintuitive" (Forrester 1971). This calls for applications to situations and problems as confronted by general management. For example, strategic issues can be modeled very efficiently and trigger important insights by means of the *System Dynamics* methodology (Sterman 2000. See also: Theme 6.63 on System Dynamics, in: EOLSS–The Encyclopedia for Life Support Systems, edited by UNESCO, available under: www.eolss.com/).

smaller models for diverse purposes. The whole process led to a convergence of the management of the company toward a new paradigm of management, in which decision support through dynamic simulation models became crucial. The process and its results are documented in Schwaninger/ Janovjak/ Ambroz 2006.

Third, the MSC can help avoid one of the main traps, namely, insufficiently underpinned decisions. This is particularly important in strategic and normative management. As the "soft factors" are prominent at these levels, the decisions taken are often vague. Assumptions have not been sufficiently examined and discussions lack rigor. The MSC framework, but also SD models, make the pertinent issues – e.g., the examination of assumptions, the answers to "What-if" questions, etc. – more transparent and help a rigorous approach to these important matters. "Rigorous" here has nothing to do with rigidity, but stands for discipline in thinking and in discourse.

5.9 Intermediate Summary and Outlook

In this chapter the Model of Systemic Control has been presented. The MSC outlines the three logical levels of control with their pre-control relationships. These are the three different "languages" to be mastered by a control system of any organization, in order to deal with dynamic complexity effectively: Intelligent organizations keep the variables of all three levels under control simultaneously.

Today the potential of the MSC to enhance organizational intelligence is higher than it has ever been. The world of private firms in particular is plagued by a high degree of disorientation, which after all is the preeminent form of organizational "dementia".

Research by A.T. Kearney Inc., a renowned consulting firm, indicates that large companies' efforts have been focused dominantly on the short term, as opposed to the long term. The CEO of A.T. Kearney summarizes, "We have learned that despite an 8.5 per cent increase in R&D investment in recent years by the top Fortune companies, their 10-year-average revenue gain generated by that investment is less than one percent. Why? Because most of it goes towards meeting the incremental needs of today's customers instead of creating tomorrow's customers by investing in breakthrough products." (Steingraber 1998: 106). Similarly, Helmut Maucher, the former president of the International Chamber of Commerce and chairman of Nestlé, alerts us in an interview to the drawbacks of an increasingly „short-term perspective" and the „excessive power of the financial people" in contemporary firms (Maucher 1998: 29).[37] And Harvard's Michael Porter adds that "the single biggest error that most companies make is to focus on operational excellence" only, "rather than true strategy" (Porter 2002).

These signs do not differ much from earlier, equally alarming ones. A team of leading researchers from M.I.T. at the end of the eighties observed that American industry had been "handicapped by shrinking time horizons and a growing preoccupation with short-term profits" (Berger et al, 1989: 25). All of these statements might seem too old to be cited. However, in the new century and millennium, everything appears to be going on in the same way. Thomas Dohonue, president of the US Chamber of Commerce, warned the practice of companies' quarterly guidance on earnings had fostered short-term thinking among both analysts and companies: "Together, we have all allowed a system where everyone's incentives – those of analysts, management, and investors – are designed to produce results today at the expense of tomorrow."[38]

The iron law still holds, that *short-termism damages corporations*. But investors misguided by their short-term thinking continue leading the fates of companies astray. The authors just cited asked why firms are "less willing than their rivals to live through a period of heavy investment and meager returns in order to build expertise" back in the eighties Yet this question is more up-to-date than ever. The speculative spree in the U.S. culminated at the end of the nineties. At the end of 1999, an analyst cited in the Wall Street Journal declared: "In a knowledge-based economy, there are no constraints to growth" (Krugman 2001). In early 2000 the stock market, as measured by Standard & Poor's 500 Index, traded at 39 times profit, i.e., three times the average of the period between 1946 and 1996 (Samuelson 2001). Yahoo stocks, which hit a high of $250, fell to about $25 in late 2000. The NASDAQ, an index of technological stock values, hit its high at 5.048,62 points on March 10, 2000; it fell below 2000 within one year (1.966,41 by March 12, 2001).

By early 2001, the physical consequences of this boom-and-bust pattern had already hit the economy hard. To quote just one example (Krugman 2001), California suffered a crisis of power supply costing the state $8 billion or more. This resulted from pervasive market manipulation by energy companies creating power shortages in order to drive up prices and profits,

---

[37] An impressive case in point was analyzed by the Britisch economist John Kay, who attributed the crisis at both Railtrack and Marks and Spencer's to the common pattern "that growth in earnings won at the cost of long-run competitive advantage" (Kay 2001: 12).

[38] Financial Times, March 8, 2006, p. 22.

as a report of the U.S. Federal Energy Regulatory Commission showed[39]. But it was also a crisis of underinvestment, "a booming state economy undone because nobody built the power plants and gas pipelines it needed. And at least part of the reason for that underinvestment was the excessive enthusiasm of the financial markets for all things tech.[40] .... The tech bust and the energy crisis are two sides of the same coin. Both reflect the fallout from an infatuation with the new that made people unmindful of the old" (ibidem; see also Ford 2001). In the early 2000s, a number of spectacular declines and collapses of corporations happened, which were causally linked to short-termist management approaches: Enron, Marconi, Tyco and ABB are just a few examples from the long list of corporate declines due to a rigid financial logic driving out sound business practice.

All of this may remind one of John Ruskin's lament, put forward one and a half centuries ago: "We pour our whole masculine energy into the false business of money-making" (1865: 88). Well, private firms always have to "make money", but that is not their business. Organizations are in *the business of solving customer problems*, be they individual needs such as nutrition, health or locomotion, or the social and ecological problems faced by our world. These kinds of functions and purposes bestow upon organizations their very *raison d'être*.

Firms have an inherent tendency to keep themselves alive. They survive if they are not brought to ruin by a destructive force. More often than not this destructive force is management itself. Conversely, good management can build marvelous organizations which create value for their customers and owners, being excellent employers and "good citizens" at the same time. Much of this ability hinges on the models by which these companies are managed. It is less a lack of leadership skill than a shortage of conceptual understanding and wisdom on behalf of its managers, which triggers organizational decay. Sometimes the reason is unfettered greed (paired with hubris) driving out reason.

Models, knowledge, wisdom and the higher logical levels of management have been emphasized in this chapter. It would be wrong to conclude that efficiency at the operational level is unimportant. Only prolific execution can close the virtuous cycle that runs from viability to potential to value and so on (Figure 5-5).

---

[39]   New York Times, March 28, 2003, p. A17.
[40]   This factor adds up with regulatory failures.

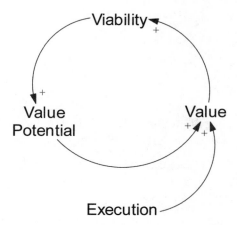

Fig. 5-5. A virtuous cycle connecting operative, strategic and normative levels

The scheme in Figure 5-5 is a specification with respect to the circular aspect of the MSC, as already visible in Figures 5-1 and 5-2. It visualizes the fact that high performance on the execution side is a crucial feature of intelligent organizations. The scheme is quite instructive: If the link from Execution to Value would be multiplicative, with Execution being zero or negative, the achieved Value would equally be zero or negative, independently of the level of Value Potential[41]. In this case strategic volition would be completely powerless.

The MSC indeed has a great deal to contribute to a higher level of organizational intelligence in practice.

---

[41] A more realistic approximation would be as follows: Let us assume 1 as the default value–denoting a normal situation–for all four variables in the scheme, and a multiplicative relationship between them. If Execution is inferior to 1, then Value will deteriorate, and so will Viability and Value Potential. As a dynamic simulation would show, the deterioration can be incisive and catastrophic.

Chapter 6 Structure – Preconditions for Effective Action

"Form ever follows function."

Louis Sullivan, American architect[1]

This chapter is about the second dimension of our framework, namely structure. The previous chapter dealt with the control parameters required for managing complexity. That picture still begs the question of how an organization must be structured to make its (self-) control and (self-) development possible. Organizational Cybernetics offers a model for this very purpose, the Viable System Model by Stafford Beer. This model has been extensively documented and widely applied. It will be briefly outlined at the outset (Sections 6.1. and 6.2.) and then be brought together with different concepts that are important for the organizations of the future (Sections 6.3 to 6.11.) – these include network organization, heterarchy, the virtual organization and project management. To date in the literature all of these topics have been tackled very much in a pragmatic sense. I am convinced that Organizational Cybernetics and the VSM, which are rather theoretical in nature, will be necessary components for dealing with these concepts in a fertile manner. As such a combination had been missing, I have explored these concepts in the light of cybernetic models over the last years, to leverage them on the basis of innovative theoretical grounds. The major part of the present chapter is a synopsis of the most important results of this effort in applied research, which has involved multiple applications across all kinds of organizations, private, public, large and small, as well as in different countries and continents.

6.1 The Viable System Model (VSM)

In search of a robust general approach for the design of organizations, Stafford Beer, the father of Management Cybernetics, came up with a set-theoretic model (Beer 1962) in which he defined the organizational pre-

---

[1]   Quoted in The Economist, March 24th, 2001, p. 114.

requisites for the viability of systems. This was later operationalized in a topological model, known as the VSM – Viable Systems Model (Beer 1979, 1981, 1985). In this model a set of management functions is distinguished which provide the „necessary and sufficient conditions" (Beer 1984) for the viability of any human or social system (Figure 6-1). These functions and their interrelationships are specified in a comprehensive theory, the propositions of which can be summarized as follows:

1. Components of the model:

An organization is viable if and only if it exhibits a set of management functions with a specific set of interrelationships, identified and formalized in the model:

- *System 1:* Regulatory capacity of the basic units (A, B, C, D), autonomous adaptation to their environment, optimization of ongoing business (e.g., the business areas of a company).
- *System 2:* Amplification of self-regulatory capacity, attenuation of oscillations and co-ordination of activities via information and communication (e.g., information systems, service units and co-ordination teams, standards of behavior, knowledge bases).
- *System 3:* Management of the collective of primary units (basic units with regulatory capacity), establishment of an overall optimum among basic units, providing for synergies as well as resource allocation (e.g., the executive corporate management).
- *System 3*:* Investigation and validation of information flowing between Systems 1-3 and 1-2-3 via auditing/monitoring activities (e.g., operations analysts, special studies and surveys).
- *System 4:* Management of the development of the organization, dealing with the future – especially the long term – and with the overall outside environment, diagnosis and modeling of the organization in its environment (e.g., corporate development, strategy, research and knowledge creation).
- *System 5:* Balancing present and future as well as internal and external perspectives; moderation of the interaction between Systems 3 and 4; ascertaining the identity of the organization and its role in its environment; embodiment of supreme values, norms and rules – the ethos of the system (normative management).

In this structure, the primary units (basic units with the regulatory capacity supplied by System 1) must dispose of high autonomy in order to be able to adapt to their respective environment or milieu. The combined activities of Systems 1, 2 and 3 (including 3*) provide for management of the present and short term, while System 4 is the fulcrum for long-term adaptation and System 5 is the embodiment of the ethos – the basic principles governing the orientation of the organization as a whole.

Systems 1-2-3 (including 3*) comprise the operative level, System 4 in interaction with System 3 the strategic level, and System 5 the normative level of management. These correspond to the three logical levels of management as outlined under the Model of Systemic Control (Chapter 5).

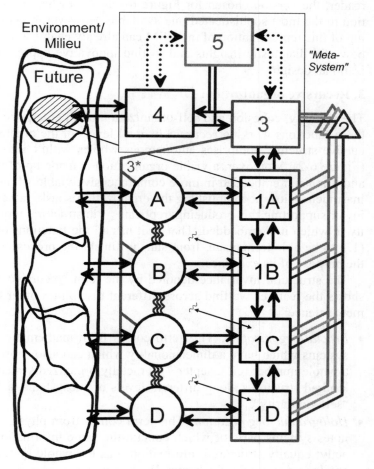

Fig. 6-1. The Viable System Model – Overview[2]

---

[2]   This is a slightly adapted version. For the full-fledged original please see: Beer 1985: 136; Beer 1979, 1981.

2. Diagnostic power:

Any deficiencies in this system, e.g., missing functions, insufficient capacity of the functions and faulty communications or interactions between them, weaken or jeopardize the viability of the organization. The VSM can be represented in different degrees of detail. To avoid overloading the reader, the version chosen for Figure 6-1 is somewhat simplified in relation to the most sophisticated one available. However, a good understanding of this representation of the VSM can already enable a manager to gain powerful diagnostic insights and to find innovative approaches to organizational design.

3. Recursive organization:

The viability, cohesion and self-organization of an enterprise depend upon these functions working *recursively at* all levels of the organization. A recursive structure comprises autonomous wholes within autonomous units (Figure 6-2). Moreover, a viable organization is made up of viable wholes and it is itself embedded in more comprehensive viable wholes. Each unit, inasmuch as it is accomplishing the organization's task, rather than servicing or supporting this producing, replicates – in structural terms – the totality in which it is embedded. That is, it has all the functions outlined under (1.), to be able to manage, from start to finish, the processes which serve the purpose of its existence.

The structural invariance denoted by the term "recursive organization" shows the features we find across different disciplines other than management science:

- *Fractal organization:* This term comes from mathematics and denotes systems which have a dimensionality which can also show a fraction of a whole number (cf. Chapter 7). Fractally organized systems perpetuate kindred structures along different levels of subsystems, a feature called "self-similarity".
- *Holographic organization:* This term comes from physics, where it denotes systems parts of which contain the same information – more exactly: equally structured information – as the whole system, albeit in a condensed fashion (cf. Chapter 7).

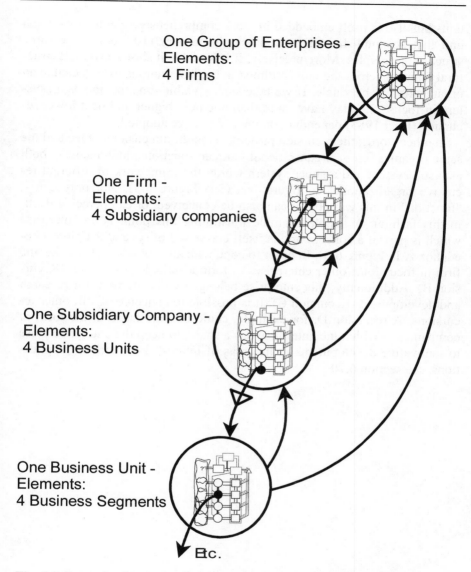

One Group of Enterprises -
Elements:
4 Firms

One Firm -
Elements:
4 Subsidiary companies

One Subsidiary Company -
Elements:
4 Business Units

One Business Unit -
Elements:
4 Business Segments

Etc.

Fig. 6-2. Recursive Structure of Viable Organizations (after Beer 1979)

6.2 On Recursive Organization Design

A recursive structure comprises autonomous units within other autonomous units. Moreover, a viable organization is not only made up of viable units but also is itself embedded in more comprehensive viable units. Each unit that accomplishes the organization's primary tasks obeys the same structural principles. More precisely, if it is viable it shows invariant structural features across the units outlined in the last sections, which enable an organization to be viable. If we take such a viable organization as a „system-in-focus", it „may have more than one next higher and next lower recursion (Beer 1985) depending on the perspective adopted.

In other words, the recursion principle is multi dimensional. One and the same organization or organizational unit can function simultaneously both as a sub system and a super system within the framework of different recursive organizational configurations (See Figure 6-3). Not only can it "function" in this way, but it can also be conceived, or can perceive itself, in this fashion. A simple example illustrating this point is an enterprise which is part of a concern and is itself composed of several divisions (Recursion A in Figure 6-3). In order to cope with an ecological challenge, the firm in focus joins other enterprises to form a suitable association (Recursion B). Additionally, this enterprise belongs to a consortium for research and development (Recursion C). It is possible to conceive of still other recursions. A recursion D, for example, could be introduced in the form of companies in which the enterprise has a share, to keep the enterprise close to innovative developments in its areas of interest. For pertinent applications, see section 6.10.

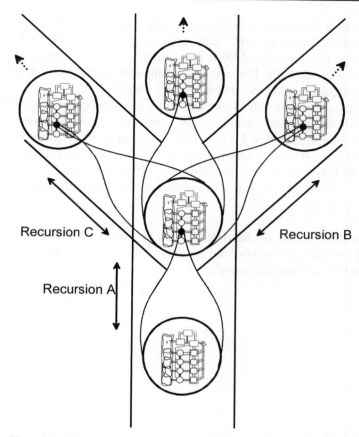

Fig. 6-3. The concept of recursion is multidimensional (Schwaninger 1994, 2000b)

According to the VSM all three levels of management – operative, strategic, normative – are distributed functions, with aspects such as control, intelligence and ethos being properties of the system as a whole, inherent in all levels of recursion.

6.3 Recursion and Heterarchy

Finally, recursions do not necessarily run "from top to bottom"; they can also be circular. In other words, recursive and heterarchical relationships are compatible (Schwaninger 1994, 2000b). In a system of concerted mutual controls, e.g., in the context of alliances and holdings, it is possible to have a configuration as illustrated in Figure 6-4. This scheme, which shows one subset of a more comprehensive network, illustrates how companies can be "locked" into each other across the recursion levels V to Z. The company at the recursion level W is a subsidiary of the company at the recursion level V, and so on. The company at the recursion level Y is a joint venture of companies at the recursion levels X1 and X2.

A paradox crops up in this scheme in the sense that company 1 is at once "great grandmother" and "daughter" of company 5. An analogous situation characterizes companies 2 to 5. This situation is in conformity with the paradox of the recursion levels relating to each other as follows. The following formula says that V contains W, which contains X1 etc. Summing up, Z is contained in V and at the same time V is contained in Z:

$$V \supset W \supset X1 \supset Y \supset Z \supset V$$

It is obvious that the solution of the paradox lies in the fact that here we have a case of a circular recursion (from a certain point of view, this can also be called a self referential recursion).

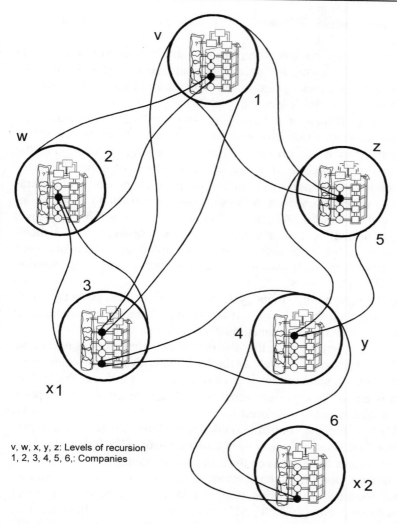

v, w, x, y, z: Levels of recursion
1, 2, 3, 4, 5, 6,: Companies

Fig. 6-4. Recursive and Heterarchical Relationships of Control are Compatible
(Schwaninger 1994, 2000b)

6.4 Embodiments of Recursive Management

At this point, the *Model of Systemic Control and the Viable System Model*
can be tied together. It will be shown that this linkage enables the distrib-

uted management which is implicit in the notion of organizational intelligence.

The most important consideration in this context is as follows: there is an inexorable need not only for operational but also for strategic and normative management to take place in any subsystem of an organization, in so far as it has to meet the criterion of viability.

The cybernetic theory of organization advocated here contradicts the oft-encountered opinion that "vision is the concern of the entrepreneur" or "strategy is the duty of the board of directors". Vision is a function of the meta-system – to be precise, it is one of the functions of normative management which must be part of the meta-system of every viable unit. Strategic thinking is necessary even in the smallest units, if such units are conceived as viable wholes. All three "languages" – those of operative, strategic and normative management – must be "spoken" in the meta-system of any one of these units. This is the structuralist foundation for humanistic postulates such as autonomy, meaningful work, participation and self-fulfillment.

It is also the reason why "meta-systems" of management have to turn to orientators other than those of the corresponding "systems" of management (i.e., the units in charge of managing the individual basic activities). In small units, it is often the case that the operative, strategic and normative functions of management as well as the basic activities are discharged by the same persons. In spite of this, it is vital for any unit in focus that it does not restrict itself to the operating functions (always under the assumption that the unit concerned is supposed to be viable). Such a system must be led in such a way that the control variables of all three levels are taken into consideration and simultaneously kept under control. This holds true even when contradictions arise between these control variables.

It is incumbent upon the management at each recursion level to define for its purposes the specific orientators in a level-appropriate manner and to realize a correspondingly "integral" leadership. Figure 6-5 illustrates this aspect, which is a key to *recursive management*. Starting from the MSC (Figures 5-1 and 5-2), a scheme of the regulatory variables and orientators is presented in terms of examples for three recursion levels consisting of an enterprise, a subsidiary company and a business unit.

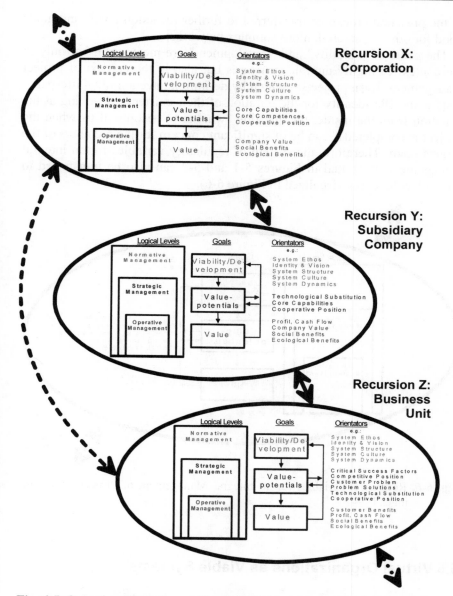

Fig. 6-5. Operative, Strategic and Normative Management as Distributed Functions (Schwaninger 2000a)

The dotted line illustrates the point that for a given unit, information about units at recursion levels other than those in the immediate neighborhood can also be of relevance. This line also indicates that in principle the logic of the presentation can be transferred to further recursion levels and holds good for other structured, more complex networks.

The goals of "viability" and "development" are meaningful not only in the context of highly durable structures but also in the context of project management. Even projects – which by definition have a limited lifespan – need a specific identity for the duration of their existence. Looking at the situation from the inside, the question "what is to become of us when the project is completed?" can be of significant concern for the members of the project team. Therefore, the system of regulatory variables for an integral management illustrated in Figures 5-1 and 5-2 can also be transferred to the project level (as visualized in Figure 6-6).

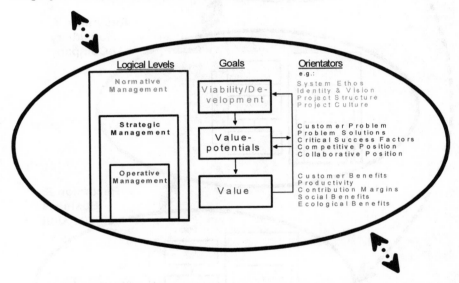

Fig. 6-6. Reference Variables for an Integral Management of Projects (Schwaninger 1994)

6.5 Virtual Organizations as Viable Systems

The same logic also applies to "virtual organizations". Colloquially this term is mostly used with regard to non-bricks organizations. However, it is useful to clarify the concept.

Virtual stands for "existing or resulting in essence or effect though not in actual fact, form, or name" or "existing in the mind, especially as a product of the imagination."[3] The term is derived from the Latin word "virtus" meaning virile force or manly spirit, and later "virtue". In principle, a virtual organization is capable of manifesting its potential through the most diverse variants. This would mean, for example, that from available resources project teams are formed in many different constellations, tailor made according to the task that needs to be accomplished. With this definition the meaning of the word "available" can be expanded almost indefinitely. What is not available "in house" can be acquired through outsourcing, partnerships and co-operation.

The definition of the Virtual Corporation refers to "a temporary network of independent companies – suppliers, customers, even erstwhile rivals – linked by information to share skills, costs and access to one another's markets." (Byrne/ Brandt/ Port 1993). To transform this idea into realistic ventures, the concept of the *Virtual Factory (VF)* has emerged (Schuh/ Millarg/Göransson 1998). In distinction from the extreme of a lack of any structural framework, the VF is based on a durable cooperation platform. From this stable pool of partner firms multifarious configurations are formed flexibly in order to fulfill specific tasks (orders or commissions). This is shown in Figure 6-7.

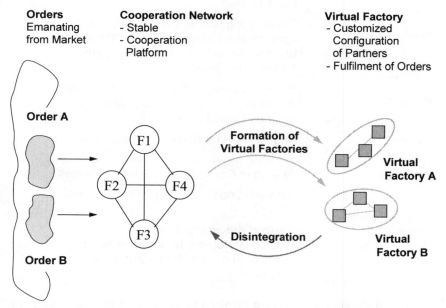

Fig. 6-7. The Concept of the Virtual Factory (in extension of Schuh 1997)

---

[3]   The Free Dictionary.com.

In the case of the "Virtual Factory Euregio Bodensee" which was formed among 25 firms located in the region of Lake Constance – in Austria, Germany and Switzerland – a number of organizational roles to be assumed in the network was defined (for details see Schwaninger/ Friedli 2002). At a later stage, a diagnosis realized on the basis of the VSM was carried out. This primarily helped to clarify the different roles. Then it led to a theory-based reorganization, the outline of which is briefly summarized in Table 6-1.

Table 6-1. Embodiments of the Functions of a Viable System in a Virtual Factory with 25 Partner Firms (after Schwaninger/Friedli 2002)

Components & Management Functions of Viable Systems	Embodied by ... at First Level of Recursion of the Virtual Organization
Basic Units	Partner Firms or Parts thereof (n=1-25)
System 1	Managements of Participating Firms or Parts thereof
System 2	Rules of the Game, Broker, Order Manager, Network-Coach, Quality Standards, Budgeting- and Information Systems, Technology Database
System 3	Product Manager, Executive Committee (Management by Objectives, Management by Exception)
System 3*	Auditor, special studies and investigations
System 4	Executive Committee, Innovation Circles, Network-Coach, Strategic Planning and Control
System 5	General Assembly, Statutes, Identity & Mission Statement (and pertinent discourse), Supreme Norms and Shared Values

The new organizational structure on the one hand entailed huge gains in terms of the efficiency and effectiveness of the cooperation among the partner firms. On the other hand and even more importantly, a new identity of the VF emerged. Not only did the cohesion of the network grow and the coherence of its image in the market improve substantially. Beyond this, what had started as a mere stock exchange of capacities grew into a powerful, integrated enterprise, all within four years.

6.6 Networks as Viable Systems

Increasingly, enterprises or parts of them are constituting themselves as networks, which tend to replace the traditional hierarchical forms (cf. Malone 2004). Figure 6-8 provides a schematic illustration of an example. This scheme represents an enterprise where five subsidiary companies are united under one holding. The diagram shows that not all command emanates from the holding but rather that many directive functions affecting the entire enterprise are located in the subsidiaries. Thus, the subsidiary *company* S3 has the overall responsibility for *branch A* and *region II* and also leadership in marketing as far as customer *group i* is concerned; the subsidiary *company S1* is responsible for *branch C* and *region I*, and so on.

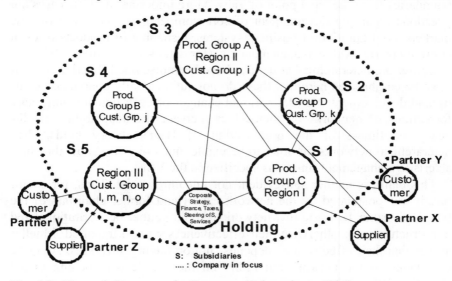

Fig. 6-8. Network Structure of a Company (Schwaninger 1994)

The networking in this enterprise is not "total" in the sense that any unit can be coupled with any other unit arbitrarily, but it is still rather structured. This means that there are well-defined points of emphasis and linkages, which, however, can still shift to form new configurations. The principle of structured networking is crucial to the fitness of an organization. As Vester visualizes with the help of examples from biology (Vester 1978: 88), unstructured networks are pathological. I have shown that optimal organizational structures show a fractal dimensionality which is equal to that of higher living organisms (Schwaninger 2001c; see also 7.7).

The dotted line represents the boundaries of the organization as legally defined. To express this idea in system-theoretical language, the limits are determined by system-internal connections which outweigh the system-external connections. For illustrative purposes reference is made to a few partners such as suppliers and major customers lying beyond these narrow limits of the organization. They will not be discussed further at this point.

The network can be subject to constant alterations. In the course of time the boundaries that define branches, regions and customer groups may change, new sub-systems may be added on, others may fuse or differentiate themselves, new holdings and alliances can be entered into, etc. The boundaries of the system itself can undergo changes, too. When for example, suppliers are bought up, the system boundaries are extended. If they are disposed of, the boundaries are correspondingly drawn closer. For the purpose of strategic analysis, it is usually not optimal to draw the system boundaries from the legal point of view. More important in these cases are questions regarding development of core competencies, conquest of new markets, configuration of business systems, reshaping of products or even entire industries, value management etc. (for details see: Gomez 1993).

Earlier on, heterarchical structures have been discussed (Section 3.5.). It must be emphasized here that these do not automatically guarantee viability and development. Nor do marginal changes or even fundamental transformations of networks by themselves increase the adaptability, intelligence or fitness of the organization. If Beer's theory holds, then heterarchical networks, in order to be viable, must likewise show the characteristic management functions specified in the VSM.

This claim is neither self-evident nor uncontroversial. Thus, for example, it was postulated by the network expert and former chairman of the board of Arthur D. Little that networks should neither be institutionalized nor structured, for otherwise their effectiveness will be impaired. Mueller argues that their effectiveness depends "not on the organizational structure or scheme of the network but rather on the people who belong to it." (Mueller, 1986: 203).

Here, however, this postulate must be considered as invalid, at least as far as intra- and inter-company networks are concerned. Every enterprise is an institution (from "instituere" - to arrange), at least to some extent. Furthermore, any social system, formed in order to fulfill a specific function or to achieve a certain goal, needs to maintain its identity and therewith its viability as long as this function remains intact. On the premise of the validity of the Theory of Viable Organizations discussed here, it is imperative that networks be structured in accordance with the principles of the VSM if they too are to be viable.

The question now arises whether structuring, which is a conscious creation of order, is not in contradiction to the *imperative of self-organization*. Indeed, there must be a lot of room for spontaneous organization within an enterprise (e.g., through the establishment of electronic markets). However, even spontaneous order, if it is to be capable of functioning effectively, needs the background of a more general framework which establishes certain rules of the game. For the rest, active structuring should be limited to the necessary, i.e., minimized.

Table 6-2 shows in broad outline how the example of an enterprise taken from Figure 6-8 can be conceived as a viable system at the first recursion level (the whole corporation).

Table 6-2. Embodiments of the Functions of a Viable System for the Firm from Figure 6-8

Components & Management Functions of Viable Systems	1. Embodied by ... at the Corporate Level
Basic Units	Subsidiaries 1, 2, 3, 4
System 1	Managements of Subsidiaries 1, 2, 3, 4
System 2	Coordination Teams/-Networks, Management Information Systems, Standards, Selected Service Functions in Holding Company
System 3	Operating-Committee (-Network)
System 3*	Corporate auditing, „Management by Walking Around"
System 4	Strategy-Team (-Network), Strategic Principles, Corporate Strategy
System 5	Policy-Team (-Network), Corporate Charter, Ethos/ Basic Values, Management and Leadership Philosophy

6.7 Networks of Viable Systems

If systemic intelligence, entrepreneurial initiative and organizational learning are to develop at all levels of a corporation or network, it is necessary that all the sub-systems be conceived as viable systems in themselves. This means that each unit (Ui), be it a firm or a subsidiary, division etc., must, in the sense of the recursion principle, possess all the management functions specified above. This is presented schematically in Figure 6-9. The "partners" can be individual firms or whole networks.

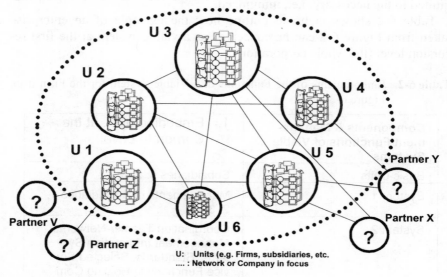

Fig. 6-9. Stylized Network of Viable Systems

Each one of these sub-systems is a network in itself and is in turn part of superordinate ones, which are not shown in the figure, however. In this sense, we are talking about networks of networks (see the abstract scheme in Figure 6-10).

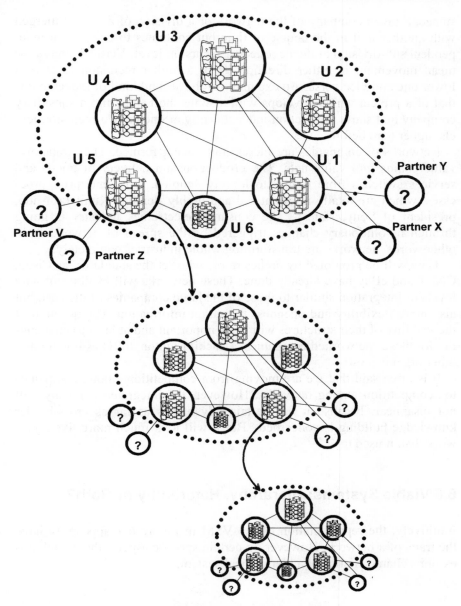

Fig. 6-10. A Network of Networks (Stylized Format)

This way of seeing things can in principle be applied to inter-organizational networks, but equally to all levels of an organization.

The levels of such a multi-layered network are subject not only to horizontal transformations, but often to vertical alterations as well. For instance, a given company of the network or a division of a firm is merged with another unit in the course of time but continues to exist as an independent sub-division at the next deeper recursion level. Vertical alterations mean movement in either direction, from a higher recursion level to a lower one and vice versa. An example for the second kind of movement is that of a project which develops within some short time into a subsidiary company and starts to function independently at one or two recursion levels higher than before.

Networks of companies are increasingly being formed. They transform value chains into value nets. The production and delivery of goods and services switches from tightly to loosely coupled, cross-enterprise processes, which are totally informatized and highly flexible. Kunitake Ando, president of Sony, states: "The consumer electronics industry is going through revolutionary changes triggered by the spread of networks."[4] In other words, networks are transforming whole industries completely.

They will be promoted by orchestrators who set the standards, as Cisco, CNET and eBay have already done. These networks will exhibit not only levels of integration similar to those of the large companies of the past, but also more flexibility and openness to market information. The question of the viability of their structures will be as important and at least as challenging for these "networked companies" (Häcki/ Lighton 2001) as it is for any other organization.

It is often said that we are moving from competition among companies to competition among networks. However, the integrated company will not disappear, because it has certain advantages as far as cross-border knowledge building is concerned.[5] But it will look much more like a network than it used to.

6.8 Viable Systems: Hierarchy, Heterarchy or Both?

Intuitively, the representation of the VSM in Figure 6-1 appears to have the traits of a network. However, in certain specific aspects the model also exhibits characteristics of a hierarchical system.

---

[4] Financial Times, February 10, 2003, p. 11.
[5] E.g., by using multiple mechanisms of knowledge transfer simultaneously and flexibly, to move, integrate and develop technical knowledge. (Almeida/Song/ Grant 2002).

1. System 1 regulates aspects which the homeostat[6] "basic unit-environment" cannot regulate. System 3 regulates what cannot be regulated within system 1, and system 5 what the homeostat "system 4 - system 3" does not regulate.
2. Viability is a recursive principle, i.e., viable organizations are themselves sub-systems of superordinate viable systems and in turn, they are themselves composed of viable subsystems (Figure 4). In mathematical terms, the recursion principle embodies the current application of a formula to itself, according to the following pattern, as in the case of, e.g., the Julia sets. In this case, a sequence of complex numbers is generated by means of the following algorithm (cf. Peitgen et al. 1998:148):

$$X \rightarrow x^2 + c \rightarrow (x^2 + c)^2 + c \rightarrow \dots,$$
where c is a constant.

A recursive construction can be regarded as a special case of a hierarchy.

Are these aspects of a hierarchical system incompatible with the new "paradigm" of heterarchical network organizations? Here certain careful distinctions must be made.

Ref. 1.) "Hierarchy of homeostats":

The hierarchy referred to here is not a social but a logical one, in the sense that at each of the three levels of management, namely operational, strategic and normative, different control variables and orientators are crucial. The control variables of a given superordinate level fulfill a function of pre-control with regard to the levels below it (for details, see MSC, Chapter 5). The viability of an enterprise depends upon the control variables of all levels being kept under control simultaneously and over time. This is difficult to achieve, given that a) each of these logical levels must be separately directed, b) each of these levels requires a "language" of its own, and c) conflicts arise between the regulatory requirements of the different levels. It is often not understood that despite the necessity for separate control at each of the levels, these controls need not necessarily be carried out by different persons. The three distinct levels of control must also be intact, for example, in a viable one-person-business.

Ref. 2.) 'Recursive structure':

Basically, the recursion principle can be realized down to the individual workplace or to the working team or the individual project. However, de

---

[6] In abstract terms, an homeostat is a device that holds critical variables within desired limits in the face of unexpected disturbance or perturbation (cf. Beer 1981: 402).

facto this is not always the case, because it is often not understood that the recursion principle as conceived in Beer's model constitutes the factual and logical underpinnings of humanistic postulates such as "autonomy", "self-development" and "meaningful work".

Compared to the traditional hierarchical structures, the recursive structures of viable systems exhibit a significantly higher capacity for information processing and effective action, since the complexity along the "fronts" it unfolds is mastered in a decentralized and yet coherent manner. The coherence results from a combination of local autonomy (basic units, systems 1), coordination/ monitoring (systems 2,3*) and the regulatory functions of the entire system (systems 3,4,5) at each level of recursion.

6.9 Criticisms and Beyond

In spite of the features outlined in the last section, the VSM has been criticized by some authors as being a plan for a "machine," in which goals are imposed from the higher levels upon the lower ones (Ulrich 1982). A careful study of Beer's original writings together with more recent interpretations of the VSM (see especially Espejo/Harnden 1989; Espejo/ Schwaninger 1993; Schwaninger 2004) leads cogently to the following counterarguments.

1. At a given recursion level, *all the constituencies* of the system-in-focus are adequately represented[7] in the highest directive organ of that system at a given recursion level.
2. Furthermore, the *recursion levels are interlaced* with each other in such a way that members of subordinate levels of recursion are represented in the directive units of the levels above them.

   For example, the metasystem (3-4-5) of each unit at a given recursion level forms at the same time a system 1 for the next higher recursion level. Although this arrangement does not entirely eliminate disequilibria of power between "above" and "below", at least it minimizes such imbalance. In addition, six different channels are available for the members for influencing the system through information (for details see Beer 1985).
3. In his latest book, Beer puts forward a model for a democratic design of organizations, which was specially conceived for the structuring of the

---

[7]   This representation can be an actual or a virtual one. For example, if future generations cannot actually participate, their position must be simulated.

communication processes in the 3-4-5-homeostat (Beer 1994). This will be an important subject of Chapter 7.

As an intermediate summary, we can state that the VSM embodies a network structure. The model was conceived by Beer as an arrangement with *heterarchical traits*. However, this fact has not spared the VSM from being misinterpreted or even perverted. Therefore one must consider that even a use of the model as hierarchical machinery for suppression cannot be excluded.

Another criticism has addressed the functionalist approach of the VSM, adverting that the underlying rationale is characterized by two assumptions:

1. Inherent harmony of the viewpoints present in an organization,
2. One rational designer's perspective.

This critique is more applicable to the state of some of the applications published to date than to the intention of the model's author himself. In fact, Beer has advocated the VSM as a model for *democratic government* (Beer 1979). A small number of publications have also shown that it can be used as a device to explore alternative organizational identities by elaborating their distinct structural implications. Espejo (1989b) developed a pertinent heuristic, and respective applications have already been documented (see section 6.11).

6.10 Autonomous Agents in Viable Organizations

It should have become clear throughout this chapter that the autonomy of agents is a crucial concept in the context of the VSM. I have also emphasized that this autonomy is not absolute but always relative, and that it stands in complementarity with control. What still needs to be discussed is the varied nature of the agents themselves.

In a socio-technical system, forms of agents appear along a continuum from human/social to technical (Figure 6-11).

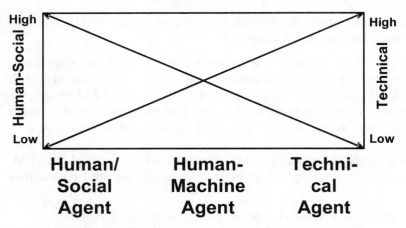

Fig. 6-11. Continuum from human to technical agent

There is always a whole spectrum of agents, from purely human to purely technical, with all kinds of combinations in between. The two extremes are abstractions, because in reality the human agent practically always supports himself with some artifact – a computer, furniture, a factory and the like. On the other hand technical agents are not only conceived by humans (directly or indirectly), but they are usually linked to the activity of a human being, a team or the like.

Automation, especially robot-based support, has progressed, particularly in the domain of information and communication technology. Robots optimize the transport and routing of bits and bytes. Humans in call centers are supported by information robots („Ibots") which lead off conversations with calling clients. Routine decisions are delegated to automatic agents with features of „machine intelligence"; the term „intelligent agents" is often used in this context. Markets or other complex systems are simulated by means of cellular automata and genetic algorithms (cf. Holland 1995, Axelrod 1999). Agent-based simulations, e.g., of internal markets, can improve decision-making and resource allocation (cf. Henoch 2003). For example: Infineon, a producer of semiconductors, increased the throughput of its production line. The Danish postal service optimized its delivery routes. A pharmaceutical company increased its operational efficiency drastically – to 50% in the case of clinical trials (Buchanan 2005). In all three cases, agent-based simulations were at the core of these improvements.

Speaking about information systems in general, their role is to support agents and the processes in which they act. That role implies making any information they need available to these agents. The approach should be one of customization, and rather of a demand-pull than of a supply-push type. In other words, the information systems should be able to respond to the information demands of the organization's people rather than inundating them with data.

The issue here is supporting the agents in their (limited) autonomy. Information and communication technologies should be conceived as enablers for purposeful action. The task of conceiving information systems so that they are naturally embedded in the structures of a viable organization, as vehicles of distributed intelligence, is a challenge. That challenge can be mastered better if the systems are designed along the lines of the Viable System Model.

6.11 An Application Perspective

The Viable System Model has been translated into the language of business and applied to organizations of all kinds, as documented in several books (e.g., Espejo / Harnden 1989, Espejo / Schwaninger 1993, Espejo / Schuhmann / Schwaninger 1996, Christopher, forthcoming), and on a CD-ROM edited as a "Festschrift" (commemorative volume) for Stafford Beer (Espejo/ Schwaninger 1998). In particular, the aspect of recursive management and an underlying cybernetic theory of human action in organizations have been elaborated in detail by Espejo/Schwaninger/Schuhmann (1996), with reference to real-world applications.

The VSM has also been used in the design of national government (Beer 1989) and public institutions (Reyes 2000). One of my doctoral candidates has based a diagnosis of the Swiss democracy on the VSM, and has arrived at important insights (Willemsen 1992).

In addition, the concepts presented in this chapter have been tested in multiple applications. The scheme in Figure 6-5 emanated from applications, mainly one case, in which I designed a management framework for a large publishing house, together with members of the corporate board and the corporate development function. The scheme in Figure 6-6 has been applied in practical designs for project management. A pertinent application in the context of complex development projects is documented in Schwaninger/Koerner 2004.

The example about the virtual factory (Section 6.5.) comes from a pioneering initiative in Swiss Industry; more details about this have been published in Schwaninger/Friedli 2002. The corporate example about heterarchical structures (Sections 6-6, 6-7) is an abstraction going back to cases in European corporations, in which I figured as an external partner.

As far as the exploration of different organizational identities and the discernment of their structural implications are concerned, a respective application to the Energy Authority of Gothenburg, Sweden, has been realized and published in a dissertation (Björkqvist 1996). Also, an exploration of different organizational concepts for a broadcasting corporation, in terms of the VSM, has been published by Leonard (1989).

In relation to the criticisms outlined in the preceding section, the important point has been made that "the functionalist paradigm certainly does not exhaust the possibilities opened up by the VSM" (Jackson 2000). This far-seeing statement points to the large territory of interpretive readings of the VSM and also to pertinent applications in both pluralist and coercive organizational contexts. This territory has been charted in a theoretical work by Harnden (1989), who emphasizes the potential role of that model in supporting the ongoing organizational discourse in which new realities can be created.

Some of the most common defects of organizations are a) that agents do the wrong things, b) that they fail to do the right things, and c) that they do necessary things at the wrong time. A very practical example: When Pierre Bouleze, one of the most influential composers of the second half of the 20th century, accepted a mandate from the management board ("Conseil de direction") of Centre Pompidou, a prominent cultural institution in Paris, he was obliged to participate in board sessions, "which often limited themselves to the discussion of the functioning of the elevators and similar things, which from the beginning were not at the centre of my interest." (Boulez 2001: 37). In that organization as in many others, a look through the lens of the VSM would have helped managers to sort out tasks, relationships and structural configuration, and to redesign the organization into a much more effective one. And that is the basic concern of any organizational diagnosis.

The VSM has been applied not only to organizational diagnosis and design for whole organizations. Practitioners and researchers have relied on it as a conceptual orientator for reinventing the design of different areas of firms as well. Over the last few years, I have supervised a number of studies in which organizational concepts for product development (Prinz 2001), marketing (Einhorn 2005), knowledge communities (Frost 2005), production systems (Thiem 1998, Moscoso 1999), and public institutions (Türke 2006) have been reviewed and redesigned on the basis of the VSM. Colleagues at other Universities (e.g., Raúl Espejo at Lincoln, Alfredo Moscardini at Sunderland, Maurice Yolles at John Moores Liverpool, Stuart Umpleby at George Washington, Allenna Leonard at York, Canada, Tom Ryan at Cape Town, Rod Sarah at Monash, Australia, Alfonso Reyes at Universidad de los Andes, Bogotá, Colombia) and their associates have made comparable efforts, creating a rich corpus of knowledge on VSM applications.

A software called VSMod has been developed at the University of Valladolid under the direction of Professor José Pérez Ríos, to support VSM-based diagnosis and design (Schwaninger/Pérez Ríos/Ambroz 2004). This software is generally available[8] and it is also useful for integrating VSM and System Dynamics-based modeling and problem-solving. Such an integration of methods has been advocated elsewhere under the title "Integrative Systems Methodology" (Weber/Schwaninger 2002, Schwaninger 1997, 2004).

Finally, the VSM has also been crucial for an innovative, market-based conception for a shop-floor system, elaborated in a doctoral dissertation which I co-supervised together with Professor Hans Jakob Luethi from the Institute of Operations Research at the Swiss Federal Polytechnic, Zurich (Henoch 2003). In this case the operative management functions (Systems 1 to 3 in terms of the VSM) were designed based on the principle of recursiveness and implemented with bidding and scheduling procedures executed by "intelligent agents". The results validated in the context of a semiconductor production facility led to an amazing increase of efficiency in comparison with traditional shop-floor decision algorithms and heuristics.

6.12 Intermediate Summary and Outlook

In this chapter, the structural conditions for the viability and development of any organization have been outlined in terms of the VSM. The Viable System Model is the structural core for the architecture of adaptive organizations. The principle of recursive structuring is a powerful response to complexity; it enables an organization to build up eigen-variety in a decentralized way, along the fronts at which complexity manifests itself. The VSM gives a more substantive guidance to decentralization than those traditional approaches, which merely postulate the need to decentralize. In addition, this model specifies the necessary and sufficient structural features which make the viability of organizational units at different levels possible. Also, these preconditions of viability, defined in terms of the set of management functions (denominated "System 1" to "System 5"), contain crucially important "instructions" for achieving a number of organiza-

---

[8]   VSMod is made available at the following address: http://157.88.193.41/msv/

tional properties which are universally desired and acclaimed today, but which have in general not been well understood:

1. the complementarity of decentral and central controls, or practically speaking, of decentral responsibility linked up with the corporate center;
2. the achievement of a balance between the short and long terms through adequate structural design;
3. the unity of thought and action at all levels of the organization, which enables a company to "live up to its vision".

"Viable" as understood here means more than "autopoietic" (self-producing). For intelligent organizations "viability" stands for more than survival at any price; such organizations are committed to the goal of "development". In borderline cases, they eliminate themselves when, with their given identity, they are not capable of fulfilling meaningful functions in the service of the more comprehensive whole. An alternative in such cases would be either a search for a new environment or the incorporation into a new recursion.

Organizational viability is recursive and so is organizational intelligence. Therefore if organizational viability is a recursive property, it requires recursive organizational intelligence as a necessary prerequisite. This is also the foundation, in structural-theoretic terms, for humanistic postulates such as autonomy, meaningful work, participation and self-fulfillment.

The VSM has also been discussed in the context of the new approaches to heterarchical, network and virtual organizations. Not every heterarchical network structure results in a more effective organization. It has been shown here:

1. That it is necessary to conceive of heterarchies as viable entities and
2. How heterarchical networks can lead to more intelligent organizations.

Whenever networks fail to meet the criteria provided by the theory of viable systems, their organizational "intelligence" and ultimately their "fitness" will predictably be impaired, or even endangered.

To conclude this chapter: Organizational Cybernetics (OC), and Stafford Beer's VSM in particular, have ushered in a new era of both the science and the practice of organizing. Even though most leaders, managers and professionals who design or develop organizations may not yet be aware of it, this OC/VSM factor is changing their trade completely. It changes diagnosis and design as much as it alters the approaches to the change and transformation of organizations of all kinds.

However, it has been necessary to bring the theory of the VSM together with the concepts of circularity, recursion, network, heterarchy, virtual organization and project management. This chapter has been a first attempt to proceed with such a synthesis in a conceptual way, giving a synoptic account of some applied research done on the basis of the VSM over the last two decades. This is one of several contributions in the present book which I hope will reach beyond the current state of the art in Organizational Cybernetics.

Chapter 7   Behavior – The Control of Cognition and Emotion

"The function of organizations is to make knowledges productive. ... Knowledges by themselves are sterile. They become productive only if welded together into a single, unified knowledge. To make this possible is the task of organization, the reason for its existence, its function."

Peter Drucker, Austro-American management thinker[1]

"Habia subordinación de todos al pensamiento común, y un instinto maravilloso para conocer la estrategia rudimentaria que las necesidades de la lucha a cada instante nos iba ofreciendo."

Benito Pérez Caldós, Spanish writer and author
of The National Episodes[2]

"Bill Evans ... offered a whole new way for the players in a piano trio to work completely cohesively with each other. ... I was amazed to see how well the stuff was organized. Yet, hearing it played, you weren't aware of the mechanics of it at all. ... Sometimes the structure can close doors. But not in Bill's case. And to hear his technique and his sense of structure serving only as a tool for the expression of the human qualities of tenderness, clarity, and balance, all played with a great creative depth – that's Bill Evans' legacy."

Herbie Hancock, American pianist and composer,
about the music of Bill Evans[3]

This chapter is about the third dimension of our framework-behavior. This subject can be of interest at different levels, namely the behavior of indi-

---

[1]   Drucker 1993: 49-50.

[2]   Zaragoza, Madrid: Alianza Editorial, 2000: 126. Translation: "All of us were subordinated to our shared thinking, and a marvellous instinct of knowing the rudimentary strategy which the necessities of the fight [defense of the city of Zaragoza] offered us at any moment."

[3]   Liner notes to the CD "Ultimate Bill Evans, selected by Herbie Hancock", Verve 1998, No. 557 536-2.

viduals, teams, organizational units, an organization as a whole, inter-organizational networks, etc. If we consider the principle of recursion expounded in the previous chapter, any unit at any one of these levels can exhibit observable behavior which is meaningful in terms of organizational intelligence.

A mere description of specific behaviors would be of little value in this context. Therefore the emphasis in the following chapter will be on the relationship between structural arrangements and the behaviors they can bring about. This is very much in the tradition of cybernetics (see Braitenberg 1959).

7.1 Behavior In and Of Organizations

We shall concentrate on behavior in organizations here, i.e., on the human side of enterprise, namely the cognitive and affective factors and their linkages with behavior. Why do I not say "... cognition's impact on behavior"? The usual view is that behavior is controlled by cognition, period. The systemic view taken here deviates from this common sense knowledge in several ways. This can be expressed graphically as visualized in Figure 7-1, and described as follows.

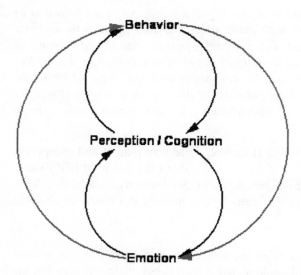

Fig. 7-1 The relationships between perception, emotion and behavior

First, this systemic view conceives behavior as an organism's mode of controlling its perceptual signals. As Powers (1973) showed on the basis of experiments, behavior operates on two perceptual signals, one for the actual and one for the desired (reference) position, to bring them into a state of zero error. In opposition to behaviorism (Skinner) he claims that "behavior exists only to control consequences that affect the organism. From the viewpoint of the behaving system, behavior itself, as output, is of no importance" (op. cit.). The approach emanating from behaviorism, which treats people as machines, is refuted by Powers: "In natural control systems, there are no externally manipulable reference inputs. There are only sensory inputs. Reference signals for natural control systems are set by processes inside the organism and are not accessible from the outside. Another name for a natural reference signal is purpose" (op. cit.).

This concept of "natural control" is perfectly in line with the view of organisms as operationally closed systems that is also applicable to social systems, i.e., organizations and societies (see Luhmann 1995). Being operationally closed means that these systems are self-referential in the sense that their self-production (autopoiesis) is a function of production rules and processes by which order (structure) and identity are maintained. Furthermore these rules and procedures cannot be modified directly from outside. This is different from the concept of materially, energetically or informationally closed systems, which does not apply to organizations.

Second, behavorial parameters control not only percpetion but also cognition as a whole, in the sense that the affective or emotional conditions of the system moderate its cognitive processes (Ciompi 1997). Take a situation in which relationships are based on mutual trust versus a case in which the climate is spoilt by mistrust. In the first instance arguments will be constructive, while in the second differences of opinion will persist and a rational exchange of ideas will be rare and difficult. Trust is essential to facilitate effective coordinated action in organizations[4].

The other side of the coin – as will be shown – is that the cognitive structures of organizations can impinge on the "emotional" state of an organization. For example, an arrangement in which information processing takes place via a network of interactions is more appropriate for building a culture of trust and mutual support than a system in which the flow of information is essentially one of top-down command or autocratic control.

Finally, the complementary view that cognition / perception controls behavior continues to be valid[5], but it has to be seen in combination with

---

[4]   Trust is in part cognition-based and in part affect-based (McAllister 1995).

[5]   There are even "automatic effects" of social perception triggering social behavior, as has been extensively corroborated (Dijksterhuis/Bargh 2001).

the other two aspects, as visualized in Figure 7-1. The main point here is that this circular relationship is what keeps an organization going (cf. Von Foerster 1984a: 215).

Given this circular relationship, it can also be claimed that intelligence has two components which affect each other. Ideally, "thinking" intelligence and emotional intelligence are one.

Let us for a moment concentrate on the organizational aspect of emotion, which has traditionally been given insufficient consideration. Randall Collins (1993) conceives of emotions as „social energy". This social energy manifests itself in variables which behavioral scientists have tried to measure. Some of them – such as the general levels of commitment, loyalty, cooperation, cohesion but also a sound degree of openness and flexibility – are crucial for the achievement of a common purpose. On the other hand, social energy can also be channeled into defensive routines, resistance to change and all kinds of power games and intrigues, all of which are detrimental to achieving common aims.

All of this only holds "in principle". For example, high cohesion is obstructive to the achievement of goals if the actors do not accept them, i.e., if a "common purpose" disliked by a group is imposed on it from outside or if the attitude of the group towards the organization is negative (Seashore 1954, von Rosenstiel et al. 2005). Furthermore, motivation theory could tell a lot about the finesses in the linkage between the attitudes, skills, goals and behavior of individuals.

Leadership theory has identified energy and focus as the drivers triggering effective behavior in leaders (Bruch 2003). And it has shown, on empirical grounds, that there is a cogent relationship between behavioral complexity and leadership effectiveness: "The more effective executives exhibit a greater variety of leadership roles than their less effective counterparts, and ... these roles are much clearer to their subordinates" (Denison/Hooijberg/Quinn 1995: 524). This apparently underpins the law of requisite variety introduced in the second chapter.

Finally, sociological theories have explored in detail the aspects of power, oppression, groupthink[6], etc. Most of these studies may somehow be relevant in this context. If this book were about the methodology of motivation and leadership, it could deal with all of these aspects.

In the specific context of organizational intelligence, however, the emphasis of this chapter will be on the question: "How can the potential of social energy be actualized in a way so that

---

[6]   Groupthink is a mode of thinking which occurs in cohesive in-groups, "when members' strivings for unanimity override their motivation to realistically appraise alternative courses of action." (Janis 1972:9).l

1. The purpose of an organization emerges in fact as a common purpose of its members, and
2. The behavior of the actors involved converges toward a joint action meaningful in terms of both the organization and its constituent individuals?"

In the tradition of the behavioral wing of organization science, extensive efforts to "integrate the individual and the organization" (Argyris 1964) have been made. In particular the importance of factors such as respect for the individual's intrinsic value, appropriate degrees of autonomy, meaningful work, self-control and alignment of individual and organizational goals has been fleshed out in specific theories.

According to Jeffrey Pfeffer from Stanford University, "there are probably 100 studies out there showing that you get a 30 to 40 per cent productivity lift by treating people right."[7] Treating people right appears to be crucial, because it can provoke organizations and individuals to "propel each other into a virtuous spiral of success" (Lawler 2003). Jeff Chambers, vice-president for human resources at the SAS Institute translates this into practical terms: "How we treat employees is a mirror image of how we treat customers. We have a customer retention rate of 98 per cent and an employee turnover rate of about 4 per cent. It is all about long-term relationships."[8]

The Systems Approach can complement these efforts with a valuable contribution of its own that focuses on the interlinkage between behavior and structure. Just as a principle of recursiveness underlies the organization of viable systems, there is also a holographic principle immanent in the behavioral dimension of intelligent organizations.

Holography, discovered by the Hungarian physicist Dennis Gabor, is a two-step coherent image-forming process in which an intermediate record is made of the complex optical field associated with the object. In more general terms this is a mode of *representing a system in a way that the parts include general information about the whole.* The hologram analogy has been applied to the brain, which is known to have a holographic organization. In the following section, a model of holographic organization will be explored, the *Team Syntegrity model* (TSM). A large number of experiments (see below) shows that this model is more powerful than alternative models *in fostering self-organized behavior* of organizational members and teams which converges toward growing coherence, *shared mental models and joint action.*

---

[7]   Quoted in London 2003b.
[8]   Quoted in London 2003.

Before we look at the Team Syntegrity model, the issue of participation will be appreciated with regard to leadership and authority.

7.2 Participation and Authority – Social Behavior for Complexity Absorption

It can be taken for granted that participation by all employees is necessary to keep performance high in an organization in the knowledge economy. But this is not sufficient. Worse than incomplete participation, if the mode of participation adopted is ill-conceived, it can damage or even ruin a business. In 2003, British Airways, global carrier and self-named "favourite airline", got into serious trouble because thousands of employees engaged in a strike to reverse a minor administrative change – the introduction of automated time-keeping. At about the same time, in troubled companies across Germany[9], employee representatives voted for not making concessions toward higher wage cost flexibility to keep those firms going. Other cases, which are very frequent, are those in which a weak management has everybody participate in virtually everything, i.e., too many people intervene into things for which they are short on either competence or concern.

What makes the difference here is the leadership of competent managers. The already mentioned Peter Drucker conceptualized the role of managers in organizations: "The enterprise can decide, act and behave only as the managers do. By itself the enterprise has no effective existence." (Drucker 1974). For him, managers should be the pivot around which organizational activity revolves, rather than directors controlling from the top down or officers leading from the front. They have to harness the resources, design systems of value creation and even, as he calls it, "create a customer." In this context, Drucker emphasizes: "Markets are not created by God, nature or economic forces, but by the people who manage a business" (*op. cit.*). He further stresses managers' responsibilities, which according to him are threefold *(op.cit.)*:

- To think through and define the specific purpose and mission of the organization
- To make work productive and the worker achieving

---

[9]   One was the case of a shipbuilder. The management, to enable the troubled company to take on a huge order of four ocean liners, had proposed a contract by which weekly worktime should be prolonged from 35 to 38 hours, while the weekly salary should be cut by ten percent.

example, can be enacted as a principle, and so it makes sense to anchor it in a corporate charter. However, the respect manifest in relationships with customers, staff and other stakeholders, demonstrated by opinion leaders, has a more powerful influence than any formal statement.

So far, so good. But people are not robots, and they should not merely imitate their bosses. Certainly, learning via emulation and stimulus enhancement takes place. Meaning, however, cannot be given; it must be found by each agent him- or herself. This also applies to teams or organizations as wholes. In this vein, the processes of reflection postulated by ethicists, as already mentioned, are of paramount importance. Organizational intelligence manifests itself in a broad participation of all members of the organizations in these processes of reflection and joint construction of meaning.[25]

So far, organizational ethos has been discussed with a special emphasis on normative management. These are long-term and in part even timeless issues. The same emphasis and wide extent also apply to the next subject, organizational identity.

8.2 Organizational Identity

"Companies often get in trouble, because they lose a sense of who they are." This diagnosis by a Mercedes-Benz executive, during a recent conference at our university, shifts the issue of organizational identity to the center.

It makes sense to start with a definition. Identity is a set of enduring characteristics which make a whole distinguishable from other wholes, i.e., recognizable in different instances (François 1997). The term derives from the Latin word "identitas", which stands for consubstantiality, based on "idem" – "the same". *Sameness* or *being itself* are good proxies for identity. In mathematics, an identity is an operand that remains the same after undergoing transformations ($a = a' = a''$, and so forth).

In the context of this book, we define *identity* (with Leonard, forthcoming) as the mark of an organization that can be consistently recognized, or

---

[25] It appears that this kind of joint sense-making is even more powerful if it can be realized in the context of collective ownership and democratic structures. An impressive example is Mondragón, a cooperative in the North of Spain with 53'000 members, which has built strong companies (e.g., Caja Laboral, one of the best-rated financial institutions in the country) and made extraordinary cultural contributions, namely the Bilbao Guggenheim Museum (Whyte 1991, Schafer 2001).

which persists over time, therewith making it distinguishable or unique.[26] Core aspects of organizational identity are the vision, the characteristic mindset, the lasting values, and the paradigm to which the members of the organization adhere.

Asking questions such as "What kind of organization are we?", "What business are we in?" and "What is our mission?" has been acknowledged as fundamental for any solid management and leadership (See next section). Strictly speaking, only the first one is about the identity of an organization. The answers to the latter two are already derivatives of the identity issue. A reflected organizational identity is expressed in the concept of self as well as the respective mental models held and shared by the members of that organization.

Just as in the case of organizational ethos, identity can be more or less explicit. It always makes itself felt as an implicate order (or lack of order), which delimits the potential modes of behavior of the organization. Nevertheless, a substantive and continuing reflection by the members of the organization upon what that identity is about is most important. The immediate answer of Todd Stitzer, the CEO of Cadbury Schweppes, to a pertinent question was: "What is unique about Cadbury Schweppes is that it was founded on a set of principles and has acted consistently with those values ever since".[27]

The corporate set of potential activities is in principle determined by corporate identity. It delimits which businesses the organization should engage in and which not. Confusions and inconsistencies at the level of strategies almost invariably have to do with a deficient understanding of the organization's identity by those who make the strategic decisions.

Notwithstanding these factors, in practice the act of asking the question "Who (or what) are we?" often entails enormous difficulties, especially if the question is asked for the first time. That is why, since early on in my career as a consultant, I have always advised firms to ask both questions: "*Who* (or what) *are we?*" and "*Who* (or what) *are we not?*" I propose asking them in both senses, the descriptive as well as the volitional, and ultimately in the normative sense. The volitional dimension introduces the aspects of ideal and design: "Who do we *want* to be?" and "Who do we *not want* to be?"

---

[26] One distinction which has been made is that between identity and image – identity expressing the concept of self shared by the members of an organization, and image being its appearance in the environment (Fombrun 1996, Dowling 2001). This differentiation is fruitful in certain contexts, but will not be pursued further here.

[27] The Guardian, December 4, 2004, p. 34.

Two insights have emerged from this practice: First, in many cases the tactic of starting off with the negative enumeration ("Who are we not?") proves to be more fruitful. There is a similarity here with individuals, especially people in their maturation stage, who may not really know who they are or want to be but know pretty well who they are not or do not want to be. Management teams, too, often show more fluency in characterizing their organization if they start confronting themselves with the "not"-questions. For example, they know if their organization is not of the "Jack of all trades" or of the "cheap and disposable" type. Why is this so? Because (negative) preclusion is more powerful in absorbing complexity than (positive) enumeration is.

However, as claimed in Chapter 5, normally a firm should strive for more than distinguishability: Distinctiveness, inconfoundability, uniqueness are the stronger features to be aimed for, always within the bounds of the criteria of effectiveness and legitimacy. Being inconfoundable is not necessarily to be achieved in relation to anyone (any observer) but in relation to relevant stakeholders – potential and actual customers in particular. To put it in abridged form, the issue is becoming unique and "irresistible" in one's market.

Intelligent organizations develop a "conscience" around a set of extraordinary traits which (can) make them unique. By honing and combining these traits they can gain unmatched strength. In this way they can reach outstanding levels of robustness, viability and performance. To take one example, a host of small and even very small firms not only survive in markets dominated by giant players but also show remarkable viability. A case in point are the large numbers of thriving micro-breweries which have emerged over the last decade or so in oligopolistic markets[28], e.g., in the U.S. and Switzerland.

Finally, identity is not necessarily something fixed. Identity is subject to changes as a function of external stimuli. The development of identity is therefore part of a process of co-evolution of the firm with its environment. Think of the examples from Chapter 5: Nokia, the company which evolved from a sawmill to one of the main players in mobile communication, or Preussag, which transformed itself from an industrial corporation to a travel organization. The changes involved in these cases were more than those of size, but included markets, locations, etc. On the contrary, the identities of these companies developed over time in mutual alignments with their environments.

---

[28] An oligopoly is a constellation in which a very small number of firms dominates a market.

8.3 Theory of the Firm

The behavior of a system is fundamentally shaped by its ends, i.e., goals, objectives and ideals.

The volitional and normative conception of what the organization wants to or should be is linked to another set of basic parameters – vision, purpose and mission of the organization, in short the broadest aims of the firm. One can also call them the "theory of the firm", together with the business model.

No one has insisted more strongly on the need for a clear, explicit *theory of the firm* than Peter Drucker: "All the great business builders we know of – from the Medici of Renaissance Florence and the founders of the Bank of England in the late seventeenth century down to IBM's Thomas Watson ... had a clear theory of the business which informed all their actions and decisions. Not intuition, but a clear, simple, and penetrating theory of the business characterizes the truly successful entrepreneur, the person who not just amasses a large fortune but builds an organization that can endure and grow" (Drucker 1977: 68).

The business model is that part of the theory of the firm which is strategic. A business model is a realistic architecture for the functioning of a business, which includes:

1. Value proposition (what specific value do we offer to the customer?)
2. Design for value-added (product-market-technology strategy)
3. Revenue model (where does the revenue come from and where does it go?)

Coming back to the level of normative management, vision is someone's conception, idea or imagination related to the future state or developmental path of a system. The working definition here conceives of vision as a creative anticipation of, or a complex insight into, the possible or desired future of an organization by an observer – "Let there be vision: and there was light" (von Foerster 1984a: 204).

Vision in this sense plays an essential part in the viability and development of a social organism. Solomon (970-928 B.C.), the sage among the kings of antiquity, is quoted as saying: "A nation without a vision has no future." Indeed, vision is not only the outcome of creative thought; it also spurs imagination, fires social energy and inspires innovation.

For example, the vision of Reuters Group PLC "to make the financial markets really work on the Internet" has given rise to a strategy of linking information supplies with traditional solutions in order to meet the needs of e-commerce. In this way, internet technologies have been extensively applied to the distribution of information and news in connection with global solutions for the financial markets, including enterprise-wide integration, market information, data distribution, risk management, etc. Another example is Honda's mission "to make environmentally friendly products that our customers want to buy because the products are easy to own and fun to drive", which is reflected in what the company actually does and strives for. Kodak's new motto of "leading the way in digital imaging with innovative ways of taking and using pictures" triggered a reorientation of the company and spurred its adaptation to a changed marketplace, where it went after a leading role in reshaping the "digital future". Estée Lauder's vision to offer women "jars of hope" was a convincing argument for both millions of customers and thousands of her company's employees. The underlying ideal of "tools for creative minds" has enabled Apple to overcome all setbacks due to multiple management failures in that company.

Can a vision be wrong? The ultimate validation of a vision is its ability to stand the test of time. However, it can and must be examined carefully in advance, including its strategic implications. Swissair's top management, which led the company to its "grounding" in 2001, may have had a vision, but the evidence suggests that the vision of Swissair becoming a global player was not only too vague, it was also flawed from the outset. First of all, becoming a global player is neither an original purpose to start with, nor is it a valuable proposition to anybody. Second, when the so-called "Hunter strategy" was presented in 1996, its flaws were already visible. The "strategy" was predicated on the unrealistic ambition of establishing Zurich as a metropolis on the global map of aeronautics. Swissair was about to follow a catastrophic path of expansion via minority stakes in rival airlines. Within five years, the prosperous company which had also been called a "flying bank" was ruined.

What is implicit in Solomon's gnomic wisdom just quoted points to the necessity of a vision being shared by the members of the nation or – in our case – the organization. Visions simply invented within some ivory tower and then imposed on the community have been shown to induce all sorts of pathologies – schisms, reluctance, quarrels and intrigue – often founded on "good reasons" or "good intentions".

Moreover, change and transformation can only ensue if the *purpose* and *mission* of the organization are visible and understood: "Today's theory of the business always becomes obsolete – and usually pretty fast. Unless the basic concepts on which a business has been built are visible, clearly understood, and explicitly expressed, the business enterprise is at the mercy of events. Not understanding what it is, what it represents, and what its basic concepts, values, policies, and beliefs are, it cannot rationally change itself" *(ibidem)*.

In principle, identity, vision and ethos can be a basis for stability and re-silience. They are a source of focus, facilitating the concentration of forces. But they can also become the most powerful levers for development and change. If not shared, however, they will tend to be obstructive barriers to transformation and innovation. If imposed they can even cata-lyze obstinate resistance and ultimately become the drivers of decay. In the first case the members of the organization are the first beneficiaries, in the latter the foremost victims.

The reflection of the basic parameters – ethos, identity and vision – is a necessary ingredient to creativity. Vision is the creative component of finding better ways of relating to the environment, and possibly coming up with improved forms of that relationship. If necessary, the organization must even generate the picture of a new environment it targets or with which it can (re-) configure itself.

The great new mental creations of this kind do not usually occur at the culmination of mental effort, but rather as a flash after a period of relaxa-tion or distraction (Polanyi 1964: 34). This insight, confirmed by many great scientists, should also be taken into consideration when working on the design of a corporate future. The endeavor needs continuity, but also – at the levels of generating ideas and of conceptualization – a playful ap-proach should be paired with disciplined thinking. An idealized design of the system-in-focus should be the reference point of any effort to reinvent or develop an organization (for details, see Ackoff 1981, 1999).

One question remains: What distinguishes a "good" from a "bad" vi-sion? A provisional answer can be given here at least via negative enu-meration. What should be shunned are visions that are immoral, narrow-minded, unrealistic or too vague. The first category concerns offenses of ethical principles. The second is about too shortsighted an outlook, e.g., one that aims at maximal advantage for one single group of stakeholders at the expense of the others. The third relates to visions which are based on wishful thinking rather than a cogent logic. One fallacy of this kind of vi-sion is that it counts on developments which are neither technologically feasible nor operationally viable (cf. Ackoff 1981). Finally, the trap of a vague vision is very dangerous, as the Swissair case just outlined illus-trates.

8.4 Some Empirical Evidence

In the time ahead, the intelligence of organizations will be decisively marked by the basic parameters outlined in the preceding sections of this chapter. An increasing demand for control by development, control by learning or control by transformation will be manifested, and indeed it already is. Each of these kinds of control will have to be essentially organizational *self-control*, enabled by *self-reference*. More than in past decades, organizational intelligence will be grounded in the ability of organizations to learn to develop. This implies higher levels of learning – learning to learn and double-loop-learning, which both have an essentially ethical dimension.

Three empirical studies and several related examples can furnish relevant insights and underpin at least some of the claims made in this chapter.

The first study is an inquiry into the successful habits of "visionary companies" by two researchers from Stanford and McKinsey. The results were published under the title "Built to Last" (Collins & Porras 1994). The authors observed, over several decades, the evolution of a set of what they classified as "visionary companies". These are the premier institutions or "crown jewels" in their industries, widely admired by their peers and having a long track record of making a significant impact on the world around them. They compared these with a control set of companies that also enjoy the reputation of being above average but "don't quite match up to the overall stature of the visionary companies" (op. cit.: 2).

The main result of that study in relation to the topic of ethos is summed up as follows by the authors: "Through the history of most of the visionary companies we saw a core ideology that transcended purely economic considerations. ... They have had core ideology to a greater degree than the comparison companies in our study" (p. 55). Most important, these companies in their visions generally adhere to *high ideals*. Examples[29]:

- "improving human life" (from: Merck & Company Management Guide)
- "respect for each individual" (from: Walmart's Core Beliefs)
- "our first responsibility is to the doctors, nurses and patients, to mothers and fathers and all others who use our products and services" (from: Johnson & Johnson, Our Credo)
- "honor our obligations to society by being an economic, intellectual and social asset to each nation and each community in which we operate." (from: Hewlett-Packard's Corporate Objectives)

---

[29] These examples are not limited to the set of companies from the referred study.

- "to enrich society through car making. ... to be a good corporate citizen, ... strive for cleaner and safer car making, and work to make the earth a better place to live. ..." (from: Toyota, Company Profile).

Recently, IBM came up with a set of three core values for the 21st century, which were elaborated in a 72-hour online real-time conversation among employees from all parts of the company: "dedication to every client's success", "innovation that matters, for our company and for the world", and "trust and personal responsibility in all relationships."

The results of the Collins & Porras study are surprising insofar as the high ethical standards of the "visionary companies" are all but counterproductive in economic terms, while on the contrary these organizations "are more than successful. They are more than enduring ... Visionary companies [as defined by Collins and Porras, can[30]] attain extraordinary long-term performance." (op. cit.: 3f.).

The second study is a survey by Booz Allen Hamilton and the Aspen Institute, which ascertained that an increasing number of companies are making their values explicit (van Lee et al. 2005). Normally, there is some distance between the formulation of basic values in a value statement and the alignment of a strategy with those values, which again is distant from a commitment to those values by all actors in the organization.

According to the study, the financial leaders among these firms have at least come further in the understanding of how to progress from maintaining values to performing better. Among the financial leaders' subset, many more than the rest of the sample[31] include ethical behavior / integrity, commitment to employees, honesty / openness, drive to succeed, and adaptability in their value statements.

As far as practices are concerned, there is relatively little agreement about "best practices" in aligning values with strategy and in embedding values in management processes. However, according to the study, explicit CEO support to reinforce values is considered one of the most effective practices for reinforcing a company's ability to act on its values. The study does not specify any differences in this regard between financial leaders and the rest of the sample.

Summing up, it would be insufficient to formulate principles, values, and the like, without sufficient consideration of how these will be put in practice. Operational goals and programs must follow and realization care-

---

[30]   Addendum by the author. It must be mentioned that Collins and Porras do not refer to "defective", i.e., "unhealthy" or pathological visions. These shall not be pursued further in this section, but – as they are a matter of fact – will be referred to in section 8.5.

[31]   The whole sample was made up of 365 public companies.

fully taken on hand. Johnson and Johnson, for example, to whose corporate value statement I have referred, makes its "beyond compliance philosophy" tangible by means of clear and binding goals. Some of these are Compliance, Understanding and Training in Environmental Aspects, Transparency, Product Stewardship, Water Consumption, and Reduction of Waste.

The third study conveys insights into the nature of "healthy" versus "unhealthy" value orientations. In a large inquiry, Harvard professors John Kotter and Jim Heskett (1992) aimed to ascertain the links between corporate culture and performance. As their research demonstrated, the prominent theorem that proclaims "Strong cultures lead to high performance"[32] is actually incomplete and therefore spurious. A *strong culture*[33] can have detrimental effects on performance if the value system adhered to obstructs adaptation.

How – according to Kotter and Heskett – should the theory be amended? Their results indicate that the main discriminator between strong and weak performers is the organizational ethos in terms of the attitude and behavior towards stakeholders.

Firms with cultures that emphasized all the key constituencies (customers, stockholders and employees) and leadership from managers at all levels outperformed firms that did not have those cultural traits, and did so by a huge margin. This study led the authors to specify the characteristics of two ideal types of culture – *adaptive* (Ideal Type I) and *non-adaptive* (Ideal Type II) – set out in the following Table 8-1.

---

[32]   See for example: Peters/Waterman 1982.

[33]   "Strong" cultures were defined by Kotter and Heskett (1992: 15) as follows: "In a strong culture, almost all managers share a set of relatively consistent values and methods of doing business. New employees adopt these values very quickly. In such a culture, a new executive is just as likely to be corrected by his subordinates as by his bosses if he violates the organization's norms."

Table 8-1. Two types of organizational culture (source: Kotter /Heskett 1992)

	Ideal Type I - *Adaptive*	Ideal Type II – *Non-Adaptive*
Core values	Most managers care deeply about customers, stockholders, and employees. They also strongly value people and processes that can create useful change - e.g., leadership up and down the management hierarchy.	Most managers care mainly about themselves, their immediate work group or some product or technology associated with that work group. They value an orderly and risk-reducing management process more highly than leadership initiatives.
Common behavior	Managers pay close attention to all their constituencies, especially customers, and initiate change when needed to serve their legitimate interests, even if it entails taking risks.	Managers tend to behave in a somewhat insular mode - politically and bureaucrati-cally. As a result, they do not change their strategies quickly in order to adjust to, or take advantage of, changes in their business environment.

The results of this study point to the importance of a normative framework which emphasizes a more sophisticated stakeholder-value orientation than a narrow profit or shareholder-value orientation, as well as a constant quest to bring about the necessary changes. Considering the properties of the ideal types laid out in Table 8-1, it becomes clear that adaptive cultures are more apt

1. to bring forth a constructive discourse about the ethos which underlies corporate behavior, and
2. to bring forth innovations.

In addition, the Kotter and Heskett study provides an important insight linked to the content of Chapter 6. In pleading for "leadership from managers at all levels" they underline the argument in favor of recursive management. In a viable and sustainable organization, ethical principles and values must be anchored recursively, i.e., they will be grounded in the operational domains of all units and members of the organization. In other words, principles and values must be put in practice recursively.

This shall be illustrated through an example. The Hilti corporation is a firm which has become famous for its strong values, innovation and customer orientation. It is a group seated in Liechtenstein, which specializes in fastening technology. A number of core values and principles condensed in a corporate charter (originally called "Leitbild", later named "Vision" and "Mission Statement") have shaped the extraordinary and unique profile of that company since its foundation in 1941. Hilti became and has remained the leading provider of high quality fastening technology to professional customers in the construction and building maintenance industries throughout the world. Hilti has also cultivated a high commitment to their stakeholders. The firm's corporate policy is expressed in a concise statement: "Hilti's corporate policy aims to build stakeholder value. Only by integrating the interests of all the company's partners, at home and abroad – 1employees, customers, suppliers and the financial community – can we create the foundation of confidence on which Hilti constructs its long-term success." (Hilti Corporation 2002a).

The mission statement emphasizes a set of core values – commitment, integrity, responsibility, trust, tolerance and respect for others, readiness to learn and change, embracing duties to society and environment, market penetration rather than entering new markets, independence and freedom of action (Hilti Corporation 2002b). One secret of the company's success has been that these values are more than an espoused theory.[34] They are components of a genetic code, originally coined by Martin Hilti, the founder of the firm (and his brother Eugen as co-founder), further endorsed by his son Michael, his successor as chairman, and over time clearly imprinted in the minds of Hilti's staff at many levels. In daily practice[35] the charter is often quoted, and when important decisions have to be taken managers at all levels of the company reflect with their staff: "What does this decision mean in the light of our corporate values and principles?" One remarkable feature of that enterprise is its exceptional solidity; equity has reached about two thirds of total capitalization over the last few years (Hilti 2002).

At this point one must interject that all of the studies quoted here are insufficient in the sense that not all of the organizations claimed as being adaptive, viable etc. as a function of specific features or "successful habits of visionary companies" (Collins/ Porras 1994) have necessarily survived in the long run.[36] I have looked closely to see if this argument holds in rela-

---

[34] In many firms there is a large gap between *espoused theory* an *theory-in-use* (see the theoretical and empirical work by Argyris/Schoen 1978).

[35] The author has maintained contacts with Hilti for many years and at different levels.

[36] A notorious case in point is the sample of "excellent Firms" from the Peters and Waterman (1982) study, among which several companies went out of business soon after the book was published.

tion to the Collins and Porras study. What I have found is that by 2005, i.e., 11 years after the study, all companies of the original sample but one[37] were still in business. Even though some of them had undergone difficulties, overall these firms had shown much more robustness than those of the samples in other studies. Probably the study was founded on a better research methodology. However, it will be necessary in the future to rely not only on examination of the intentional, adaptive behavior of the companies themselves. Rather, a view of environmental forces at the macro level should be integrated into the picture as well (cf. Volberda/ Lewin 2003).

8.5 Immoral Organizations

Are there organizations which, albeit viable, are not worth having around? In this context, the following questions arise:

Are all viable organizations intelligent?

The fact that an organization survives is a necessary but not sufficient condition for proving that it is intelligent. First of all, viability is more than mere survival. Second, it is not something that can be achieved absolutely or maximally but only to a relative extent or to a certain degree. We know organizations which are not virtuous at all – or even immoral in their ends or in their behavior – and yet which have co-evolved with their milieu and developed remarkable skills of adaptation. Examples can be found in the illegal drug industry. For example, Anatol Rapoport, the pioneering systems theorist already mentioned, has presented profound studies on "parasitical institutions," which thrive on war and perpetuate it (Rapoport 1989, 1992b). Parasitical organizations follow a path of self-reproduction, evolution and often growth on their own, and they can even become so strong as to threaten the existence of the very system they exploit. This has occurred in the case of certain guerilla organizations. Also, if we scan the private sector, we can certainly identify a host of criminal firms – organizations which, in either a hidden or open mode, exist for the sake of an immoral purpose. The production and trade of illegal goods or services (e.g., pyramid saving schemes) is only one example. However, there are variants and degrees of immorality here at which we shall take a closer look (see below). And by the way, not everything that is illegal is necessarily immoral and vice versa.

---

[37] Nordstrom had merged with Travelers Group in 1998 to form Citigroup.

Are all virtuous organizations intelligent?

A virtuous organization is not necessarily intelligent or viable. It may prove to be non-viable or non-adaptive. Expressed in terms of the models discussed in this book (MSC and VSM), it may have a normative management in place which embodies a powerful ethos, and still founder on a lack of strategic acumen or operative laxity.

However, an organization designed and managed so as

- to uphold values such as autonomy, responsibility, respect, fairness and justice and
- to avoid situations in which its component individuals or external co-players have to face contempt, humiliation, degradation, injustice, repression, exploitation or coercion[38],

will also be more healthy and adaptive where the action is[39].

Are all non-viable organizations also non-intelligent?

No, a pathological environment may be so destructive that it also puts highly intelligent organizations out of business. A society may be badly in need of the products provided by a firm, but the market may be blind to that need. For example, many producers of organic food went out of business when the market was not yet sensitive enough to the benefits they provided. Similar cases can be found in "green car" production.

One could argue that the third faculty of intelligent organizations named in Chapter 1 excludes such an excuse – the ability of a firm to find a new environment if necessary, or to reposition itself anew within the extant environment. In real life, however, there may be cases in which that hurdle is simply too high. External – especially market – pressures can be very strong indeed.

The immoral organizations addressed above require a more differentiated treatment. Which organizations are to be qualified as immoral? A straightforward answer is that any organization which offends the morals of a society can be subsumed under this term. In the first place, these are the ones that violate the law. Given the complexities in the international context, natural law is becoming more prominent as a standard for judging corporate behavior (see Kokott 2000). In the second place, however, those organizations which fail to abide by less formalized – unlegislated – socie-

---

[38] "Institutional humiliation is independent of the peculiarities of the humiliating agent." (Margalit 1996: 129).

[39] See for example Margalit's concept of "Decent Society", in which decency has been established alongside justice as a distinctive ethical ideal (Margalit 1996).

tal requirements, such as imperatives for ecological and social responsibility, must also be qualified as "immoral" to a greater or lesser extent. While the first group is to be judged by legal institutions, the latter is increasingly submitted to the scrutiny of consumer initiatives, including ratings, admonitions and sanctions by consumer organizations, as well as ecological and social initiatives. The formal power of these sanctions is inferior to those of the courts, but, as history has shown, they can be very effective nevertheless[40]. The "greening of the industry" has been one remarkable effect, not only of environmental legislation, but also of consumer pressure.[41]

Obviously, both sides must be emphasized. On the one hand, the "machinery" which controls what is produced ticks in the head of the consumer. This statement will certainly provoke the objection that consumers are apathetic, non-critical, decadent, and that they are manipulated by publicity. In the same vein, some claim that immoral organizations are to be abolished. In fact, decadence and immaturity are issues of societal concern. On the other hand, I maintain that society and the state should rather invest in education, culture and ethics than decide centrally which organizations are immoral and which are not. A society gets those organizations which it deserves. In a mature and healthy society immoral organizations are bound to lose territory in a natural way.

8.6 More Empirical Evidence

The evidence condensed here is based on case studies. It is difficult to find systematic empirical studies about incidences of ill corporate ethos. Without doubt, it is more fashionable to cultivate the positive and successful examples (see Section 8.3.). Yet there are different degrees of moral-

---

[40] This is not the place to judge the adequacy or justice of these sanctions. In principle, they are not necessarily of high moral or ethical stature.

[41] Several firms have scrutinized their supply policies under social aspects, partly in response to accusations (not all of which were well-founded) of inhuman or illegal practices. In 1998, Nike, the producer of sports articles, decided it would set the "industry standard" for sweatshop reform. Phil Knight, the founder and chairman, announced a package of reforms which included a minimum working age of 16, a maximum work week of 50 hours and inspectors to police the new rules. Similarly, several multinationals have responded to public pressure on social issues. IKEA, the Swedish furniture producer, already added a clause to its supply contracts forbidding child labor in 1992. By 2000 this enterprise even started to support UNICEF in fighting the roots of child labor, like poverty and poor education, by donating resources for the setting up of schools and other programs in the "carpet belt" of India (Piore/Theil 2001).

ethical and immoral-unethical behavior. This section will therefore be limited to a brief set of examples which indicate that an ill ethos or an erosion of ethical standards are in principle strong indicators of imminent danger. Three ideal types of ill ethos derived from my observations will be sketched out.

1. Ideal-type More of the same:

The preference for more of the same over innovative approaches to business is a danger endemic to successful businesses. A comment of The Wall Street Journal about the crisis in one of the American corporate giants speaks for many: "[The company's] efforts to redefine itself through acquisitions has redefined it as a deeply troubled company."[42]

2. Ideal-type Disrespect of Heritage:

In certain cases, the efforts of companies to give themselves what they consider "cool" names are a symptom of forgetfulness and disrespect in relation to their heritage – in short, of cultural decay. One example is the Swissair group, which renamed itself with the nebulous SAir label in the mid-nineties, therewith carelessly giving away a brand name which had been zealously projected over decades. Five years later – taking the path of an incoherent strategy – this airline, which had been a symbol of Swiss quality, underwent a shameful collapse.

3. Ideal-type Greed to Corruption:

The adoption (and "veneration") of corporate growth and managerial power as ends or "positive" values in themselves, drove the quest for size in some spectacular cases of the stock boom in the nineties. Cases of business fraud, in which unscrupulous greed was the main driver and where illegitimate opportunities for personal enrichment by top managers remained unchecked, led to spectacular collapses of firms: Enron, WorldCom, Arthur Andersen, etc. After the Enron debacle, experts "cleaning up the mess" and chroniclers ascertained that a literal *culture of corruption* with fraudulent, ruthless, reckless and destructive features had evolved in that corporation.[43]

---

[42] Wall Street Journal Europe, November 16/17, 2001, p. 7.
[43] Lawyers have alleged that the banks which underwrote Enron's debt issues and lent money took part in the fraud (The Wall Street Journal Europe, April 9, 2002, p. A5).

Integrity, Communication and Excellence were the declared core values of Enron, designated by its chairman Ken Lay. These words were emblazoned on huge banners that hung in the lobby of its headquarters in Houston. In retrospect, former employees have stated that "Mr. Lay's interest was performance. The flaw was that performance, as defined by Enron, was limited to actions that boosted ... its stock price." (Chaffin/Fidler 2002). The dominant behavior of Enron people evolved organically, from smart and ambitious to greedy and obsessed with stock prices, thence to arrogant, conceitful and prankish, and finally to criminal. Destruction of value was the end of the road (cf. Fox 2003).

Enron was the "domino stone" whose fall set off a spate of corporate scandals, and it marked, in a psychological sense, the end of one of the great bull markets in economic history[44] (Smith/Emshwiller 2003). Following the Enron debacle, the global auditing firm Arthur Andersen became mired in the Enron scandal and finally went out of business.[45] Later on, KPMG, one of the remaining "big four" accounting firms, was involved in a tax-fraud case that might have threatened its very existence, had it not been settled with the American government.[46]

The evidence from companies fallen from grace – including Arthur Andersen after the Enron scandal (cf. Martin 2002) – teaches a valuable lesson: In the end, firms are judged on what they do, not on what they say they do.

It is an insightful exercise to place these observations (and the points made about deficient visions, in section 8.3) in the mirror provided by empirical work from a related domain, the cultural-historical studies on the collapse of societies carried out by Diamond (2005). In a nutshell, the answer to the question, why do societies destroy themselves, rests in a number of factors identified in this study: Ignorance, false analogies, self-

---

[44] This crisis of the private economic sector spurred governments to undertake reforms of corporate governance, which it otherwise probably would not have done.

[45] Arthur Andersen was accused in January 2002 at a federal court in the U.S. of having obstructed justice by shredding documents in connection with Enron, who was its client for auditing and consulting services. As a consequence, Andersen got into the heaviest crisis of its 89 year history, which soon led to the corporation's demise. Two months after convictions were handed down against Andersen in June 2002, only 3'000 of its roughly 28'000 employees were left; of more than 1'200 public-company audit clients none would remain. The terminal tasks of the once-proud firm were to cope with its remaining obligations and shut itself down (Glater 2002).

[46] The Economist, September 3rd, 2005, p. 66.

interest and prioritizing short-term aspirations at the expense of the long term.

A great many firms, however, stand on the better side. Ethical standards, but also regulatory measures, have contributed to keeping companies "clean". Higher social responsibility, the abolishment of corruption, better working and living conditions for the workforce in developing countries, are just a few keywords in the relevant lexicon. Even showpieces of excellence are discernible. Here are two examples:

- Bosch, the leading supplier of the automotive industry, exhibits a remarkable corporate culture, centered upon trust and a very long-term perspective[47] (cf. Fehrenbach 2005)
- Home Depot, the second largest retailer in the U.S. and the largest home improvement retailer in the world, known for its ethos of service[48], which is paired with a culture of passion – joint commitment and enthusiasm – as well as efficiency-driven, human-centered management (Griffith 2005).

And there are millions of small and medium sized businesses around the world in which values of high stature and an impeccable ethos govern the organization.

8.7 Immoral Actors in Organizations

After the instances of ill ethos reported in the last section, one can reasonably infer: What kills such firms is not environmental turbulence but forces that come from inside, namely greed and addiction to growth. But the corruption of the ethos of an organization is not only a top-down or inside-out problem, which can be tackled at the level of the whole by means of sound ethical principles and the good example of leaders. It is just as much a bottom-up or outside-in problem.

According to an old saying, one mangy sheep infects the whole herd. The immorality of the "mangy sheep" meant here is not only embodied in greed, hate, jealousy and envy. In the worst cases these vices tend to exacerbate each other, and they corrupt organizations in different ways:

- By the half-truths they proclaim and the intrigues they spin,

---

[47] Otherwise, the development of the new high-compression diesel injection system, which took a 15-year effort, would have been out of reach.

[48] This includes pioneering work in the do-it-for-me market, which increasingly complements the do-it-yourself market.

- Via the negative projections which such actors impute to their colleagues,
- By way of the mobbing they engage in,
- Through the laziness by which they pursue the easiest path instead of the best one, and
- By the vaingloriousness or greed for which they are ready to sacrifice (almost) anything.

This list covers only some variants of behavior which lead to a sluggish job at best, but often to the work of active destruction.

The cybernetic principle to adopt in dealing with these people is one of distance – Keep them out of the loop, i.e., "Do not deal with them at all". Filter them out before they get into the organization, and if they are already in there, open for them a brilliant way out.

8.8 Intermediate Summary and Outlook

In this chapter the basic parameters of our framework – organizational ethos and identity, and in conjunction with them vision – have been highlighted. From a cybernetic stance, organizational *identity*, ethical *virtues* and *norms* are important attenuators of complexity.

As identity and ethos have a founding function, they are also the most powerful levers of change in organizations. This view is also shared by other systems thinkers. According to Dana Meadows, a leading protagonist of the System Dynamics and the Sustainability Movement, the *mindset* or *paradigm* to which an organization adheres is the strongest leverage point for transformations available to organizations. It is more powerful than such levers as stocks and flows, information and the goals of a system (Meadows 1998[49]). It must be added that a change of beliefs often presupposes changes in behavior; i.e., the adoption of a new frame of reference – if at all – is hardly possible any way other than through learning-by-doing.

---

[49] Meadows expounds ten "places to intervene in a system", in the following sequence of pertinent interventions arranged in order of growing impact: 9. Numbers, 8. Material stocks and flows, 7. Regulating negative feedback loops, 6 Driving positive feedback loops, 5. Information flows, 4. The rules of the system (incentives, punishments, constraints), 3. Self-organization, 2. The goals of the system, 1. The mindset or paradigm out of which the system arises. Finally, she makes the crucial point that even the paradigms must be transcended, i.e., remain open to being changed once they are obsolete.

Poor mindsets are mostly coined by the vices of their holders. If the vice[50] is "only" a cognitive one (e.g., ignorance) it can usually be overcome more easily than if it resides in the affective domain (e.g., arrogance, dishonesty and the like).

Moreover, this functional conception of ethos is complemented and transcended by the inherent value of virtues, i.e., the virtues are ends in themselves (Aristotle, *passim*). They are practiced for their own sake, but the individual is free to adhere to them.

The empirical study by Collins and Porras cited in this chapter shows that enterprises which stand out for their excellent performance in the long run are also generally driven by high ethical values. These values are not imposed by any authority external to the organization, but are the expression of a characteristic mindset or paradigm. They have often led to the foundation of the organization, coined its identity and shaped its ethos. The financial results these firms attain are not an exclusive goal but rather a side-effect of their general orientation.

Finally, the Kotter and Heskett study has provided a valuable clue about the superiority of a relatively broad stakeholder-orientation, by showing that the concept of recursion is a prerequisite for viability not only in structural terms (see chapter 6) but also in cultural terms. In this context it makes sense to revert to a specific concept of recursion – *self-similarity*. This term comes from fractal geometry (Mandelbrot 1982), where self-similarity is defined as the resemblance between the parts of a shape and the shape as a whole[51] . We have met the concept of recursion as related to structure earlier, in Chapter 6. Recursion, and especially self-similarity in the context of the current chapter imply that a replica of the overall organizational culture and ethos can also be identified in arbitrarily small units of the organization (e.g., in a division or in a work group).

Higher values can catalyze innovation and superior performance, triggering processes of organizational learning. To avoid hollow consensus about sublime values which everybody can subscribe to but nobody acts on, these guiding aims need specification according to the individual contexts of the individual members in the organization. In these processes of concretization the quest involves translating them into objectives and measures via recursive conversations and implementing those through multilevel action. Organizational viability is recursive; *organizational intelligence* and *ethos are recursive* as well.

---

[50] Vice is used in broad terms here, meaning "a weakness in some part of a system" (Compact Oxford Dictionary, 1996: 2232).

[51] This is a more general feature than holography, which is a special case of self-similar representation.

In this chapter virtues and values have been treated in terms of the cultural-religious and philosophical traditions best known to the author. This discussion of course is not complete, but it serves a representative purpose, and within its limits is relevant to organizational intelligence. The dialogue between different traditions that is needed for amplifying this framework will certainly bring to the fore new insights in the future.

As an outlook, the following example can shed some light on the potential of science to contribute to this dialogue. This example comes from game theory and simulation. Simulation is often considered a technique relevant only to the domain of operative management. As this example will show, however, it can also reveal new insights into the implications of different ethical principles.

Adam Smith stated over 200 years ago that we do not get our bread due to the *altruism* of the baker but due to his *self-interest*. The theory of cooperation has made the point that altruism is not necessarily an enemy of self-interest, but that – in the long term – it can even serve it. In this vein, the principle of "live and let live" comes off as the more prudent alternative in comparison with selfish principles (Axelrod 1984, 1997). Our example originates from basic research: From his earlier studies in mathematical modeling applied to biology, Anatol Rapoport derived two principles:

1. that co-operations among actors can be either stable or unstable, and
2. that co-operation can entail a "dividend".

Subsequently, Rapoport carried out extensive theoretical and empirical studies (in part with A.M. Chammah)[52], with special emphasis on non-zero-sum games. One of his theoretical "harvests" is a general strategy of interaction for iterated prisoner's dilemma games[53], denominated *Tit-for-Tat*. In essence, this is a meta-strategy based on the principles of *cooperativeness* ("goodwill") and *forgiveness*, combined with the principle that *betrayal* is sanctioned ("retaliation"). Although classified as "semi-weak", Tit-for-Tat won two tournaments against multiple other strategies, outperforming all the other – aggressive ("strong") as well as "weak" – counter-

---

[52] See especially the classical book by Rapoport and Chammah (1965). More recent empirical work by and large corroborates the results found by that study, e.g., Clark/Sefton 2001.

[53] Prisoner's Dilemma is "a non-zero-sum game" which illustrates the failure of both the minimax principle and of the dominating strategy principle" (Rapoport 1969: 311). It is represented in a standard situation of two agents along the following lines. Two prisoners are accused of a crime and will be interrogated separately. If both cooperate, their payoff will be 5 for each. If both defect, their payoff will be -10 for each. If A cooperates and B defects, their payoffs will be 0 and 10 respectively, and vice versa.

parts. The most important theoretical result of those tournaments was that although the Tit-for-tat-strategy cannot possibly win the iterated Prisoners' Dilemma in an encounter with another single strategy, it is more likely to win in a "war of all against all" among different strategies (for details, see Axelrod 1984, Rapoport 2000). This result is in line with the biblical prophecy that "the meek... shall inherit the earth" (Matthew 5.5; Rapoport, 2000).

Chapter 9 Time and Organizational Dynamics

"Todo lo que nos pertenece en realidad a nosotros es el tiempo; aun aquellos que no poseen otra cosa tienen tiempo. "
Balthasar Gracián, Spanish Philosopher, 17th century[1]

"Time is a sort of river of passing events, and strong is its current. "
Marcus Aurelius, Roman emperor and philosopher (121-180)[2]

The fifth dimension of our framework is time. Some readers may find a chapter on this subject redundant. After all, time is a well-established dimension of physics. We know what it is. We also know how to express it. Additionally, we are able to measure it very precisely. We are not concerned when Einstein's Relativity Theory tells us that time is relative. Time changes for objects which move very fast - close to the speed of light. This has no impact on the delays experienced by human beings. Therefore we are impressed if Harvard astrophysicists report that they have succeeded in slowing down and even stopping light by means of specially prepared gases (Lightman 2001), but we could not care less. In daily life this fact is of no direct practical importance.

Information scientists have even abolished physical time from their considerations. For the Abstract State Machines (AST)[3], probably a core concept of the computers of the future, physical time does not exist.[4]

For organizations however, physical time is of prime importance. Organizations are webs of relationships which evolve over time. These processes are bound to *duration*, which is not the same as, but which has something in common with, the *time constants* in physics – they can not be changed arbitrarily. In fact they are closer to the time constants encountered in chemistry and biology. As in those domains, processes of organ-

---

[1] In English: "All that really belongs to us is time; even those who possess nothing else have time." Gracián 1993.
[2] Wordsworth Dictionary of Quotations, 1996, 27.
[3] An AST is a generalized machine that can model any algorithm, no matter how abstract, very closely and faithfully (Gurevich 2000).
[4] On the other hand, an abstract concept of time is used in the AST, namely in the form of sequences of events.

izational development can be accelerated or decelerated to a certain extent by catalytic forces.

In physiology, one example is the kind of medicines which change blood viscosity to improve circulation (blood flow/time). Another case is that of psycho-pharmaceuticals, which modify the behavior of neurotransmitters to avoid depressions, phobias, etc. (via hormone flow/time). Comparable instances in organizations can be either external pressures or forms of internal leadership which mobilize social energies and trigger faster change. This will be illustrated by a concrete example in the next section.

9.1 Transformation over Time

Before we revert to that example, several general issues which emerge from the current state of knowledge shall be highlighted.

The first issue concerns the question if there is a necessary *correlation between change and progress*. Among practitioners it is often assumed that the mere fact that a system evolves is a guarantee for its improvement. However, studies in the self-organization of social systems have shown that this assumption is misleading. The "natural evolution" of a system does not necessarily raise its efficiency[5] (cf. Allen 1997), nor is organizational change a panacea for malfunction or a sure path toward progress. On the contrary, the fashionable adherence to "constant change" has rather become a destructive force. In many firms managers have become addicted to change projects, promoting superficial change for the sake of change, often to compensate for their incapacity to genuinely innovate. This mode of behavior jeopardizes organizational culture and destroys value (London 2002).

Secondly, *resistance to change* and the extended lengths of time needed to change anything in organizations are already proverbial. Accordingly, much of the discussion about organizational development revolves around overcoming obstacles to learning, namely organizational defensive patterns (Argyris 1990). A systematic treatment of the issues pertinent to organizational transformation and learning has been given in one of my earlier books (Espejo/ Schuhmann/ Schwaninger/ Bilello 1996).

A third aspect is that transformation over time has different *degrees of profoundness*. As emphasized in Chapter 8, the most powerful triggers of transformation are changes of the mindset or paradigm, which are superior to other levers such as goals, self-organization, rules, information flows,

---

[5]   Similarly, free markets do not necessarily lead to optimal economic structures.

feedback loops etc. Whenever a bifurcation in the evolutionary path of an organization is close at hand, it is the dominant mindset which can and does switch the points. The paradigm sets the course. It is problematic to generalize about the time needed for different kinds of transformation. Yet, as will be shown in the next section, some insights about *time constants* concerning the duration of the processes of fundamental change have emerged from empirical studies.

A fourth issue is the *speed of change*. Much has been said about the advantages of being fast and the dangers of being too slow. There is empirical evidence as well that organizational change processes can be speeded up impressively - by a factor of 5 or so[6] - even though a cumulative body of research results about the whys, whens and hows of such accelerations is still lacking. Nevertheless, at least an insightful example can be provided in the following section.

9.2 A Practical Example

Our example is one in which the speed of transformation was multiplied to a magnitude of the order just mentioned. The cases in point are two factories, a frozen food plant in Listowel and the Toronto soup can plant, both of Campbell Canada[7]. In the early nineties, in the face of cutthroat competition, the viability of these plants suddenly became questionable. The evidence as provided by both accounting figures (namely excessive cost) and strategic diagnosis (in particular concerning the competitive position in terms of relative quality and price) suggested that the situation was very dangerous. Campbell had fallen behind its competitors, and seven out of eleven Campbell plants in Canada had been closed or sold in the previous years.

The process of transformation which then evolved despite the initial situation can be reconstructed in terms of our framework from Chapter 4. In brief, the occurrences were as follows; references to the categories of the framework are made in brackets.

CEO David Clark, with the help of an outside motivational expert, undertook an effort "to transform the way Campbell's workers relate[d] to their jobs and their company" (Trueman 1993: 30). Kick-off workshops were realized in each of the four plants remaining at that time, after closure

---

[6]   See for example the organizational transformation process with a large insurance company reported in Schwaninger 2005, as well as the following practical example.

[7]   The following case is documented in Trueman 1993.

of the seven others, and the whole of the top and middle management of Campbell Canada was formed into "power teams" supported by external facilitators. According to Clark, these teams "had to commit to unreasonable, irrational achievements" in terms of cost and quality improvements.

Let us look at the Listowel plant, the worst performer of all, and the similar Toronto plant, the only two factories of Campbell Canada, since both have remained in operation as of 2006. A series of motivational workshops became crucial in turning the company around because the whole workforce of about 400 suddenly understood what was at stake – their own employment. Enormous social energy (motivation→behavior) emanated from that understanding. The personnel formed itself into self-managed teams which completely reshaped the production process (→structure and activities). Within less than a year (→time) the doomed factories rose like a phoenix from the ashes. The work ethic had changed completely (→basic parameters) and the organization presented itself as a competitive (in both, cost and quality) and successful player in a new game where the Canadian factories were to serve the much larger U.S. market, too. For details see Trueman (1993).

For a start, this example at least illustrates the relevance of a claim which is at the core of this book – a virtuous transformation leading to ever more vigorous viability and development requires guided, synchronized evolution and transformation over time, in all three domains – activities, structure and behavior[8], in alignment with the fourth dimension – the underlying basic parameters[9].

In fact, it has often been claimed by different authors that the dimensions of strategy, structure and behavior of organizations interrelate. However, in the mainstream of organization research little has been done to study the dynamic patterns of systemic behavior that emerge as a function of that interaction.

As an initiative taken toward closing this gap, simulation models have been developed by the author which enable one to explore these aspects. The following section reports on some of the results and insights emanating from simulations with one of these models.

---

[8]   For some empirical evidence – even though collected in more specific domains – to support this argument, see: Pettigrew/Whipp 1993, and Rudolph 1999.

[9]   These basic parameters (referring to organizational ethos, identity and vision) can be operationalized by means of constructs such as *values, norms or lead distinctions*, which are logically superordinate to the distinctions drawn in the three other dimensions (cf. Model of Systemic Control, Chapter 5).

9.3 Lessons from Computer Simulations

The model we are drawing on here represents the interaction of the components of our framework over time. It was elaborated by means of System Dynamics – a modeling and simulation methodology developed by Jay W. Forrester, Professor at MIT, which is particularly useful for applications to social systems[10]. The model is a conceptual-theoretical one, elaborated with the purpose of visualizing the dynamic links between the dimensions of our framework (Figure 9-1). It is not validated with detailed data from real organizations, because it is too broad and too abstract. However, more specific models have been realized which specialize in partial aspects included in this model and therefore have also been carefully validated (e.g., Rockart 2001 for the Strategy-Behavior link, Weber/ Schwaninger 2002 for the strategy-structure relationship).

The model was implemented by means of VENSIM software[11] and has been called the Transformation of *Organizations Model (Trafo Model)*. The details of that model and multiple simulation results are documented elsewhere (publication planned). Here we can limit ourselves to taking a look at the basic structure of the model, which is depicted as a high-level map in Figure 9-1.

---

[10]   The characteristics of System Dynamics have already been described in Chapter 5.

[11]   Producer: Ventana Systems, Massachusetts, U.S.A.

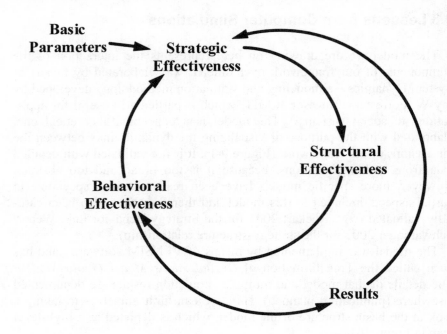

Fig. 9-1. Structural map of the simulation model

This structural map of the simulation model contains a number of variables linked by arrows denoting causal relationships, and a set of fundamental parameters which essentially represent the organizational identity and ethos. The structure of the model is a closed-loop structure of two feed-back-loops. The inner loop links strategy, structure and behavior. All three concepts are brought into an operational form by referring to their effectiveness. For example, structural effectiveness would be high if the structure of the organization under study would be adaptive and well aligned with the needs of the organization. The behavioral effectiveness would be high, if it would lead to a high measure of goal achievement, etc. All three concepts are causally related: The higher strategic effectiveness the better the ensuing structures, and the higher structural effectiveness the better their support for behavior. Behavioral effectiveness then feeds back into strategic effectiveness. All three links of the loop contain time delays. The outer loop simply denotes that behavior leads to results, which impinge on strategic effectiveness.

We can abstract from the technicalities of the simulation model[12] and concentrate on the results of simulations concerning our subject matter in focus – how the organizational dynamics evolve over time, as a function of the *interaction of the dimensions* depicted in our framework: Activities, Structure, Behavior and Basic Parameters. For the underlying theory see especially Hurst (1995).[13]

I shall now address a number of questions, which were also posed to orient the design of the model and the exploratory computer simulations:

Is there anything like a reaction time?

We know that social systems have their own time constants. This was ascertained by the studies of technological substitution carried out by researchers of the International Institute for Applied Systems Analysis, Laxenburg, Austria, for example. These authors found out that the time needed for a society to learn something fundamentally new runs in the neighbourhood of fifty years (Marchetti 1982, Gruebler 1990). Similar regularities – albeit with time constants varying across industries – were found concerning the time needed for a new technology or product generation to replace an established one (cf. Heizmann 1990, Eggler 1991).

The delicacy of managing an organizational transformation is in large part due to the fact that the time constants (i.e., the time needed to effectuate fundamental change) inherent in each one of the domains mapped out in our framework are different. The established Strategies can often be reinvented fairly quickly, whereas structural transformation takes more time. The variables that change most slowly are the deep-seated behavioral ones. Even though behavior may adapt superficially, the basic pattern tends to remain the same. Also, variable features essentially shaped by human behavior, such as knowledge, competence etc., cannot be changed arbitrarily. It takes substantial time and effort to build them up (See Chapter 5).

Consequently, the process of organizational development faces discrepancies of the following kind: In order to realize a certain strategy a competence may be needed whose evolution is more time-consuming than developing the strategy itself. The usual approach adopted is typically viewed as a panacea – acting faster – but it does not solve the problem. The only solution is to anticipate needs at an earlier stage. But how can anything be

---

[12]   This is a model designed for didactical purposes, not a corporate simulation mode. It can be obtained from the author.

[13]   The base run with the simulation model replicates the Hurst model of organizational change, even though this is only possible in a qualitative mode, because Hurst has not specified the amplitudes and frequencies of his model quantitatively.

anticipated if everything changes so fast? These contradictions can be solved only with the help of an orientation system of a higher order; for strategic management this higher order system is normative management.

First conclusion:

In managing organizational transformation,
different time constants must be taken into account.
Contradictions can be solved only at a higher logical level.

Is it true that combined or synchronized measures are superior to punctual ones?

Combination and synchronization are two different concepts. It is necessary, as a first step, to look at these two aspects separately. Then it must be ascertained whether there is a relationship between the two.

The first claim to be examined is that multi-dimensional interventions are superior to uni-dimensional ones. The superiority of combined interventions has been shown both theoretically and with computer simulations (Reither 1997, Schwaninger/Powell/Trimble 2002) and there is much practical evidence to corroborate it. For example, the failures of several spectacular mergers have often been the consequence of uni-dimensional thinking. In the case of the "fusion" of Daimler-Benz and Chrysler in the late nineties, it appears that the only dimension considered was the logic of product-market-strategy, and even that consideration was not flawless. The dimensions of structure and behavior were almost neglected, and ethics appeared only much later and in the negative sense – the famous lie of one of the Chairmen[14].

As far as the question of combined versus punctual interventions is concerned, several scenarios were simulated:

1. Intervention only in the Activities (Strategy) Dimension – "Scenario S"
2. Intervention only in the Structural Dimension – "Scenario Str"
3. Intervention only in the Behavioral Dimension – "Scenario B"
4. Simultaneous intervention in both the Activities and the Structural Dimensions – " Scenario CombS&Str"
5. Simultaneous intervention in all three dimensions, Activities, Structure and Behavior – Scenario "CombAll".

The simulations showed results which at a first sight contradicted the anecdotal evidence. The combined interventions in two or more dimensions, e.g., Activities and Structure, did not unequivocally breed better cumulated

---

[14]   He had officially treated this case as a merger. After the accomplished deal he alleged that for him it had always been a takeover.

performance than interventions limited to a single dimension. The scenario which generates the best performance data combines measures in two dimensions, while the scenario where all measures are combined significantly underperforms when compared to the base, uni-dimensional one.

Second conclusion:
The combination of measures
is not in itself superior to the application of punctual measures.

This appears to be a paradox. As paradoxes need names, I called it *Markus' Paradox*. However, I surmised that the aspect of the synchronization of measures plays an important role. Therefore, in the next step the role of synchronization was examined. Only thereafter are we going to be able to deal with Markus' Paradox successfully.

What is meant by synchronization and how important is it?

To answer this question, different scenarios were set up. Besides the Default scenario 1., in one case all interventions are realized simultaneously, i.e., at the same time 2. In two cases, the sequence of the interventions was synchronized (i.e., staggered in coincidence) with the pattern of delays along the chain of variables (scenarios 3 and 4). In detail, these scenarios were defined as follows:

1. *Default*: In this case no intervention is made.

The other three cases simulate the impacts of the same combination of three measures but following a different chronology:

2. *CombSameTime*: In this scenario all three interventions (on Strategy, Structure, and Behavior) are realized at the same point in time (t=10),
3. *Combsynch*: In this scenario the measures are staggered in accordance with the specific rhythm of the system under observation. The three measures are put in effect at t=10, 16 and 18 in accordance with the delays of six and two months following in the chain of variables (Strategy-Structure-Behavior).
4. *CombSynchCareful*: In this case the synchronization followed an even more sophisticated timing than in the Combsynch scenario (t=10, 36, 56).

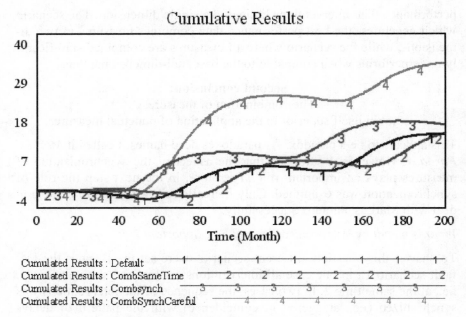

Fig. 9-2. Comparison of the Synchronization Scenarios

The results show that it pays off to consider the time constants or patterns inherent in the system – that is, the results achieved under the Combsynch scenario (line 3) are better than those under Default 1 and CombSameTime 2. The more sophisticated – in terms of synchronization – CombsynchCareful scenario 4 generates significantly better results. It is also remarkable that the CombSameTime scenario 2, despite all the efforts (three interventions, same as in Combsynch) does not lead to any better results than the Default scenario (no interventions, 1).

Third conclusion:
Synchronicity must not be confounded with simultaneity.

The patterns exhibited suggest that the relatively good performance of the Default scenario – relative to CombSameTime[15] – may hinge on the fact that it follows the rhythm of the system better[16]; its reference line 1 runs

---

[15]   The level of cumulative results, which are gross figures, i.e., calculated before deduction of intervention costs, is similar for both scenarios. However, a high intervention cost characterizes the CombSameTime scenario, while the Default scenario is without such a cost.

[16]   Further analysis would be needed in order to answer the question of whether this is true.

less delayed and almost in parallel with the one of CombSynch 3, while the CombSameTime scenario 2 is "out of step". The most famous practical examples in this context come from the cyclical markets (e.g., the "pork cycle"). Producers who do not understand the pattern produce more whenever the price is high. This leads to an excess of supply and a decline in prices, etc. Anti-cyclical behavior in this case is preferable to following the herd instinct.

Fourth conclusion:
Follow the rhythm of the system!

Finally, the superior results attained under the CombSynchCareful scenario 4 visualize the potential leverage of careful timing. The importance of timing is undisputed. Simulation exercises can be used to train managers for better timing (cf. Thorelli 2001). Relevant theory on the subject is scarce, but some principles have been elaborated, e.g., with respect to innovation processes (Gälweiler 2005, Schwaninger 1989).

Fifth conclusion:
Careful timing can breed exceedingly good results.

This may be something that has entered conventional wisdom, but it is less intuitive a) how big the payoffs are, b) how strongly this can compensate for shortcomings, e.g., on the resource side, and c) how expensive it can be not to understand the dynamics of the system.

Therefore **the sixth conclusion** is:
Try to understand the dynamics of the system!

How can the Paradox be solved?

Let us revert to Markus' Paradox – the combination of measures is not in itself superior to the application of punctual measures. The question is whether our paradox can be solved by integrating the combination and the synchronization aspects. Examining this question calls for running a set of scenarios, but with a more sophisticated timing (Figure 9-3). We shall use the timing (t=10, 36, 56) – already selected for CombSynchCareful scenario and proven successful (Figure 9-2).

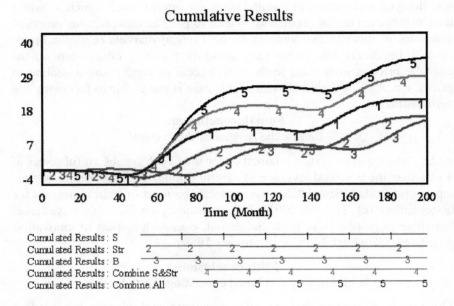

Fig. 9-3. Results of Five Scenarios Integrating Combination and Synchronization of Interventions

The scenarios are:

1. A combination of interventions in all three dimensions, Strategy, Structure, and Behavior, which are also synchronized. – "Scenario Combine All"
2. A combination of interventions in the Strategy and Structure dimensions, which are also synchronized – "Scenario Combine S&Str"
3. Intervention only in the Behavioral dimension – "Scenario B"
4. Intervention only in the Structural dimension – "Scenario Str"
5. Intervention only in the Strategy dimension – "Scenario S".

The message conveyed by the patterns in Figure 9-3 is clear. Two-dimensional synchronized measures (Scenario Combine S&Str) generate better results than do one-dimensional measures (Scenarios S, Str, B), and they are even surpassed by the results from three-dimensional synchronized measures (Scenario Combine All). This cogently leads to our

Seventh conclusion:
Combined measures are more successful than punctual ones,
if they are also synchronized appropriately.

The explanation of why theory and empirical evidence have often suggested the superiority of combined measures over isolated ones is that these claims already imply the notion of synchronization. Herewith Markus's Paradox is solved. For theory see Schwaninger/Powell/Trimble (2002), and for empirical studies Reither (1997) and Doerner (1997).

What is more important, long-term orientation or short-term adaptation?

Additional simulations reported elsewhere (Schwaninger 2003b) show that both long-term orientation and short-term adaptation are vital. Intelligent organizations excel at combining perseverance in pursuing their ethos and strategy on one hand and acting fast and flexibly on the other. In other words, they hone both short-term adaptiveness in current processes and long-term persistency, as complementary capabilities.

The best strategy is only as good as its implementation. However, the highest efforts at the operative level are futile if they cannot build on prerequisites created beforehand through a long-term effort. Path-dependence – the inescapable restrictions due to omissions in the past – can hit hard, if these prerequisites are absent (cf. Arthur 1994).

In this sense the main conclusion of this chapter can be condensed into which I call the Principle of Time Management:

Eighth conclusion:
The basis of effective time management is starting earlier, not acting faster.

9.4 Intermediate Summary

At this stage we can summarize the lessons of this chapter:

1. In managing organizational transformation different time constants must be taken into account. Contradictions can be solved only at a higher logical level.
2. The combination of measures is not in itself superior to the application of punctual measures.
3. Synchronicity must not be confounded with simultaneity.
4. Following the rhythm of the system enhances performance.
5. Careful timing can breed exceedingly good results.
6. Understanding the dynamics of the system and acting upon it improves performance.
7. Combined measures are more successful than punctual ones, if they are synchronized appropriately as well.

8. The basis of effective time management is starting earlier, not acting faster.

The principle "start earlier" expressed in the eighth lesson links the time aspect back to the first dimension of our framework – activities – treated in the context of the Model of Systemic Control in Chapter 5. There we laid the foundation for this principle when introducing the notion of pre-control. Here we have been able to support it by means of computer simulations.

All of the above lessons hold *only if* the improvements in insight and understanding are put into practice effectively and efficiently. This is the link between normative, strategic and operative management as outlined in Chapter 5.

What we have not simulated here is macro-level "natural" selection. Observing these processes of selection by environmental forces, at the population level, can become very important. Reverting, then, to the Law of Requisite Variety: A fundamental and effective approach to variety engineering is to shun those environments where the selective forces are against you.

Chapter 10 The Framework Revisited

„Philosophy teaches us to act, not to talk. "
Lucius Aenneus Seneca, Roman Philosopher, Playwright and Politician[1]

"Act always so as to increase the number of choices. "
Heinz von Foerster, Austro-American Cybernetician[2]

In this chapter we shall revisit our Framework for the Design and Development of Intelligent Organizations, in order to introduce the integrative connections that can only be made at this stage – that is, after having discussed each one of its dimensions in detail.

For this purpose, we once more revert to the overview presented in Chapter 4 (Figure 4-1). However, at this stage we link the three models outlined in Chapters 5, 6 and 7 with the dimensions to which they are primarily related (Figure 10-1).

This chapter is an attempt at tying the components from the preceding chapters together, and so is rather theoretical. Sections 10.1 to 10.4 can be skipped by readers mainly interested in practical aspects. Section 10.5, however, which deals with applications of the framework, will be of interest to them.

---

[1] *Epistulae*, no. 20, in Seneca 1993.
[2] Von Foerster 1984b: 308.

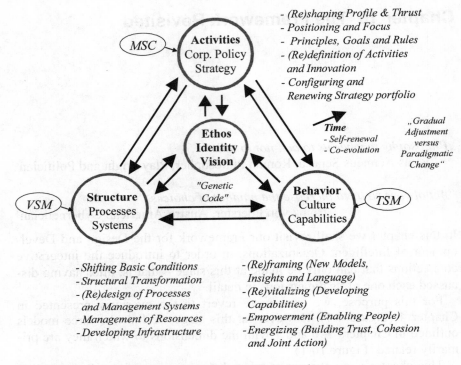

- (Re)shaping Profile & Thrust
- Positioning and Focus
- Principles, Goals and Rules
- (Re)definition of Activities
  and Innovation
- Configuring and
  Renewing Strategy portfolio

Time
- Self-renewal
- Co-evolution

„Gradual
Adjustment
versus
Paradigmatic
Change"

- Shifting Basic Conditions
- Structural Transformation
- (Re)design of Processes
  and Management Systems
- Management of Resources
- Developing Infrastructure

- (Re)framing (New Models,
  Insights and Language)
- (Re)vitalizing (Developing
  Capabilities)
- Empowerment (Enabling People)
- Energizing (Building Trust, Cohesion
  and Joint Action)

Fig. 10-1. Cybernetic Models Linked to the Framework

10.1 Systemic Features

When presenting the Framework, we discerned four of its systemic features (Cf. Section 4.2.):
1. The *integrative* nature of the Framework,
2. Its *design* orientation,
3. Its *multidimensionality* and
4. The *dynamic interrelationship* of its components.

As the Model of Systemic Control, the Viable System Model and Team Syntegrity have been introduced in relation to the dimensions of Activities, Structure and Behavior, two additional systemic features of the Framework have come to the fore:

5. In logical terms, management is conceived as a *multi-level process* with
   - Normative management fulfilling the foundational function, embodied by System 5 in the VSM;

- Strategic management, the orientational function, embodied by System 4 and the interrelationship between Systems 3 and 4 in the VSM;
- Operative management, the function of realization, embodied by Systems 1, 2 and 3 (including System 3*) and their interrelationships in the VSM.

6. Management is conceived as a recursive process. The principle of recursiveness is applicable to all three models. Also, the whole framework is applicable to any level of recursion in an organization, even though some of the terms may contain a certain bias towards the higher levels of recursion.

10.2 Organizational Principles in the Framework

At this stage the Framework has to be reflected in terms of the organizational principles it incorporates; an overview of the crucial categories is given in Table 10-1.

Table 10-1. Different Organizational Principles Incorporated in the Dimensions of the Framework

Dimensions of Framework	Organizational Principles
Activities	Hierarchy
Structure	Recursion
Behavior	Holography
Fundamental Parameters	Self-similarity
Time	Continuity

It is important to comment on these categories because they convey a more differentiated picture of what intelligent organizations are about than do the simplifications inherent in much of what is recommended in the literature for the design of organizations. The discussion will proceed sequentially through the five dimensions of the Framework (Cf. Chapters 5 to 9):

Activities:

The control of activities as conceived by the Model of Systemic Control (Chapter 5) transcends the simple feedback cycle. The web of operative, strategic and normative variables of control shows the property of pre-control, besides conventional control. The knowledge of these interrelationships – which is one of *logical hierarchy* – is crucial for managers coping with the dynamic complexities they must confront. In this context, the abhorrence of anything labeled as hierarchy, which is characteristic of the spirit of our time, would be misleading.

Structure:

The concept of *recursion* immanent in the Viable System Model (Chapter 6) is an utterly powerful principle for the design of organizations. The theory of the VSM is more rigorous and effective than similar models[3] which have been proposed. The pragmatic merits of those models are in no position to define the necessary and sufficient preconditions for an organization to be viable. Please note that the principle of recursion has been conceptualized as multidimensional; therefore it is perfectly compatible with the concept of heterarchical structure.

Behavior:

The organizations of the future will depend on the ability of their members to make sense of the organization they are part of, more so than those of the past. This is precisely what the principle of *holography* is about: In a holographic organization the parts include information about the whole. Team Syntegrity has been expounded as both a model and a protocol (Chapter 7). It embodies a very close approximation to this structural principle.

Basic Parameters:

The Chapter on basic parameters (Chapter 8) has focused on aspects of ethos and identity and therewith on the selfhood of organizations. The empirical evidence cited there indicated the necessarily *self-similar* nature of adaptive cultures. In other words, a constructive orientation towards the different stakeholders is necessary but not sufficient. For a culture to qualify as adaptive, this orientation must be discernible at many levels of the social organism, as the Kotter and Heskett (1992) study has shown.

---

[3]   E.g., a model denominated as "Fractal Factory" (Warnecke 1992). The similarity with the VSM stems from the fact that this model loosely refers to recursive structure, insofar as fractals are recursive: A formula is recursively applied to itself (cf. Peitgen/Richter 1986).

Time:

Over time, the evolution of an organization that strives for viability and development requires continuity, but it does so, however, only at a meta-level. This is a *continuity* which also opens space for discontinuities where they are necessary. This factor implies not only controls for stability but also the admittance of instability. This applies in a well-defined sense only. According to Nobel Prize laureate Ilya Prigogine's Order-through-fluctuation Principle (Prigogine/Stengers 1984), the fluctuations which lead to innovation or higher levels of order[4] must be allowed.[5] These fluctuations can originate from both sides, internal (intentional forces striving for adaptation) and external (environmental forces driving selection).

A reference of interest here is Kauffman's (1996) design principle, which says that: the complex systems best able to adapt by mutation and selection are those constructed in a way that places them on the boundary between order and chaos.

10.3 An Integrative View of the Dimensions and Models

The three models outlined in Chapters 5 to 7 can in principle leverage, facilitate and improve organizational transformation substantially, if they are used in an integrated and synchronized manner. In Figure 10-2 the three models are integrated graphically, but further elucidation of this rather impressionistic image is necessary. In this respect two points must be made.

---

[4]   The concept of control through instability must not be confounded with two utterly destructive modes of management that have been observable frequently over the last few years, namely Management by laissez-faire and Management by destabilization (via power games, intrigues, etc.).

[5]   In this context, the findings of Cheng and Van de Ven (1996) are of interest: From their analysis of innovation processes these authors found that both action and outcome events exhibit chaotic patterns during the initial period of innovation development, and more orderly periodic patterns during the end of the innovation process. The term *chaotic* here refers to a nonlinear system which is neither totally predictable nor completely random.

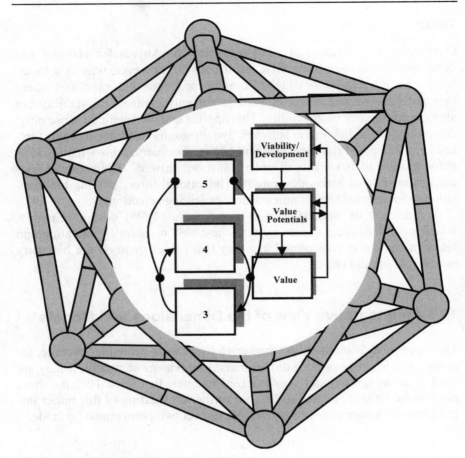

Fig. 10-2. Integrative View of the Models (I)

First, an *integration of the three models* is neither artificial nor arbitrary, as they are bound together by strong and cogent conceptual links (cf. also figure 10-3).

The MSC and the VSM are *intrinsically connected* by the equivalence of three logical levels - operative, strategic and normative. For competent applications it is necessary to understand these relationships thoroughly. In the case of the MSC the three logical levels are represented by the respective referents for conceiving and controlling what the organization does, while in the case of the VSM they are represented by the structure of the management functions which embody these three logical levels. The TSM is *complementary* to both the MSC and the VSM. It was conceived for the optimal design of communications and interactions in the managerial metasystem of organizations (Systems 3/4/5 in terms of the VSM, in particular the homeostat of Systems 3 and 4[6], in which the checks and balances between "Inside and Now" and "Outside and Then" occur). This design turned out to be necessary: On one hand, the number of people involved in the issues at stake in such a metasystem usually transcends the size of face-to-face groups. On the other hand, there was no theoretically well-founded protocol available to provide for an optimal design of communications in large groups (cf. Beer 1994).

These inherent logical relationships provide a *naturally integrative* force, which may not be recognized by outside observers who are unfamiliar with the links made explicit here. It can be argued that the effectiveness of any combined application will significantly depend on the knowledge of these relationships on the parts of the key actors, particularly the facilitators involved in relevant projects of organizational transformation. One must add that a combination with other models is not in principle excluded from consideration. Also, in practice, methods and methodologies not explicitly specified here will necessarily be included in the repertory of change agents and facilitators of organizational transformations.

---

[6]   As specified in Chapter 6, System 3 represents the operative management of a collective of primary units (subsystems), System 4 the management for the long term development of the organization, and System 5 the normative management.

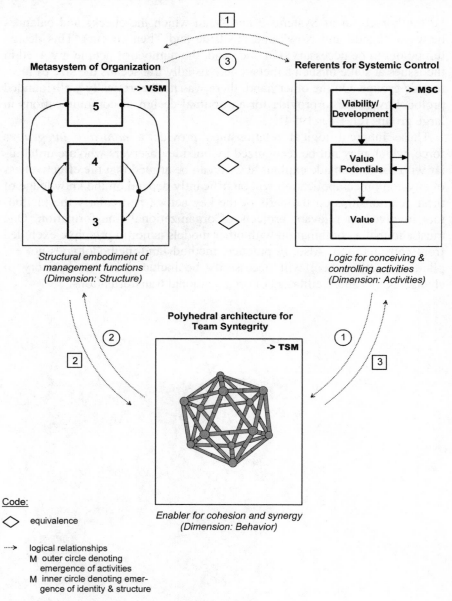

Fig. 10-3. Integrative view of the models (II)

The second point is that each one of the three models outlined has a particularly strong link to one of the dimensions of the framework:

1. The aspect of *activities:* The *Model of Systemic Control* furnishes a frame of reference which supports an integral (self-) control. It helps agents to distinguish between the three logical levels of management and orientates them in keeping the steering variables of all three levels under control simultaneously, even if contradictions occur.

2. The aspect of *structure*: The *Viable System Model* is a device for diagnosing an organization and designing it in a way that the (self-) control necessary for achieving viability and development can be attained.

3. The aspect of *behavior*: The *Team Syntegrity Model* provides a framework for developing virtuous synergetic interactions and relationships in an organization. This holds in particular for an increase of cohesion and the generation of knowledge in multi-person settings, and also in the context of reflective and innovative processes.

However, the utility of each one of these three models is not limited to any one of the dimensions of activities, structure or behavior, as this enumeration might seem to imply. On the contrary, all three of them incorporate a systemic perspective which to some extent also considers the other dimensions. And each one has a substantial contribution to make with regard to reflecting such basic issues as the ethos, identity and vision of an organization (cf.: Schwaninger 1998b).

On the other hand, organizational identity, ethos and vision can be considered *basic parameters* insofar as they shape an organization in a fundamental way. Their impact on the other dimensions – activities, structure and behavior – is in principle primordial. Insofar as that is so, it is also necessary to specify how they are tied to the concept of an intelligent organization as formulated at the outset.

A specific set of these basic parameters always enables certain modes of *adaptation* while it precludes others. For example, those firms which have established strong identities as leaders in environment-friendly problem solving, exclude toxic products and technologies from their options for adapting to market demand.

Similarly, the modes by which a company can *shape its environment* will strongly depend on these basic parameters. An ethos of opportunistic reaction will provide little space for influencing the milieu constructively. On the other hand, a strong sense of ethical responsibility is often at the root of innovation and leadership, through which firms have helped society at large in coping with problems such as disease or scarcity of resources. For pertinent empirical evidence, see Collins/Porras 1994.

Furthermore, *finding a new milieu* and, if necessary, *reconfiguring itself* with relation to its environment, can instill new vigor into an organization.

However, such a process of renewal is risky. A virtuous trajectory will be favored by a strong sense of identity, e.g., to avoid the fallacy of diversification unguided by any concept, with its potentially disastrous implications for competitiveness and economic performance (cf. Palich/Cardinal/ Miller 2000, von Werder et al. 2001).

Finally, an organization confined within a narrow perspective will not be prone to making a substantial *contribution to the larger whole* of which it is part. Responsible leaders need a sufficiently broad vision, which includes an understanding of the embeddedness of the organization (see VSM, Chapter 6) and of the requirement of legitimacy for viability and development (see MSC, Chapter 5). At this stage, it is worthwhile revisiting the fundamental parameters – ethos, vision and identity – with a perspective on change in view.

10.4 Change and the Fundamental Parameters Revisited

To start with, it must be reemphasized that the relative persistence over time of an identity does not preclude the fact that it may change, and even at a fast pace in some cases. For example, Encyclopedia Britannica, the traditional publisher and marketer of the „ultimate home library" founded in 1768 in Edinburgh, weathered its greatest crisis in the nineties of the 20th century. After several attempts at revising its business model (a huge sales campaign, and availability of contents via paid Internet services), the firm transformed itself into an electronic information center in 1999. This change has been compared metaphorically with the transformation of a time-honored steam-ship into a modern speed-boat (Weber 2000). One could argue that corporate identity in this case has not changed fundamentally; Encyclopedia Britannica always was and still remains a knowledge source. There are indeed different degrees of change in identity, some of them dramatic.

Neither is ethos or vision exempt from change; e.g., growing insight and wisdom may lead to the emergence of new ethical principles or to sharper anticipations of desirable futures.

On the other hand, there is hardly anything more destructive than careless changes in identity or ethos. These have often to do with a lack of conscience, which leads to an erosion of principles. A comparative study about the long term evolution of two industrial giants in Germany – Siemens and AEG – has shown that despite having practically the same initial conditions, these corporations have taken completely different paths of evolution (von Werder et al 2001). Both were founded in the 19th century by pioneers, and both brought innovations based on electricity to the mass market. At the beginning of the 21st century Siemens was still strong while AEG had gone out of business in 1996, after a death struggle lasting over 20 years.

The study tracks this difference back to the genetic code and its influence over time. In the case of Siemens, the pronounced values of its founder Werner von Siemens – besides innovation and social responsibility – were self-determined growth, maintenance of the influence of the founder's family, with a clear preference for self-financing and a reluctance to let power be exerted from outside. In the case of AEG the values of the founder Emil Rathenau were similar, except for a greater openness to banks. Early on, this resulted in a more rapid growth because the capital market was exploited without reservations. As far as Siemens is concerned, Werner's principles of management have continued valid over one and half a centuries. Even today, Siemens resists fashionable management practices with respect to corporate finance or asset stripping, even though this has often resulted in the exertion of strong external pressures against the company and its managers. In the case of AEG, however, the founder's principles, which by and large had also been long-term oriented and conservative, gave way to short-termism and a purely financial orientation soon after his death. As a consequence, management repeatedly failed to correct wrong causes of action and became ever more unable to liberate the corporation from its "disastrous fate." The decline of AEG is a clear case of path dependence[7] – the binding effect of past structures and decisions (von Werder 2001).

This cautionary tale serves as a strong reminder of the ethical imperative established by Heinz von Foerster (1984b: 308): *"Act always so as to increase the number of choices."*[8]

The question remains, however, if acting purposefully and adaptively is sufficient for a firm to find a path of both self-renewal (inside-out and micro view) and co-evolution (outside-in and macro view).

A first answer is that, besides taking the firm-level into account, the population-level should be carefully considered as well. Co-evolutionary models rely on the premise that both forces are fundamentally interrelated:

---

[7]   cf. section 5.4., Arthur 1994.

[8]   There are exceptions to this rule. The number of choices cannot be increased ad infinitum. There are for example limitations of cost; the marginal cost of an increase in flexibility can become prohibitive. Furthermore, in certain cases, a reduction in one's choices can be indicated, e.g., in the case where a decision to deliberately annihilate certain options can enable one to get a desirable action underway.

- Adaptation, i.e., an adjustment of the organization to internal or external stimuli, guided by the intentionality of decision-makers, and
- Selection, i.e., the process by which certain firms (at the level of the industry) or subsystems (strategic initiatives or organizational units, at the firm level) are "selected out" through environmental forces, while others are retained.

The second answer strikes a measured balance between these strategies. Research suggests that – of all options available – "managed selection" is the approach which results in the most balanced co-evolutionary journey among selection and adaptation (Volberda/Lewin 2003: 2126). In a multi-unit firm, for example, the co-evolutionary pattern emerges

- as bottom-up strategic initiatives are originated, developed and promoted,
- as a strategic context for nurturing and selecting promising renewal initiatives is created.

In this case, blind variations give way to anticipated variations based on past experience (*ibidem*; see also Schwaninger 1989).

Finally, co-evolutionary theory suggests that a set of three higher-order principles underlies an effective renewal process (Volberda/Lewin 2003: 2126)[9]. These principles are described below in terms of the processes which they oversee:

1. Managing rates of change (i.e., deliberately varying rates of change in accordance with the contextual requirements and internal capabilities)
2. Nurturing and maintaining self-organization (i.e., fostering distributed intelligence, self-control and adaptation)
3. Sustaining concurrent exploration and exploitation (i.e., building new value potentials, fostering and exploiting extant value potentials concurrently).

All of these processes are a form of context management, and they can be enabled by managed selection. If handled with the necessary continuous attention, these processes will make the difference between successful, developing organizations, which maintain their viability in the long run, and their non-developing counterparts, which are focused mainly on short-term exploitation *(ibidem)*.

---

[9] The authors use the term "second-order-renewal", therewith indicating that the principles are about "the renewal of renewal", i.e., about the general approach to renewal.

From here on out in this chapter, a number of cases shall be reported, all of which are about integrative change as construed by the proposed Framework for the Design of Intelligent Organizations. It makes sense to subject all of them to scrutiny with regard to the ethical imperative just quoted.

10.5 Applications of the Framework

To illustrate aspects of integrative change along the dimensions outlined in the proposed framework, and also to visualize the different time dimensions involved, I shall refer to four examples. The first two are about corporate transformation projects in private firms, which date back to the eighties. The advantage of this older dating is that the results of these projects have been observed and evaluated over a long period. The third example goes back to the second half of the nineties, while the last one, from the new millennium, remains an ongoing project.

Case 1

The first project – in which I served as an external consultant – was realized by a Swiss insurance company. The strategy was completely reinvented (→*activities*), and a structural transformation was carefully planned and prepared (→*structure*) over a period of 18 months. The methodological pillars of the project were the MSC and the VSM. This work led ultimately to a new vision shared within the whole group of which the company was part and had implications for its identity (→*basic parameters*). Within the team of executives carrying out the pioneering work a new quality of knowledge emerged, together with an awareness of the superior competence which the firm had in handling insurance and risk management issues for corporate customers, particularly on an international and global scale.

The lengthy preparation period could have been compressed to 6 or 9 months, and many would have opted for such a faster approach. However, it was deemed prudent to take more time so that a new mindset could emerge in the core group of 15 executives directly involved in the project. This also allowed for greater interaction with their followers in order to build up confidence in the new model of the organization and to co-align motivation to put it into practice (→*behavior*). The consequent efficiency gain revealed itself when the company was completely reorganized from being a function-oriented organization to becoming a divisional organization. This was accomplished within less than 6 months, including the transformation of the whole IT infrastructure (→structure). All of this happened without any significant resistance to change (→behavior).

As far as *effectiveness* is concerned, a longer-term horizon was necessary for assessing the consequences of the project. A first formal follow-up research was carried out about six years after the original project, and some informal inquiries were undertaken in the years thereafter (cf. Schwaninger 2005). Looking back at the project now, it must be added that it took the new vision about seven years to become an integral part of the culture of the organization, i.e., to become a "paradigm" (→*identity, ethos, vision*). The original project goes back to the early eighties, but the consequences of the organizational transformation have been palpable ever since. By the late nineties the company in question had become one of the most powerful players worldwide in the insurance and risk management business that serves corporate customers at the international level.

Finally, an interview with the Chairman and Chief Executive Officer was conducted in 2001, 20 years after the original project[10]. He remembered the project very well and stated that it was a landmark for the further evolution of the corporation. The conceptual work done at that time had triggered a new orientation in the company, which has been pursued ever since and has led to higher organizational fitness. More details of this case have been published by Schwaninger (2005).

Case 2

The second case of a combined application of both models – MSC and VSM – was a corporate development project in a private health organization, for which I served as an external consultant. This firm had different features than the company in our first case, particularly in being a smaller firm. Both corporate transformations, however, were comprehensive, and both firms shared a similar approach to the process.

Follow-up research on this second case, carried out five years after the project and carefully documented in a book (Schwaninger 1988), uncovered surprising results. The most astonishing pattern was the following: The joint work of the team on issues of strategy and structure enabled the firm to continue unswervingly to realize its strategic investments, despite a serious decrease in sales and profits between years one and three of a six year monitoring period. The company went so far as to actualize the larg-

---

[10]   The interview was conducted on June 18th, 2001 in St. Gallen. The interviewee had been a member of the project team, functioning at that time as the manager in charge of international business in the Swiss company.

est investments during a period in which, from an operative point of view, it was faring the worst.

The fruits of this tremendous effort were long-term competitive superiority and sustained economic prosperity. This can not be explained in terms of reshaped *activities* and *structure* only. The fulcrum of this amazing trajectory was consistent joint *behavior* by the management team, putting their mental models into practice, which now were shared and grounded in a new sense of organizational *identity*.

Reflection

In both of these cases, the two models – MSC and VSM – were used to orientate the projects. The MSC served as a framework to which the facilitators (internal and external) referred during plenaries and work sessions with subgroups, e.g., to make evident the differences between the strategic issues at hand and any operative questions. The VSM was used as a conceptual tool for the diagnosis of the organizational structures, and, as also in case one, served as the reference model for the redesign of the whole organization (see also Schwaninger 2005).

In these two cases, the MSC and VSM were not yet combined with the TSM or anything similar. However, teamwork was carried out in larger and smaller groups. This proved most valuable in terms of group learning as evidenced in follow-up studies (Schwaninger 1988, 1989, 2005). Also, the processes were supported in each case by a project manager and a "power promoter" (top executive or board member). In either case, the core group (about 15 persons respectively) gathered in a number of workshops. Additionally, the team members – in part supplemented by further knowledgeable individuals in the organization – engaged in smaller groups to tackle specific issues.

Furthermore, in both cases the internal project managers were pillars of strength at the behavioral level, providing extensive individual and human support all along the difficult path of transformation. In sum, the external and internal facilitators designed the work process both in and between the teams for self-organized integration of perspectives, plans and actions. This design showed several features of TSM (even though TSM was not yet available as a methodology at that time). In each case, the project was undertaken by a large-scale group with the different issues of the overall project being tackled essentially by the same set of people in varying subset compositions.

Case 3

This was a comprehensive project of organizational transformation realized at the National General Auditing Office (NGAO) of Colombia[11], in
which I was involved as one of the two international consultants for two
years, in the late nineties. The NGAO is in charge of the audit of all organizations in the public sector. Under the terms of this mandate, all gov-
ernmental organizations and public services (education, health etc.) were
subsumed, as well as the national enterprises, which included Ecopetrol, a
huge energy provider, and Telecom, the leading telecommunication enterprise.

In Colombia, the new constitution of 1991 brought about important
changes in the role and functioning of the state. One of these dealt with
regulatory mechanisms. However, the most important segment of these, as
stipulated by the new constitution, were those in public entities: "It was established that all public entities should have an internal control system. In
practice, the new constitution was recognizing the futility of [the extant]
external and police-like mechanism undertaken by organisms such as the
National General Auditing Office (NGAO), and proposing a mechanism
whereby each public entity should assume responsibility for creating its
own internal control system" (Reyes 2000: 2).

Traditionally, the effectiveness of audits had been measured by the
number of reports per year, and by an indicator of corruptive practices in
terms of the money embezzled. Under the new mandate the role of the
NGAO had to change substantially. A three-year project was designed to
establish this new role and to deal with its structural implications. For extensive reports of this project, cf. Contraloría General de la Republica,
1998, and Reyes 2000; the following is mainly based on the latter source.

The objective of the transformation project was to conceive the NGAO
as an organization "that would ensure that the public entities would use
their resources effectively instead of detecting the largest possible number
of irregularities in their use.

This new perspective implied that the main role of the NGAO was to
ensure the high quality of internal control systems within each public entity. It would, in turn, simply exercise *second-order control* over these
control systems" (Reyes 2000: 3f.). It was clear from the start that new auditing practices were necessary and that these could be brought about only
by a joint process of cultural change and the creation of new structures.

---

[11]   Contraloría General de la República.

The new auditing practices should encourage self-diagnosis as a process within the entity audited, by which structural defects would surface. Three characteristics of these practices were established:

1. They should facilitate an internal process of reflection within the audited entity. Consequently, the auditing teams were to incorporate both employees of the NGAO and the entity audited.
2. Semi-structured interviews and workshops would be primary sources of information.
3. The auditing report would be used as a vehicle for agreements between the NGAO and the entity audited, not as an end in itself. Three types of agreements were considered – operational, strategic and normative (in the sense of the Model of Systemic Control (cf. Chapter 5).

In 1997 and 1998 fifty-two organizations were audited along these lines. The audits relied on a set of tools customized to the specific needs of the case under study. The primary device was a method called VIPLAN, developed by Raúl Espejo, then a professor at the University of Humberside and Lincolnshire. This method consists of three tools, namely declaration of identity, unfolding of complexity and analysis of discretionality (cf. Espejo 1989b, Syncho 1997). These support the elaboration of a Viable System Model (cf. Chapter 6) of the entity-in-focus, for the purpose of organizational diagnosis and then design.

The project was conceived as a learning process, in which approximately one thousand employees of the NGAO were trained on their jobs. The work on the audits was prepared and accompanied by a large number of workshops which were of three types:

- Workshops of reflection, to bring about the paradigm shift in the auditors' understanding of their role and practice ("epistemological / ontological workshops")
- Workshops to train the auditors in the use of tools and concepts ("methodological workshops")
- Workshops to encourage individual self-learning, supported by the VIPLAN software ("poietic workshops").

Both the VSM and the MSC were recurrently presented and discussed in plenaries and workshops. Apart from these uses of the VSM and the MSC, the Team Syntegrity protocol (Cf. Chapter 7) was applied to support certain audits. The most important application was related to the regulation of the natural environment at the national level. Early on in the project (November 1996) an infoset of 32 individuals gathered for a syntegration to work on the question: "How can we organize the state and the population to preserve Colombia's environment?" That group included the leaders of the newly created Ministry of the Environment and the Ministry of Agriculture, directors of institutions for environmental issues, congressmen, representatives of the indigenous and the black populations, members of ecological movements, university professors, etc. The result was a set of inter-institutional agreements known as the Gorgona Manifesto, which became a milestone in the environmental policy of Colombia. This event also was an exemplar for later discussions of complex topics within the broader context of the new control discourse.

The results achieved in this sophisticated project were thoroughly analyzed in detail by Alfonso Reyes, one of the Colombian professors who were members of the project team (Reyes 2000), and in a special number of the journal "Systemic Practice and Action Research" (April 2001).

Throughout the project the whole spectrum of models linked to the Framework for Intelligent Organizations expounded in this book was applied extensively. If one is curious about the potential of these models for large-scale applications in a cross-institutional setting, one can turn Professor Reyes, a local insider, for first-hand testimony: "The project illustrates how organizational cybernetics can greatly contribute to an understanding of complex phenomena such as corruption and state regulation, the former from a structural point of view and the latter from a conversational point of view that can encourage mutual learning" (Reyes 2000: 20).

Case 4

After his studies at the University of St. Gallen, one of my students designed a feasibility study and plan for a consulting firm that would specialize in ecological planning and the management for sustainability. Having known the Framework for Intelligent Organizations from my earlier publications, he considered this the most appropriate model on which to build a viable enterprise. He contacted me with the purpose of writing his master's thesis under my supervision. In this way he was able to engage in the conceptual design of that firm while being supported by my advice. After the successful conclusion of his thesis (Schlatter 2000) my student referred back to me in order to continue this dialogue. Together with several of his colleagues, professionals who come from different scientific disciplines – economics & management, law, engineering and the natural sciences – he founded the new enterprise, called Ecovía Consultores Ambientales[12]. That little company is still in the course of building up experience – two of the partners are still finishing their doctoral studies – and is preparing for its take-off.

---

[12] In English: Ecovía Environmental Consultants.

The whole firm is conceived on the basis of the Framework for the Design and Development of Intelligent Organizations presented in this book. The business plan relies mainly on the Model of Systemic Control with its three logical levels (Chapter 5). The structure of the firm is conceived along the lines of the Viable System Model (Chapter 6). The enterprise operates as a virtual firm, with two partners working in Southern Chile, one in Santiago de Chile and the other in Peru, the latter as an agent who acquires and generates relevant knowledge. Further associates can be hired as needed. Several ideas from the electronic Team Syntegrity protocol (as outlined in Chapter 7) have already been used to support some of the interactions among the team, especially ongoing, topic-centered and project-related interactions of all partners involved, which take place each week via videoconferencing. The team is considering the use of Team Syntegrity as a protocol for interactions in the operations-strategy-homeostat on a continual basis, once the number of associates grows beyond the size of the face-to-face team.

In an interview with Paul Schlatter, the spearheading founder of Ecovía[13], he informed me that the use of the Framework for the Design and Development of Intelligent Organizations is a crucial enabler which has contributed enormously to bringing this new venture to life. He also maintained that "this is the basis which enables us to run the firm with this flexible approach. Actually this is the only way to run Ecovía effectively under the present conditions." Schlatter informed me that the firm was facing a difficult environment - fierce competition in the Chilean market, regulatory and bureaucratic hurdles, as well as financial limitations. Yet, as he maintained, the robust cybernetic design of the enterprise has helped them to cope.

It is rare that a new firm is designed from scratch with such clarity and leads to an innovative and unique mode of operation – not only formally but actually - so quickly. The interviewee suggests that this would not have been possible in the case studied without the specific framework adopted. The coherence of the initial decisions made, and the cohesion which was already notable in the organization at the time of the study, appeared to be remarkable. Its systemic architecture gave this young firm a high development potential. There were good chances that the enterprise would flourish as a viable unit and would establish itself in a new market, despite all the uncertainties it faced.

---

[13]   Interview, Tuesday, March 13, 2002.

Reflection

Is there a link between the conceptual underpinnings of these four projects and their positive results? In cases one and two, members of the core teams have claimed that the positive effects can mainly be attributed to the conceptual guidance of an integrative framework with all five dimensions outlined[14], and the combined use of the reference models[15] for the process of organizational transformation. It cannot be proven, but there is substantial evidence from the follow-ups that this conceptual guidance was a major factor in enabling the virtuous processes of transformation and development in these two companies.

An overall examination of all four cases allows the following general observations:

1. In each one of cases 1 to 3 the spectrum of choices was enhanced successively. The trap of a path dependence entailing an unintentional confinement of the repertory of behaviors was avoided, given the orientation provided by powerful models. In other words the ethical imperative – "Act always so as to increase the number of choices" (von Foerster 1984a) was complied with.
2. Management in these cases was rather of the second-order type, i.e., a design of context rather than an intervention at the object level. Potential variety (complexity) makes a huge set of behaviors contingent, i.e., liable to happen. A contingency is an uncertainty of occurrence. The challenge, then, is to design a context[16] in which these uncertain or even unlikely events, if they materialize, are likely to be matched – in the sense of an absorption of complexity. This challenge was weathered effectively in cases 1 to 3.

Case 4 is still too young for a conclusive statement about it to be made; the aspects reported here are therefore only indicative and provisional.

---

[14]   Sources:
    - For Cases 1 and 2: Follow-up analysis of corporate data as well as interviews realized 5 years after the original project had been concluded (mostly published in Schwaninger 1988 and 1989), and later (cf. Schwaninger 2005).
    - For Case 3: Contraloría General de la República 1998, Reyes 2000, special issue of "Systemic Practice and Action Research", April 2001.

[15]   The concrete framework used in cases one and two was a predecessor of the one finally proposed in the present book. The models explicitly introduced in the workshops and applied together with the executives of the companies were the MSC and the VSM.

[16]   The framework presented here offers a number of dimensions for such context design.

Ongoing and forthcoming action research is about to extend the empirical evidence given here. A case in point is a project in which the Framework for Intelligent Organizations is being adapted to the specific needs of, and applied to enterprises in, the telecommunications sector (Teuta Gómez/Espinosa 2001).

10.6 Relevant Empirical Work by Other Authors

Among the empirical work done by other authors, several studies have been identified which are relevant in this context. The first source is a publication by Pettigrew and Whipp (1993). These authors, on the basis of longitudinal in-depth case studies, have identified the following "central factors" as conditions for successful corporate transformations:

- *Environmental assessment*: e.g., information processing as a multi-function activity, development of an understanding of the environment, becoming an open learning system
- *Leading change*: e.g., context-sensitive leadership, creating capability for change, linking action by people at all levels of the organization, construction of a climate for change
- *Linking strategic and operational change*: e.g., supplying visions, values and direction, implementing intentions over time, cumulative and supportive activities at various levels
- *Human resources as assets and liabilities*: e.g., raising consciousness about human resource management, demonstrating the need for change in both business and people, creating a longer-term learning process with successive positive spirals of development
- *Coherence:* e.g., consistency of goals, consonance by adaptive response to the environment, maintenance of competitive advantage, feasibility of the strategy.

These factors represent all five dimensions of the framework - activities, structure, behavior, basic parameters and time, albeit in a slightly different terminology. Additionally, the time dimension is implicit in several factors. This coincidence of findings from both researchers is quite remarkable, because both Pettigrew and I[17] arrived at roughly the same results while doing our work independently of each other. The coincidence therefore serves objectively as a triangulation that points towards a set of in-

---

[17] My colleagues at the Institute of Management are included here (cf. Bleicher 2004).

variant features of successful corporate transformation in a complex environmental setting.

10.7 Intermediate Summary and Outlook

The *Framework for the Design and Development of Intelligent Organizations* has now been revisited from an integrative perspective. First the models expounded in the earlier chapters were linked to the general scheme. Then, a condensation of the crucial organizational principles inherent in the framework followed. The number of different principles combined contradicts simplistic recommendations, which often rely on only one or two principles. Third, the logical links between the component models were brought to the fore, and an integrative picture emerged. Finally, a report on four applications showed the effectiveness of the framework proposed, but it also gives an idea of the difficulty of measuring such effectiveness. As Nobel laureate Friedrich von Hayek contended, the deeper our insights into complex systems, the more difficult is it to come up with theoretical statements about them that abide by the methodological principle of refutability[18] (von Hayek 1972).

It must be added that I have also seen successful applications of the framework in which a development took place throughout all of its dimensions even though not all of the models specified in this book were explicitly applied.[19] Apparently the framework has a usefulness in its own right.

A more extensive elaboration on the potential and the difficulties of applying the framework presented here will have to be the object of follow-on research. At this stage, I surmise, on the basis of the empirical evidence available to date and referred to in this chapter, that such a systemic approach is superior to an approach where only one of the models outlined – MSC, VSM, and TSM – is applied, or where several or all of them are used in a merely additive mode. It must be added at the same time that the systemic nature of each one of the three theories, including their conceptual interrelationships as specified above and in particular the framework proposed here, also facilitate such an integrative application.

---

[18] Hayek uses the term "falsifiability", which is the principle–after the philosopher Karl Popper–that scientific propositions must be formulated in such a way that they can be falsified (refuted) on empirical or logical grounds, i.e. submitted to systematic scrutiny.

[19] One of these cases, about a leading retail organization in Switzerland, has been documented together with the help of an executive from that firm (Schwaninger/Schmitz-Draeger 1997).

When introducing the *Framework for the Design and Development of Intelligent Organizations* in chapter 4, it was proposed that integrating these theories can provide a systemic approach which enhances organizational intelligence more than do isolated uses of one or more of these theories (Schwaninger 2001).

The case studies reported in this chapter underpin the argument of this chapter: A virtuous transformation, leading to ever more vigorous viability and development in an organization, requires synchronous evolution and transformation in all three domains – activities, structure and behavior[20], in alignment with the underlying *fundamental parameters* and the environmental forces. The continual reflection and development of those parameters and forces comes as an additional prerequisite of a higher order. In other words, the concepts of organizational identity, ethos and vision are like the other components of the model are dynamic ones (cf. Gioa/Schultz/Corley 2000).

Isolated, one-dimensional, non-aligned or asynchronous changes in any one of these dimensions are in principle less robust and subject to failure more easily. The mutual adjustment outlined above is essentially about the alignment of "strategy and organization", to use a shorthand expression. The resulting coherence is an important factor for better performance. To complete the picture, the environment of the firm – economic, social, technological and ecological – must be an integral part of that alignment. In sum, a mutual fit among all three – environment, strategy and organization – is the key to an organization's success (cf. Roberts 2004).

Change management then takes mainly place at a higher level: It is conceived as context management, not as a management which intervenes at the object level. The vantage point of context management is essentially one of designing a context for a virtuous development of the organization. Taking into account both the micro-level adaptation processes and the macro-level selection processes, this kind of management makes it possible to combine self-renewal of the organization and the co-evolution with its environment.

The difficulty and delicacy of managing an organizational transformation is in large part due to the fact that the *time constants* inherent in each one of the different dimensions are different. Strategies can often be reinvented fairly quickly, whereas structural transformation takes more time. Finally, the variables that react most slowly are the behavioral ones. That is why the alignment of all four dimensions and the quest for co-evolu-

---

[20] For some empirical evidence – even though collected in more specific domains – to support this argument, see: Pettigrew/Whipp 1993, and Rudolph 1998.

tionary adjustment over time must be subject to great care, foresight and continual attention.

Chapter 11 Outlook: The Way Ahead

"Entia non sunt multiplicanda praeter necessitatem"
William of Occam, Franciscan philosopher and theologian (1285-1350)[1]

The parsimony of this text is possible due to the transdisciplinary language used, which is inherent to the systems approach.

Compared to classical business approaches, the systemic approach to intelligent organisations advocated here can be illustrated if we revert to an analogy between the classical and systemic approaches in business and the differing approaches in classical and quantum physics.

Classical physics deals with separate systems. In quantum physics, on the other hand, everything is deeply linked. By way of our analogy, business schools have traditionally been compartmentalized according to separate functions or method oriented disciplines. Equally, management models and methods have had a strong disciplinary bias – economic, behavioral, quantitative, qualitative etc. The systems-oriented approach to management, on the other hand, which underlies the framework and models presented here, is integrative and transdisciplinary. Economic and behavioral aspects are deeply linked; qualitative and quantitative aspects of the organizations under study cannot be separated, unless for certain analytical purposes. If understanding is to ensue, however, these analyses have to be complemented immediately by synthesis.

In the 10 preceding chapters I have tried to demonstrate that the enormous potential of the Systems Approach, along with pertinent tools for dealing with high variety, work more effectively than could established disciplines or mere pragmatics. This does not disqualify disciplinary efforts in the important fields of economics, sociology, psychology etc. Nor does it deny the wisdom of practitioners. On the contrary, Systems Theory and Cybernetics are in line with natural, praxis-oriented modes of thinking. They furnish crucial knowledge about invariant features of organizations. This can help managers, specialized scientists of the different disciplines, and all members of organizations to leverage their knowledge by making

---

[1] This statement, called „Occam's Razor" today, says in paraphrase: „Do not use more categories than necessary."

new sense of it through reaching a deeper understanding. Thereby they hone their behavioral repertory, becoming more apt to serve the needs of organizations and society, while developing themselves at the same time.

People talk a great deal about the competition between firms. But ultimately the competition is between models. The organizations that survive are those with the better models. More generally, the evolution of a social system manifests itself in cultural progress. But such progress is grounded in the *evolution of models,* which conceptually guide the ongoing process by which socio-cultural reality is shaped. Models are not in the first place objective images of a reality out there, but devices which support the dialogue and the (inter-) action by which

- Organizations invent and reinvent themselves
- Desirable futures are designed and brought about.

With the work presented here I wish to contribute to the design and development of organizations so that they can attain higher intelligence. This implies a quest for more organizational cohesion, self-control and self-reference, and ultimately for more vigorous viability and development. A crucial challenge, which I have stressed in this context, is to provide better models – including theories, frameworks, etc. – which are more apt to enhance the capability of organizations to cope with the paramount and growing complexities (and contingencies) they face, and to cope in adaptive and responsive modes.

For this purpose a *Framework for the Design and Development of Intelligent Organizations* has been proposed. The concept of intelligence in which it is grounded is a systemic one. This means, among other things, that it is multidimensional. In other words, it distinguishes itself from the monistic and reductionist concepts of "intelligence" which abound in this world. Examples of those are the views, often inspired by neo-Darwinism, which suggest that any one of the dimensions available to us, such as speed or cleverness or greed or mass or protection or power, can be considered good proxies for "intelligence", as long as it does the job of self-maintenance for an actor who maximizes that single dimension.

In sum, my proposition is that a virtuous transformation of organizations can only be achieved

1. If the dimensions of activities, structure and behavior are developed in a balanced, synchronic mode.
2. If they are aligned with such underlying fundamental parameters as organizational identity, ethos and vision. The latter have to be subject to development in their own right.
3. If a balanced co-evolution with the environment is enabled.

Consequently, the power of a higher-order management has been fleshed out – a management which designs contexts for complexity-absorption rather than interfering at the object level.

I have outlined three models of Organizational Cybernetics, proven to be most helpful for triggering an evolution towards higher organizational intelligence, and I have indicated how to apply them. My point is that these models can and should be applied in a combined and integrative manner.

Such a systemic use of these models can trace the path towards superior organizational intelligence more effectively than merely punctual uses of any one or more of them. Also, the incorporation of ethics and esthetics as explicit components of design, as advocated here, should contribute to broader minded, less myopic approaches to management, and ultimately foster socio-cultural progress. On the basis of the arguments developed in this book, the proposed framework promises to be a powerful response to the needs of the new types of intelligent organizations which have already begun to emerge.

Both individual and collective actions are crucial as sources of variation in an organization's performance, and they are especially important as success factors for organizational change. As key players, managers can create contexts for better performance and catalyze collective action[2]. It is this kind of *context design* which can be improved with the help of the framework and models presented in this book.

My intention here is not to "sell" this framework or any one the models outlined. The purpose of these chapters is simply

1. to convey the need for multidimensional and higher order management approaches, by which intelligent organizational self-renewal and co-evolution can be achieved,
2. to make available a set of proven systemic frameworks and heuristics which could help the reader in coping with complexity, and
3. to trigger reflection about the status quo and about new ways of management.

In the age of complex challenges calling for inter- and transdisciplinary approaches, one final aspect must be emphasized: The systemic approach outlined here helps to enhance the connectivity and synergy of specialists from different domains by fusing their capabilities in joint efforts for organizational advancement – not just in economic terms but in a much broader sense.

---

[2]   The action of managers is increasingly in the focus of research (e.g. Bruch 2003, Pfeffer/Sutton 1999).

This will hopefully lead us beyond the technocratic, uni-dimensional, reductionist and narrow-minded modes of management which are still so often in use today. I am also convinced that it will ultimately breed the new kinds of organization so urgently needed for ensuring a sustainable future.

Appendix

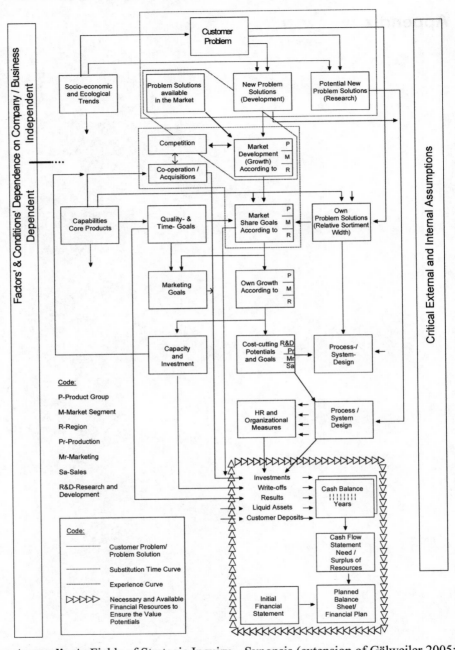

Appendix A. Fields of Strategic Inquiry – Synopsis (extension of Gälweiler 2005: 31)

DIMENSIONS		OPTIONS/MODES			
P	Products	Complete Menus	Complete Dishes	Dishes without Garnishes	Garnishes/Vegetables
PZ	Services	Fast-Food-Restaurants	Deli Shops	Home Delivery	None
PP	Price Level	High	High-Moderate	Moderate	Moderate-Lower	Low
TS	Degree of Standardization	Customized	Partially standardized		Standardized
TF	Technology / Finish	Ready-to-Eat	Ready-to-Eat, no Heat	Semi-Finished	Raw Portions
TP	Package/Format	Single Portion	Family Package		Large Package
KG	Customer Group	Singles	Families	Restaurants	Companies
KP	Customer Problem	Dining at Home	Dining out Privately	Dining out for Business	Dining in the Company
AK	Distribution Channel	Direct Distribution	Franchise Outlets	Specialized Retailers	Retail Chains	Wholesalers
AR	Regions	Diameter of ~50 Miles	East and Center	Nationwide	CH, A, GE
W	Competition	Many Local Competitors	Several Regional Competitors		Rigid Oligopoly

▬▬▬   Our Profil (Actual)

▬▬   Option A for New Business

Appendix B. Configuration Analysis (Example Catering)

Business Area: ....

	Customer Problem / need	Customer Groups	Products / Services	Technology	Distribution Channels
1 Actual					
3 Plan I					
4 Plan II					
2 Ideal / Vision					
Countries / Regions:					

Appendix C. Business Design – Layout for Configuration Design and Positioning

References

Abel, Roland (2001) Die Balanced Scorecard im Arbeitsfeld von Betriebsräten. Bochum, Düsseldorf: Hans-Böckler-Stiftung

Abraham Ralph A (1994) Chaos, Gaia, Eros. San Francisco, California: Harper

Ackoff, Russell L (1981) Creating the Corporate Future. New York etc.: Wiley

Ackoff, Russell L (1986) Management in Small Doses. New York etc.: Wiley

Ackoff, Russell L (1994) The Democratic Corporation. New York Oxford: Oxford University Press

Ackoff, Russell L (1999) Ackoff's Best. His Classical Writings on Management. New York etc: Wiley

Ackoff, Russell L (1999) Re-creating the Corporation: A Design of Organizations for the 21st Century. New York: Oxford University Press

Ackoff, Russell L, Emery FE (1972) On Purposeful Systems. Chicago: Aldine

Ackoff, Russell L, Gharajedaghi J (1984) Mechanisms, Organisms and Human Systems. In: Strategic Management Journal, Vol. 5, pp. 289-300

Ackoff, RL, Pourdehnad J (2001) On Misdirected Systems. In: Systems Research and Behavioral Science, Volume 18, Issue 3 , pp. 199-205

Ahmad, Albakri Bin (1999) A Pluralist Perspective of Team Syntegrity: Design and Intervention Strategy for Organisational Change. Ph.D. dissertation, Liverpool John Moores University

Aldrich, Howard, Ruef Martin (2006) Organizations Evolving, revised edition. Thousand Oaks: Sage

Alexander, Christopher (1979) The Timeless Way of Building. New York: Oxford University Press

Allen, Peter M (1997) Cities and Regions as Self-organising Systems. Models of Complexity. Amsterdam etc.: Gordon and Breach Science Publishers

Almeida, Paul, Song Jaeyong, Grant Robert M. (2002) Are Firms Superior to Alliances and Markets? An Empirical Test of Cross-border Knowledge Building, Organization Science, Vol. 13, pp. 147-161

Anderson, Ray C (1998) Mid-course Correction. Toward a Sustainable Enterprise: The Interface Model, White River Junction, VT: Chelsea Green Publishing

Argyris, Chris (1964) Integrating the Individual and the Organization, New York etc.: Wiley

Argyris, Chris (1990) Overcoming Organizational Defenses. Facilitating Organizational Learning, Boston etc.: Allyn and Bacon

Argyris, Chris, Schön, Donald A (1978) Organizational Learning: A Theory of Action Perspective, Reading, Mass.: Addison-Wesley

Aristoteles: Werke (ΑΡΙΣΤΟΤΕΛΟΥΣ, Greek and German), 7 Volumes, Aalen, Germany: Scientia Verlag, 1978

Arthur, W Brian (1994) Increasing Returns and Path Dependency in the Economy, Ann Arbor: The University of Michigan Press

Ashby, W Ross (1956) An Introduction to Cybernetics, London: Chapman & Hall.

Ashby, W Ross (1965) Design for a Brain, London: Chapman & Hall

Ashmos, Donde P et al. (2002) What a Mess! Participation as a Simple Managerial Rule to 'Complexify' Organizations, in: Journal of Management Studies, Vol. 39, No. 2, March 2002, pp. 189-206.

Axelrod, Robert (1984) The Evolution of Cooperation, New York: Basic Books

Axelrod, Robert (1997) The Complexity of Cooperation: Agent-based Models of Competition and Collaboration, Princeton, NJ: Princeton University Press

Axelrod, Robert, Cohen, Michael D (1999) Harnessing Complexity : organizational implications of a scientific frontier, New York: Free Press

Baer, Urs, Schwaninger, Markus (1998) Statistische Auswertung der im Mai 1998 an der Universität St. Gallen durchgeführten Team-Syntegrity-Veranstaltung, Report, St. Gallen, Switzerland: University of St. Gallen, Institut für Betriebswirtschaft

Barney, Jay B, Hansen, Mark H (1994) Trustworthiness as a Source of Competitive Advantage, In: Strategic Management Journal, Vol. 15, pp. 175-190

Barney, Jay (1991) Firm Resources and Sustained Competitive Advantage, in: Journal of Management, Vol. 17., No. 1, pp. 99-120

Bateson, Gregory: Steps to an Ecology of Mind, London etc.: Paladin Books, 1973

Bavelas, A (1952) Communication Patterns in Problem Groups. In Cybernetics: Transactions of the Eighth Conference, New York: Josiah Macy Jr. Foundation

Bavelas, A (2003) Communication Patterns in Problem-Solving Groups. In Cybernetics: Transactions of the Eighth Conference, New York: Josiah Macy Jr. Foundation, re-edited by Pias, Claus Cybernetics - Kybernetik. The Macy Conferences 1946-1953. Transactions, Zürich-Berlin: Diaphanes, pp. 349-381 (originally published in 1952)

Beer, Michael, Nohria, Nihtin (2000) Breaking the Code of Change, Boston, Mass.: Harvard Business School Press

Beer Stafford (1979) The Heart of Enterprise, Chichester: Wiley

Beer, Stafford (1981) Brain of the Firm, 2nd edition, Chichester etc.: Wiley

Beer, Stafford (1984) The Viable System Model: Its Provenance, Development, Methodology and Pathology. Journal of the Operational Research Society, Vol. 35, pp. 7-25

Beer, S. (1985) Diagnosing the System for Organizations, Chichester: Wiley

Beer, Stafford (1988) Holism and the Frou-Frou Slander, in: Kybernetes, Vol. 17, No. 1, pp. 23-32

Beer, Stafford (1994) Beyond Dispute. The Invention of Team Syntegrity, Chichester etc.: Wiley

Berger, S, Dertouzos, ML, Lester, RK, Solow, RM, Thurow, LC (1989) Toward a New Industrial America, in: Scientific American, Volume 260, June 1989, 21-29

Björkqvist, Olof (1996) Perspectives on Demand-Side Energy Efficiency. Doctoral Dissertation, School of Mechanical and Vehicular Engineering, Chalmers University of Technology, Gothenburg, Sweden

Bleicher, Knut (1994) Normatives Management: Politik, Verfassung und Philosophie des Unternehmens, Frankfurt a.M.: Campus Verlag

Bleicher, K (2004), Das Konzept. Integriertes Management, 7th edition, Campus, Frankfurt, New York

Boulez, Pierre (2001) Interview, in: Neue Zürcher Zeitung

Braitenberg, Valentino (1959) Functional Interpretation of Cerebellar Histology, in: Nature, Vol. 190, N0. 4775, pp. 539-540

Bruch, Heike (2003) Leaders' Action, Munich, Germany: Hampp

Buchanan, Mark (2005) Supermodels to the Rescue, in: Strategy + Business, Issue 38, Spring 2005, pp. 51-59

Buzzell, Robert D Gale, Bradley T (1987) The PIMS Principles, New York, London: Free Press, Collier

Byrne, JA., Brandt, R, Port, O (1993) The Virtual Corporation, in: Business Week, 8.2.1993, S. 36 – 41

Carlzon, Jan (1988) Moments of Truth, Ballinger, Cambridge, MA

Chaffin, Joshua, Fidler, Stephen (2002) Enron Revealed to Be Rotten to the Core, in: financial Times, April 9, p. 20

Chandler, Alfred D, Jr., Cortada, James W (2000) A Nation Transformed by Information, Oxford University Press

Cheng, Yu-Ting, Van de Ven, Andrew H (1996) Learning the Innovation Journey: Order out of Chaos, in: Organization Science, Vo. 7, No. 6, November-December, pp. 593-614

Christensen, Clayton M (1997) The Innovator's Dilemma: When New Technologies Cause Great Firms to Fail, Boston, Mass.: Harvard Business School Press

Christopher, William F (forthcoming 2006) The Wisdom of System Science: A New Paradigm for Management, Chichester & New York: Wiley

Churchman, C West (1968) Challenge to Reason, New York: McGraw-Hill

Ciompi, Luc (1997) Die emotionalen Grundlagen des Denkens. Entwurf einer fraktalen Affektlogik, Göttingen: Vandenhoeck & Ruprecht

Clark, Kenneth, Sefton, Martin (2001) The Sequential Prisoner's Dilemma: Evidence on Reciprocation, in: Economic Journal, January 2001

Cloke, Kenneth, Goldsmith, Joan: The End of Management and the Rise of Organizational Democracy, Chichester: Wiley 2002

Collins, Randall (1993) Emotional Energy as the Common Denominator of Rational Action. In: Rationality and Society, Vol. 5, pp. 203-230

Collins, James C, Porras, Jerry I (1994) Built to Last. Successful Habits of Visionary Companies, London: Century

Collis, David J, Montgomery, Cynthia A (1998) Corporate strategy: a resource-based approach, Boston, Mass.: Irwin, McGraw-Hill

Conant, Roger C, and Ashby, W Ross (1981) Every Good Regulator of a System Must Be a Model of that System. In:L Conant, Roger C (ed.), Mechanisms of Intelligence. Ashby's Writings on Cybernetics, Seaside, CA.: Intersystems Publications, pp. 205–214

Contraloria General de la Republica, ed. (1998) El Estado del Estado, Bogotá, Colombia: Contraloría General de la Republica.

Cosh, A.D., Hughes, A., eds. (2000) British Enterprise in Transition: growth, innovation and public policy in the small and medium sized enterprise sector 1994-1999, Cambridge : ESRC Centre for Business Research, University of Cambridge

Crosby, Philip B (1992) Completeness: Quality for the 21st Century, New York, NY: Dutton

Danesi, Marcel, Perron, Paul (1999) Analyzing Cultures. An Introduction and Handbook, Bloomington and Indianapolis: Indiana University Press

Deal, Terrence E, Kennedy, Allan A (1982) Corporate Cultures. The Rites and Rituals of Corporate Life. Reading, Mass.: Addison-Wesley

de Geus, Arie (1997) The Living Company: Habits for Survival in a Turbulent Environment, London: Nicholas Brealey

Denison, Daniel Rl, Hooijberg, Robert, Quinn, Robert E (1995) Paradox and Performance: Toward a Theory of Behavioral Complexity in Managerial Leadership, Organization Science, Vol 6, No. 5, pp. 524-540

de Raadt, J, Donald R (1997) A New Management of Life, Lewiston, New York: Edwin Mellen Press

de Raadt, J Donald R (2000) Redesign and Management of Communities in Crisis, USA: Universal Publishers, uPUBLISH.com

Deutsch, Karl W (1966) The Nerves of Government. Models of Political Communication and Control, New York, London: The Free Press, Collier-MacMillan Ltd

de Zeeuw, Gerard (1986) Social Change and the Design of Enquiry, in: Geyer, van der Zouwen, eds., Sociocybernetic Paradoxes, London: Sage, pp. 131-144

Diamond, Jared (2005) Collapse. How Societies Choose to Fail or Succeed, London: Viking

Dijksterhuis, Ap, Bargh, John A: The Perception-Behavior Expressway: Automatic Effects of Social Perception on Social Behavior, in: Advances in Experimental Social Psychology, Vol. 33, 2001, pp. 1-40

Doerner, Dietrich (1996) The Logic of Failure: Why Things Go Wrong and What We Can Do to Make Them Right, Reading, Mass.: Perseus Books

Dowling, Graham (2001) Creating Corporate Reputations. Identity, Image, and Performance, Oxford: Oxford University Press

Drucker, Peter F (1980) Managing in Turbulent Times, London: Heinemann

Drucker, Peter F (1974) Management. Tasks, Responsibilities, Practices, London: Heinemann

Drucker, Peter F (1977) Management, London: Pan Books 1977

Drucker, Peter F (1980) Managing in Turbulent Times, London: Heinemann

Drucker, Peter F (1986) The Frontiers of Management, New York: Truman Talley Books, Dutton

Drucker, Peter F (1993) Post-Capitalist Society, New York City: Harper Business

Drucker, Peter F (1999) Peter Drucker on Financial Services, in: The Economist, September 23, 1999

Drucker, Peter F (1999) Management Challenges for the 21st Century, Oxford: Butterworth-Heinemann

Eagleton, Terry: The Idea of Culture, Oxford: Blackwell 2000

Eggler, Andreas Johannes: Diffusions- und Substitutionsprozesse : Struktur, Ablauf und ihre Bedeutung für die strategische Unternehmensführung, PhD Dissertation No. 1273, University of St. Gallen 1991

Ehrbar, Al (1998) EVA <Economic Value Added>: the Real Key to Creating Wealth, New York, NY: Wiley

Einhorn, Martin (2005) Effektive und effiziente Kundenorientierung im Sortimentsmanagement: nutzerorientierte Marktforschung zur Vermeidung von Information Overload, PhD Dissertation; Nr. 3011, St. Gallen, Switzerland: University of St. Gallen

Elkington, John (1998) Cannibals with Forks: the triple bottom line of 21st century business, Gabriola Island, BC: New Society Publishers

Espejo, Raúl (1989a) The Viable System Model Revisited. In: Espejo, Raúl and Harnden, Roger (eds.), The Viable System Model: Interpretations and Applications of Stafford Beer's VSM, Chichester: Wiley, pp. 77–100

Espejo, Raúl (1989b) A Cybernetic Method to Study Organizations. In Espejo, Raúl and Harnden, Roger (eds.), The Viable System Model: Interpretations and Applications of Stafford Beer's VSM, Chichester: Wiley, pp. 361-382

Espejo, Raúl, Harnden, Roger, eds. (1989) The Viable System Model. Interpretations and Applications of Stafford Beer's VSM, Chichester: Wiley

Espejo, Raúl, Schuhmann, W, Schwaninger, M and Bilello, U (1996), Organisational Transformation and Learning. A Cybernetic Approach to Management. Chichester: Wiley

Espejo, Raúl, Schwaninger, Markus, eds. (1993) Organizational Fitness - Corporate Effectiveness through Management Cybernetics, Frankfurt, New York: Campus

Espejo, Raúl, Schwaninger, Markus, eds.: To Be and Not to Be, that is the System. A Tribute to Stafford Beer (Chapter Red), CD-ROM, Wiesbaden: Carl Auer-Systeme Verlag

Espejo, Raúl, Watt, John (1988) Information Management, Organization and Managerial Effectiveness, in: Journal of the Operational Research Society, Vol. 39, No. 1, pp. 7-14

Etzioni, Amitai (1968) The Active Society. A Theory of Societal and Political Processes, London, New York: Collier, MacMillan

Fehrenbach, Franz (2005) Who's Afraid of Globalisation? The Bosch Approach Towards Innovation and Cost Leadership, Keynote Address, ISC-Symposium 2005, St. Gallen, Switzerland: International Students Committee Approach Towards Innovation and Cost Leadership

Flood, Robert L, Jackson, Michael C (1991) Creative Problem Solving. Total Systems Intervention, Chichester: Wiley

Fombrun, Charles J (1996) Reputation. Realizing Value from the Corporate Image, Boston, Mass.: Harvard Business School Press

Ford, Andrew: Simulating the Patterns of Power Plant Construction in California, in: Hines, James H. et al., eds.: Proceedings of the 19th International Conference of the System Dynamics Society, Atlanta, Georgia, July 2001

Forrester, Jay W (1961) Industrial Dynamics, Cambridge, MA: MIT Press

Forrester, Jay W (1971) Counterintuitive Behavior of Social Systems, in: Technology Review, Vol. 73, January 1971, No. 3, pp. 52-68

Fox, Loren (2003) Enron. The Rise and Fall, Hobokern, NJ: Wiley

François, Charles (1997) International Encyclopedia of Systems and Cybernetics, München: Saur

Frank, Ken A, Fahrbach, Kyle (1999) Organizational Culture as a Complex System: Balance and Information in Models of Influence and Selection, in:ial issue of Organization Science on Chaos and Complexity , Vol 10, No. 3, pp. 253-277

François, Charles (1999) Systemics and Cybernetics in a Historical Perspective, in: Systems Research and Behavioral Science, Vol. 16, pp. 203-219

Freeman, R Edward (1984) Strategic Management: A Stakeholder Approach, London: Pitman

Frost, Benjamin (2005) Lebensfähigkeit von Communities of Practice im organisationalen Kontext, PhD Dissertation, St. Gallen, Switzerland: University of St. Gallen

Fukuyama, Francis (1999) The Great Disruption: Human Nature and the Reconstitution of Social Order, London: Profile Books

Fuller, R Buckminster, Applewhite, EJ (1982) Synergetics: Explorations in the Geometry of Thinking, New York, London: Macmillan, Collier

Gälweiler, Aloys (1986) Unternehmensplanung, 2nd edition, Frankfurt und New York: Campus

Gälweiler, Aloys (2005) Strategische Unternehmensführung, 3rd edition, Frankfurt, New York: Campus

George, Michael L, Wilson, Stephen A (2004) Conquering Complexity in your Business: How Wal-Mart, Toyota, and Other Top Companies are Breaking through the Ceiling on Profits and Growth. New York: McGraw-Hill

Georgopoulos, Apostolos P, Taira, M, Lukashin (1993) Cognitive Neurophysiology, in: Science, Vol. 260, No. 2, April 1993, pp. 47-52

Geyer Felix, Van der Zouwen Johannes, eds. (1978) Sociocybernetics, Leiden: Nijhoff

Gioia, Dennis, Schultz, Majken, & Corley, Kevin D (2000) Organizational Identity, Image and Adaptive Instability, in: Academy of Management Review, Vol. 25, pp. 63-81

Glater, Jonathan D (2002) Andersen Turning Out the Lights After 89 Years, in: Herald Tribune International, August 31-September 1, 2002, p. 11

Gomez, Peter (1993) Wertmanagement, Düsseldorf: Econ

Gomez, Peter, Zimmermann, Tim (1997) Unternehmensorganisation. Profile - Dynamik - Methodik, St. Galler Management-Konzept, 3. Aufl., Frankfurt, New York: Campus

Goold, Michael, Campbell, Andrew, Alexander, Marcus (1994) Corporate-level Strategy: creating value in the multibusiness company, New York, NY: Wiley

Gracián, Baltasar (1993) Obras completas de Baltasar Gracián, Emilio Blanco, ed., Madrid: Turner

Greenhalgh, L (2001). Managing Strategic Relationships, New York: Free Press

Gregory, Richard L, ed. (1987) The Oxford Companion to the Mind, Oxford, New York: Oxford University Press

Griffith, Victoria (2005) Winning Hearts and Minds at Home Depot, Strategy and Business, Issue 38, Spring 2005, pp. 60-71

Grübler, Arnulf (1990) The Rise and Fall of Infrastructures : dynamics of evolution and technological change in transport, Heidelberg : Physica-Verlag

Gurevich, Yuri (2000) Sequential Abstract State Machines Capture Sequential Algorithms, ACM (Association for Computing Machinery) Transactions on Computational Logic, Volume 1, Number 1 (July 2000), pages 77-111

Haeckel, Stephan H (1999) Adaptive Enterprise: Creating and Leading Sense-and-respond Organizations. Boston, Mass.: Harvard Business School Press

Häcki, Remo, Lighton, Julian (2001) The Future of the Networked Company, in: The McKinsey Quarterly, No. 3, pp. 26-39

Hamel, Gary, Prahalad, CK (1994) Competing for the Future, Harvard Business School Press

Hannan, Michael T, Freeman, John (1989) Organizational Ecology, Cambridge, Mass., London: Harvard University Press

Harnden, Roger John (1989) Technology for Enabling: The Implications for Management Science of an Hermeneutics of Distinction, Diss. University of Aston, Birmingham

Hawawini, Gabriel, Verdin, Paul J, Subramanian, G (2003) Is Performance Driven by Industry- or Firm-specific Factors? A New Look at the Evidence, in: Strategic Management Journal, vol. 24, no. 1 (Jan.), pp. 1 - 17

Hedberg, Bo (1981) How Organizations Learn and Unlearn. In Handbook of Organizational Design: Adapting Organizations to Their Environments , ed. Paul C. Nystrom and William H. Starbuck, New York, NY: Oxford University Press, pp. 3-27

Hechenblaickner, Peter P, Krafft, Andreas, Steiner, Silke (1995) Research Report on the „Kingview Syntegration" July 17-20, 1995, Toronto, Canada. St. Gallen, Switzerland: University of St. Gallen

Hedlund, Gunnar (1986) The Hypermodern MNC - A Heterarchy?, in: Human Resources Management, Spring, Vol. 25, No. 1, pp. 9-35

Hedlund, Gunnar (1993) Assumptions of Hierarchy and Heterarchy, with Applications to the Management in the Multinational Corporation, in: Ghoshal, S, Westney E, eds.: Organization Theory and the Multinational Corporation, London: MacMillan, pp. 211-236

Heizmann, Bernhard: Die Entwicklung ökologisch motivierter Substitionen : eine empirische Untersuchung der zeitlichen Verläufe und eine Diskussion der Bestimmungsfaktoren, Frankfurt a.M. ; Bern etc.: Lang, 1990

Helgesen, S (1995) The Web of Inclusion, New York: Currency, Doubleday

Henderson, Bruce (1972) Perspectives on Experience, Boston, Mass.: Boston Consulting Group

Henkel (2004) Annual Report, Düsseldorf, Germany

Henoch, Jens (2003) Towards Adaptive Management Systems in Manufacturing : an Agent Supported Approach, Berlin: wvb-Wissenschaftlicher Verlag Berlin, 2003

Hilti Corporation (2002a) Hilti Group in brief - corporate policy, http:// www. hilti.com

Hilti Corporation (2002b) Mission Statement, http://www.hilti.com

Hilti Corporation (2002c) Financial Report 2001, http://www.hilti.com

Himmelfarb, Gertrude (1994) The De-Moralization of Society: From Victorian Virtues to Modern Values, New York: Random House

Hofstede, G (1991) Cultures and Organizations. Software of the Mind. London: McGraw-Hill

Hofstede, G (1991) Cultures and Organizations. Software of the Mind. London: McGraw-Hill

Holland, John H (1995) Hidden Order: How Adaption Builds Complexity, Reading, Mass. <etc.> : Addison-Wesley

Hurst, David K (1995) Crisis and Renewal, Boston, MA: Harvard Business School Press

Jackson, M C (1989) Evaluating the Managerial Significance of the VSM, in: Espejo, Raúl, Harnden, Roger, eds., The Viable System Model. Interpretations and Applications of Stafford Beer's VSM, Chichester: Wiley, pp. 407-439

Jackson, Michael C (2000) Systems Approaches to Management. New York: Kluwer Academic, Plenum

Jackson, Michael C (2003) Systems Thinking: Creative Holism for Managers. Chichester: Wiley

Jalali, Assad (1994) Reverberating Networks. Modelling Information Propagation in Syntegration by Spectral Analysis. In Beer, Stafford, Beyond Dispute. The Invention of Team Syntegrity, Chichester: Wiley, pp. 263-281

Janis, Irving L: Victims of Groupthink, Boston, Mass.: Houghton Mifflin, 1972

Janisch, Monika (1992) Das strategische Anspruchsgruppenmanagement: vom Shareholder Value zum Stakeholder Value, PhD Dissertation, Hochschule St. Gallen, Nr. 1332

Jantsch, Erich, Waddington, Conrad H, eds. (1976) Evolution and Consciousness. Human Systems in Transition, Reading, Mass.: Addison-Wesley.

Johnson, Gerry, Scholes, Kevan (2002) Exploring Corporate Strategy, 6th ed., Harlow: Financial Times Prentice-Hall

Jonas, Hans (1979) Das Prinzip Verantwortung, Frankfurt am Main: Insel Verlag

Kaplan, Robert S, Norton David P (1996) The Balanced Scorecard: Translating Strategy into Action, Boston, Mass. : Harvard Business School Press

Kaplan, Robert S (2003) Foreword to: Marr, Bernard, Neely Andy: Automating Your Scorecard: The Balanced Scorecard Software Report, www.som.cranfield.ac.uk/som/research/centres/cbp/products/BScorecard.asp

Kauffman, Stuart (1995) At Home in the Universe, New York, NY <etc.> : Oxford University Press

Kauffman, Stuart (1996) Order for Free, in: Brockman, John, ed., The Third Culture, New York: Simon and Schuster, pp. 332-343

Kay, John (2001) High Street Homilies, in: Financial Times, April 4, 2001, p. 12.

Kay, John (2003) Why Those Who Seek Popularity Lose Their Authority, Financial Times, July 24, p. 13

Kelly, Kevin (1994) Out of Control: the New Biology of Machines, Social Systems and the Economic World. Reading, Mass. <etc.> : Addison-Wesley

Kern, Peter (1990) Ethik und Wirtschaft, Frankfurt am Main etc.: Lang

Kim Daniel (1993) The Link between Individual and Organizational Learning. Sloan Management Review, Vol. 35(1): 37-50

Kim, W Chan, Mauborgne, Renée (1999) Creating New Market Space, in: Harvard Business Review, January/February, Vol. 77, Issue 1, p 83

Kim, W Chan, Mauborgne, Renée (2005) Blue Ocean Strategy: How to Create Uncontested Market Space and Make the Competition Irrelevant, Boston: Harvard Business School Press

Klir, GJ (1991) Facets of Systems Science, New York: Plenum Press

Kokott, Juliane (2000) Naturrecht und Positivismus im Völkerrecht – sind wir auif dem Wege zu einer Weltverfassung?, in: Meier-Schatz, Christian J, Schweizer, Rainer J, eds.: Recht und Internationalisierung, Zürich: Schulthess, pp. 3-21

Koller, Tim, Goedhart, Marc, Wessels, David (2005) Valuation: Measuring and Managing the Value of Companies, 4th ed., Hoboken: Wiley

Kotter, John P (1988) The Leadership Factor, New York, NY: Free Press

Kotter, John P (1999) John P Kotter on What Leaders Really Do, Boston : Harvard Business Review

Kotter, John P, Heskett, James L (1992) Corporate Culture and Performance, New York: Free Press

Krieg Walter (1985) Management- and Unternehmungsentwicklung - Bausteine eines integrierten Ansatzes, in: Probst, Gilbert, Siegwart, Hans, eds.: Integriertes Management. Bern, Stuttgart: Haupt, pp. 261-277

Krugman, Paul (2001) The New Reality Is Old Economy Shortages, in: International Herald Tribune, January 3, 2001, p.7

Laesser, Christian, Hermann, Franz, Schwaninger, Markus (2002) Mediationsverfahren bei Verkehrs-Grossprojekten. Beobachtungen und Erfahrungen am Fallbeispiel „Gasteinertal", in: Jahrbuch 2001/2002 Schweizerische Verkehrswirtschaft, edited by Kaspar, Claude, Laesser, Christian , Bieger, Thomas, St. Gallen: Institut für Öffentliche Dienstleistungen und Tourismus, Universität St. Gallen, pp. 21-43

Lawler, Edward E (2003) Treat People Right! How Organisations and Individuals can Propel each Other into a Virtuous Spiral of Success, San Franciso: Jossey-Bass

Leonard, Allenna (1989) Application of the VSM to Commercial Broadcasting in the United States. In: Espejo, Raúl and Harnden, Roger (eds.), The Viable System Model: Interpretations and Applications of Stafford Beer's VSM, Chichester: Wiley, pp. 175-209

Leonard, Allenna (1994) Team Syntegrity: Planning for Action in the Next Century. In: Brady, B, Peeno, L, eds., Proceedings, Conference of the International Society for the Systems Sciences, Louisville, Kentucky, pp. 1065-1072.

Lewis, JD (2000) Trusted Partners, New York: Free Press

Lightman, Alan (2001) Feelings of Awe and Loss As Scientists Stop Light, in: International Herald Tribune, February 9, 2001, p. 5

London, Simon (2002) Corporations With Hard and Soft Centres, in: Financial Times, February 20, 2002, p. 15

London, Simon (2003a) Genetically Modified Business Has Arrived, in: Financial Times, June 17p. 11

London, Simon (2003b) Profit Machines Where People Come First, Financial Times September 26, p. 7

Longman Group Limited (1982) Longman Concise English Dictionary, Harlow, Essex: Longman

Luhmann Niklas (1995) Social Systems, Stanford, California: Stanford University Press

Luhmann, Niklas (1997) Die Gesellschaft der Gesellschaft, Frankfurt am Main: Suhrkamp

Luhmann, Niklas (2000) Vertrauen: Ein Mechanismus der Reduktion sozialer Komplexität, fourth edition, Stuttgart: Lucius und Lucius

MacQueen, Adam (2004) The King of Sunlight. How William Leber Cleaned up the World, London etc.: Bantam

Malik, Fredmund (2001a) Messgrössen des Unternehmenserfolges - Gewinn ist erst die halbe Hausaufgabe, in: Student Business Review, Winter 2001, pp. 28-30

Malik, Fredmund (2001b) Interview, in: 90 Jahre Heinz von Foerster. Die praktische Bedeutung seiner wichtigsten Arbeiten, a film by Margot Zoppe Filmproduktion, Vienna

Mandelbrot, Benoit B (1982) The Fractal Geometry of Nature, San Francisco: Freeman

Marchetti, Cesare (1982) Die magische Entwicklungskurve, in: Bild der Wissenschaft ,19. Jg. (10), pp.114-128

Margalit, Avishai (1996) The Decent Society, Cambridge, Mass., London, England: Harvard University Press

Martin, Peter: A Global Reputation Falls Apart, in: Financial Times, March 19, 2002, p. 15

Maucher, Helmut (1998) Daran haben die Väter der Marktwirtschaft nicht gedacht, Interview, Neue Zürcher Zeitung, 28/29 November 1998, Nr. 277, p. 29

McAllister, Daniel J (1995) Affect- and Cognition-based Trust as Foundations for Interpersonal Cooperation in Organizations, in: Academy of Management Journal, Vol. 38, No. 1, pp. 24-59

McCulloch, Warren (1988) Embodiments of Mind, Cambridge, Mass., London: M.I.T. Press, Reprint

Meadows, Donella (1998) Places to Intervene in Complex Systems, in: Whole Earth Review, Winter 1998

Meyer, Christopher, Davis, Stan (2003) It's Alive: the Coming Convergence of Information, Biology, and Business. New York: Crown Business

Meyer, Marshall W, Zucker, Lynne G (1989) Permanently Failing Organizations, Newbury Park etc.: SAGE

Miller, George A (1967) The Magical Number Seven, Plus or Mus Two: Some Limits on our Capacity for Processing Information, in: the Psychology of Communication, New York: Basic Books

Miller, James Grier (1978) Living Systems. New York: McGraw-H

Mingers John, Gill, Anthony, eds. (1997) Multimethodology: theory and Practice of Combining Management Science Methodologies, hichester: Wiley

Mitroff, Ian I (1983) Stakeholders of the Organizational Mind, San Fr. o etc.: Jossey Bass

Monmonier, Mark (2000) Air Apparent: How Meteorologists Learne Predict, and Dramatize Weather, Chicago: University of Chicago Press,

Moscoso Philipp (1999) Managementsysteme für die Shop-Floor-Logist modellbasierte Gestaltungsmethodik, Doctoral Dissertation, Nr. 132 rich, Switzerland, Eidgenössische Technische Hochschule Zürich - F Institute of Technology

Mueller, Robert K (1986) Corporate Networking: Building Channels for Info tion and Influence, New York: The Free Press (German version: Betriebl Netzwerke, Freiburg: Haufe 1988)

Müller-Stewens, Günter & Lechner, Christoph (2003) Strategisches Managemen wie strategische Initiativen zum Wandel führen, 2. überarb. u. erw. Auflage, Stuttgart : Schäffer-Poeschel

Nakicenovic, Nebojsa, Grübler, Arnulf, eds. (1991). Diffusion of technologies and social behavior, Berlin <etc.> : Springer

Nielsen, Steen, Sorensen Rene (2004) Motives, Diffusion and Utilisation of the Balanced Scorecard in Denmark, International Journal of Accounting, Auditing and Performance Evaluation, Vol. 1, No.1, pp. 103-124

Nonaka, Ikujiro, Takeuchi, Hirotaka (1995) The Knowledge-Creating Company. New York: Oxford University Press

Normann, Richard (2001) Reframing Business: When the Map Changes the Landscape, Chichester: Wiley

Novartis (2002) Annual Report, Basle, Switzerland

Ortega, Bob (1998) In Sam we Trust: the Untold Story of Sam Walton and How Wal-Mart is Devouring America, New York, NY: Times Books

Ortega y Gasset, José (1983) Obras Completas, XII Tomos, Madrid, Spain: Alianza Editorial, Revista de Occidente

Parkes, Louise P, Bochner, Stephen, Schneider, Sherry K (2001) Person-Organization Fit Across Cultures: An Empirical Investigation of Individualism and Collectivism, in: Applied Psychology: An International Review, Vol. 50, No. 1, pp. 81-108

Peitgen, Heinz-Otto, Richter, SH: The Beauty of Fractals, Berlin: Springer 1986.

Peitgen, Heinz-Otto, Jürgens, Hartmut, Saupe, Dietmar (1998) Bausteine des Chaos. Fraktale, Reinbek bei Hamburg: Rowohlt

Peters, Thomas J, Waterman, Robert H (1982) In Search of Excellence, New York etc.: Harper & Row

Pettigrew, Andrew M, Whipp, Richard (1993) Managing Change for Competitive Success, Oxford etc.: Blackwell

228   References

Pfeffer, Jeffre⟩ Sutton Robert I (1999) The Knowing-doing Gap: How Smart
Companie Turn Knowledge into Action, Boston, Mass.: Harvard Business
School p⟩ss
Piaget, Jea⟩967) Biologie et Connaissance, Paris: Gallimard
Piore, Ad⟩Theil, Stefan, et al. (2001) The Teflon Multinational, in: Newsweek,
2, 2001, pp. 26-37
Polan⟩chael (1964) Science, Faith and Society. A Searching Examination of
Polan⟩eaning and Nature of Scientific Inquiry, Chicago and London: The Uni-
ty of Chicago Press
Michael E (1980) Competitive Strategies, New York: Free Press
⟩ Michael E (1985) Competitive Advantage, Free Press, New York: Free
ress
er, Michael (2002) Crucial Importance of Clear Business Goals, Interview
with Rod Newing, in: Financial Times, June 4, 2002, p. IV
ost, James E, Preston, Lee E, Sachs, Sybille (2002) Managing the Extended Enterprise: The New Stakeholder View, in: California Management Review. Review, Vol. 45, No.1, Fall 2002, 6-28
Powers, William T (1973) Behavior: The Control of Perception, Chicago: Aldine
Publishing Company
Price Waterhouse (2001) Die Balanced Scorecard im Praxistest: Wie zufrieden
sind Anwender?, Frankfurt am Main: PwC Deutsche Revision
Prigogine, Ilya (1989) The Philosophy of Instability, in: Futures, pp. 396-400
Prigogine, Ilya, Stengers, Isabelle (1984) Order out of Chaos: Man's New Dia-
logue with Nature, New York: Bantam
Prinz, Patrick (2001) Strategische Angebotsgestaltung im Private Banking: eine
systemorintierte Betrachtung der Private Banking-Marktleistung, PhD Disser-
tation, Nr. 2526), St. Gallen, Switzerland: University of St. Gallen
Probst, Gilbert JB. (1992) Organisation, Landsberg/Lech: Moderne Industrie
Pümpin, Cuno (1991) Corporate Dynamism. Aldershot: Gower
Quine, Willard Van Orman (1964) Word and Object, Cambridge, MA: MIT Press
Quinn, James Brian (1992) Intelligent Enterprise, New York: Free Press
Quinn, James Brian (1997) Innovation Explosion : Using Intellect and Software to
Revolutionize Growth Strategies, New York, NY: Free Press
Rapoport, Anatol, Chammah, Albert M (1965) Prisoner's Dilemma, Ann Arbor:
The University of Michigan Press
Rapoport, Anatol (1969) Strategy and Conscience, New York: Shocken Books
Rapoport Anatol (1986) General System Theory. Essential Concepts and Applica-
tions. Tunbridge Wells, Kent, Cambridge, Mass.: Abacus Press
Rapoport Anatol (1989) The Origins of Violence, New York: Paragon
Rapoport, A (1992a) Weltbilder – Wissen und Glauben: Die systemische Sicht. In
Weltbilder – Wissen und Glauben, Aulavorträge, Nr. 55, Hochschule St. Gal-
len, St. Gallen, pp. 3-27
Rapoport, Anatol (1992b) Peace: an Idea, Whose Time Has Come. Ann Arbor:
University of Michigan Press
Rapoport, Anatol (1998) Decision Theory and Decision Behaviour, 2nd edition,
Basingstoke, London: Macmillan

Rapoport, Anatol (2000) Certainties and Doubts, Montreal: Black Rose

Rappaport, Alfred (1998) Creating Shareholder Value: a Guide for Managers and Investors, New York, NY: Free Press

Reither, Franz (1997) Komplexitätsmanagement. Denken und Handeln in komplexen Situationen, München, Germany: Gerling Akademie Verlag

Reyes, Alfonso (2000) An Instance of Organizational Learning: The Case of the Colombian General Accounting Office. In: Proceedings of the World Congress of the System Sciences, edited by Janet K. Allen and Jennifer Wilby (on CD ROM), Toronto, Canada

Ricard, André (2000) La Aventura Criativa. Las Raíces del Diseño, Barcelona: Editora Ariel

Richardson, George P (1999) Feedback Thought in Social Science and Systems Theory. Waltham, MA: Pegasus Communications

Rios, José Pérez (1996) Integrative Systems Modelling. Leveraging complementarities of qualitative and quantitative methodologies, in: Richardson, George P, Sterman, John D, eds., Proceedings, 1996 International System Dynamics Conference, Cambridge, Massachusetts, 21-25 July 1996, Volume 2, pp. 431-437

Roberts, John (2004) The Modern Firm: Organizational Design for Performance and Growth, Oxford : Oxford University Press

Rockart, Scott (2001) How Do Professional-Services Firms Compete?, in: Hines, James H et al., eds., Proceedings 19th International Conference of the System Dynamics Society in Atlanta, Georgia, Albany, New York: System Dynamics Society

Ross, Kelley L (2000) The "Need to Know" and the Meaning of Life, in: Encyclopedia Britannica, www.friesian.com/ethics.htm

Rudolph, Thomas (1999) Marktorientiertes Management komplexer Projekte im Handel, Stuttgart: Schäffer-Poeschel

Rüegg-Stürm, Johannes (2001) Dynamisierung von Führung und Organisation: eine Einzelfallstudie zur Unternehmensentwicklung von Ciba-Geigy 1987-1996, Bern: Haupt

Rüegg-Stürm, J (2002) Das neue St. Galler Management-Modell, Bern etc.: Haupt

Ruskin, J (First published 1865) Sesame and Lilies, 1907 edition. London: George Allen

Rykwert, Joseph (2000) The Seduction Of Place: The City in the Twenty-First Century, Pantheon Books

Samuelson, Robert J (2001) The 'New Economy' Was Foolish Optimism, in: International Herald Tribune, January 3, 2001, p.7

Sawyer, R Keith (2005) Social Emergence: Societies as Complex Systems, Cambridge: Cambridge University Press

Schafer, Thilo (2001) Mondragón Reaps the Dividends of a Co-operative Approach, in: Financial Times, June 26, 2001, p. 25

Schein, Edgar H (1985) Organizational Culture and Leadership. San Francisco, etc.: Jossey Bass

Schlatter, Paul (2000) Plan de negocios sobre la base del concepto administrativo de St. Gallen ejemplificado en una consultora chilena en el área de ecología, Master thesis, St. Gallen, Switzerland: University of St. Gallen

Schreiner, Melanie (2004) Collaborative capability in Vendor-service Provider Relationships: construct development and empirical analysis in the software service industry, Doctoral Dissertation No. 2956, University of St. Gallen, Switzerland

Schuh, Günter (1997): Virtuelle Fabrik - Beschleuniger des Strukturwandels, in: Schuh, Günter, Wiendahl, H J (eds.): Komplexität und Agilität – Steckt die Produktion in der Sackgasse?, Berlin etc.: Springer, pp. 293-307

Schuh, Günter, Millarg, K, Göransson, Å (1998), Virtuelle Fabrik - neue Marktchancen durch dynamische Netzwerke, München, Wien: Hanser

Schwaninger, Markus (1987) A Practical Approach to Strategy Development, in: Long Range Planning, Vol. 20, No. 5, 74-85

Schwaninger, Markus (1988) Anwendung der integralen Unternehmungsentwicklung. Beurteilung von Konzept und Methodik anhand einer Pilotstudie. Bern, Stuttgart: Haupt

Schwaninger, Markus (1989) Integrale Unternehmungsplanung. Frankfurt, New York: Campus

Schwaninger, Markus (1993) A Concept of Organizational Fitness, in: Organizational Fitness - Corporate Effectiveness through Management Cybernetics, Espejo, Raúl, Schwaninger, Markus, eds., Frankfurt, New York: Campus, pp. 39-66

Schwaninger, Markus (1994) Die intelligente Organisation als lebensfähige Heterarchie, Diskussionsbeiträge des Instituts für Betriebswirtschaft an der Hochschule St. Gallen, Nr. 14

Schwaninger, Markus (1997) Integrative Systems Methodology: Heuristic for Requisite Variety, in: International Transactions in Operational Research, Vol. 4, No. 4, pp. 109-123

Schwaninger, Markus (1998a) Management Knowledge and Knowledge Management: A Case for Cybernetics, in: Espejo, Raúl, Schwaninger, Markus, eds.: To Be and Not to Be, that is the System. A Tribute to Stafford Beer (Chapter Red), CD-ROM, Wiesbaden: Carl Auer-Systeme Verlag

Schwaninger, Markus (1998b) Are Organizations Too Complex To Be Understood? Towards a Framework for Intelligent Organizations, Discussion Paper No. 32, University of St. Gallen; Institut für Betriebswirtschaft

Schwaninger, Markus (1998c) Anatol Rapoport, http://www.isss.org/lumrapo.htm

Schwaninger, Markus (2000a) Managing Complexity - The Path Toward Intelligent Organizations, in: Systemic Practice and Action Research, Vol. 13, No. 2, pp. 207-241

Schwaninger, Markus (2000b) Distributed Control in Social Systems, in: Parra-Luna, Francisco, ed.: The Performance of Social Systems, New York etc.: Kluwer Academic, Plenum Publishers, pp. 147-173

Schwaninger, Markus (2001a) System Theory and Cybernetics: A Solid Basis for Transdisciplinarity in Management Education and Research, in: Kybernetes, Vol. 30, No. 9/10, pp. 1209-1222

Schwaninger, Markus (2001b) Intelligent Organizations: An Integrative Framework, in: Systems Research and Behavioral Science, Vol. 18, Issue 2, pp. 137-158.

Schwaninger, Markus (2001c) Optimizing Organizational Structure: Hausdorff Benchmark for Complex Social Systems, in: Moreno-Díaz, Roberto; Buchberger, Bruno; Freire, José-Luis, eds.: Computer Aided Systems Theory – EUROCAST 2001, Berlin etc.: Springer, pp. 182-195.

Schwaninger, Markus (2001). The Role of System Dynamics within the Systems Movement, in: Encyclopedia for Life Support Systems, UNESCO, Chapter 6.63.2.4, published under: WWW.EOLSS.COM

Schwaninger, Markus (2003a) A Cybernetic Model to Enhance Organizational Intelligence, in: Systems Analysis Modelling Simulation. A Journal of Mathematical Modelling and Simulation in Systems Analysis, Taylor & Francis, Vol. 43, No. 1, January 2003, pp. 53-65

Schwaninger, Markus (2003b) Long Over Short Term: The Example of Ecological Management, in: Organisational Transformation and Social Change, Vol. 1, No. 1, pp. 11-26

Schwaninger, Markus (2004) Methodologies in Conflict: Achieving Synergies between System Dynamics and Organizational Cybernetics, Systems Research and Behavioral Science, Vol. 21, pp. 1-21

Schwaninger, Markus (2005) Design for Viable Organizations: The Diagnostic Power of the Viable System Model, World Congress of Cybernetics and Systems, Proceedings, Maribor, Slovenia: University of Maribor

Schwaninger, Markus (forthcoming) Saving a Valley: Systemic Decision-making Based on Qualitative and Quantitative System Dynamics, in: Qudrat-Ullah, Hassan, Spector, J Michael, Davidsen, Paal I, eds., Complex Decision Making: Theory and Practice, U.S.A.: Springer

Schwaninger, Markus, Friedli, Thomas (2002) Virtuelle Organisationen als lebensfähige Systeme, in: Scholz, Christian, Hrsg., Systemdenken und Virtualisierung. Unternehmensstrategien zur Vitalisierung und Virtualisierung auf der Grundlage von Systemtheorie und Kybernetik, Berlin: Duncker & Humblot, S. 57-81

Schwaninger, Markus, Ambroz, Kristjan, Olaya, Camilo (2006) A Model of Systemic Control, in: CASYS-Computing Anticipatory Systems '05, Proceedings, Liège, Belgium (to be published with the American Institute of Physics)

Schwaninger, Markus, Janovjak, Matej, Ambroz, Kristjan (2006) Second-order Intervention with System Dynamics: Enhancing Organizational Competence and Performance, in: Systems Research an Behavioral Science, forthcoming

Schwaninger, Markus, Koerner, Markus (2004) City Planning- „Dissolving" Urban Problems. Insights from an Application of Management Cybernetics, in: Kybernetes, Vol. 33, No. 3/4, pp. 557-576

Schwaninger, Markus, Laesser, Christian (2000) Volkswirtschaftliche Auswirkungen des Neubaus einer Hochleistungs-Bahnverbindung der ÖBB auf das Gasteinertal, Gutachten, St. Gallen, Switzerland: Universität St. Gallen, Institut für öffentliche Dienstleistungen und Tourismus

Schwaninger, Markus, Pérez Ríos, José, Ambroz, Kristjan (2004) System Dynamics and Cybernetics: A Necessary Synergy, Kennedy, Michael, et al., eds., Proceedings 22nd International System Dynamics Conference in Oxford, England; Albany, NY: System Dynamics Society

Schwaninger, Markus, Powell, Steve, Trimble, Chris (2002) Modeling a Control System for Organizational Processes, in: Cybernetics and Systems. An International Journal, Vol. 33, No. 7, pp. 675-721

Schwaninger, Markus, Schmitz-Dräger, Ralph (1997) Organisatorische Herausforderungen eines integrativen Handelsmanagements am Fall der EPA AG, in: Thexis - Fachzeitschrift für Marketing, 14. Jg, Nr 4, S. 48-52

Schwarz, Eric (forthcoming) Une histoire du mouvement systémique (provisional title), Paris: Editions du Seuil

Seashore, SE. (1954) Group Cohesiveness in the Industrial Work Group, Ann Arbour: University of Michigan Press

Seghezzi, Hans Dieter (2003) Integriertes Qualitätsmanagement: Das St.Galler Konzept, 2nd edition, München: Hanser

Seneca, Lucius Annaeus (1999) Philosophische Schriften (Latin and German), Darmstadt: Wissenschaftliche Buchgesellschaft

Senge, Peter M. (1992). The Fifth Discipline. The Art and Practice of the Learning Organization. London: Century Business

Senge, Peter M (2000) The Puzzles and Paradoxes of How Living Companies Create Wealth, in: Beer, Michael, Nohria, Nitin, eds.: Breakind the Code of Change, Boston, Mass.: Harvard Business School Press, pp. 59-81

Sernetz, Manfred (2000) Die fraktale Geometrie des Lebendigen. Spektrum der Wissenschaft, July 2000, 72-79

Shannon, Claude, Weaver, Warren (1949) The Mathematical Theory of Communication, Urbana, Chicago, London: University of Illinois Press

Sharma, Sanjay, Henriques, Irene (2005) Stakeholder Influences on Sustainability Practices in the Canadian Forest Products Industry, in: Strategic Management Journal, Vol. 26, pp. 159-180

Slywotzky, Adrian J, Wise, Richard (2003) How to Grow When Markets Don't. New York: Warner Business Books

Smith, Rebecca, Emshwiller, John R (2003) 24 Days, New York: Harper Business

Soderquist, Donald (2001) How Companies Can Be Successful by Holding Up Values Instead of Seeing Them as Obstacles, in: Balance of Power, 31st ISC Symposium at the University of St. Gallen, Switzerland, St. Gallen: ISC-International Students Committee, pp. 41-45

Stacey, Ralph D, Griffin, Douglas, Shaw, Patricia (2000) Complexity and Management: Fad or Radical Challenge to Systems Thinking? New York : Routledge

Stanford Business School (2002) The GLOBE Initiative. www.gsb. stanford. edu/ globe

Steingraber, Fred G: The Paradox of Successful Growth, in: Success in Times of Paradox, St. Gallen: ISC – International Management Symposium St. Gallen, 1998, pp.103-109

Sterman, John D (2000) Business Dynamics. Systems Thinking and Modeling for a Complex World, Boston, Mass.: Irwin, McGraw-Hill

Sternberg, Robert J (1987) Intelligence. In Gregory, Richard L., ed., The Oxford Companion to the Mind, Oxford, University Press, pp. 375 – 379

Stückelberger, Christoph (2001) Ethischer Welthandel. Eine Übersicht, Bern etc.: Haupt

Sull, Donald N: Why Good Companies Go Bad, in: Harvard Business Review, Vol. 77, No. 4, July-August 1999, pp. 42-52

Surowiecki, James (2004) The Wisdom of Crowds, New York: Doubleday

Syncho (1997) VIPLAN, software package, available in English and Spanish, Birmingham, U.K.: Syncho Ltd

Teuta Gómez, Guillermo, Espinosa S, Angela (2000) Hacia las Organizaciones del Siglo XXI: Transformación integral de las empresas de telecomunicaciones en Colombia, Research Report, Santafé de Bogotá: Universidad de los Andes - Departamento de Ingeniería Industrial

Teuta Gómez, Guillermo, Espinosa, Angela S (2001) Hacia las Organizaciones del Siglo XXI: Transformación integral de las empresas de telecomunicaciones en Colombia, Working Paper, Santafé de Bogotá: Universidad de los Andes - Departamento de Ingeniería Industrial

Thiem, Ingo (1998) Ein Strukturmodell des Fertigungsmanagements: Soziotechnische Strukturierung von Fertigungssystemen mit dem „Modell Lebensfähiger Systeme". Doctoral Dissertation, Fakultät für Maschinenbau, Ruhr-Universität Bochum, Shaker Verlag: Aachen

Thorelli, Hans B (2001) Ecology of International Business Simulation Games, in: Simulation and Gaming, December 2001, Volume 32, Issue 4, pp. 492-506

Trueman, Wendy: Alternate Visions, in: Canadian Business, March 1991, pp. 29-33

Truss, J, Cullen, C, Leonard, A (2000) The Coherent Architecture of Team Syntegrity®: From Small to Mega Forms, In: Proceedings of the World Congress of the System Sciences, edited by Janet K. Allen and Jennifer Wilby (on CD ROM), Toronto, Canada

Türke, Ralf-Eckhard (2006) E-Governance: An Integrated Framework to Promote Governance, Doctoral Dissertation, St. Gallen, Switzerland: University of St. Gallen (forthcoming)

Ulrich, Hans, ed. (1981) Management-Philosophie für die Zukunft: gesellschaftlicher Wertewandel als Herausforderung an das Management, Berne, Switzerland: Haupt

Ulrich, Hans (1984) Management. Bern, Stuttgart: Haupt

Ulrich, Hans (2001) Gesammelte Schriften, 5 volumes. Bern, Stuttgart: Haupt

Ulrich, Hans, Krieg, Walter (1974) St. Galler Management Modell, 3rd. ed., Bern: Haupt

Ulrich, Peter (1993) Transformation der ökonomischen Vernunft: Fortschrittsperspektiven der modernen Industriegesellschaft, 3rd edition, Bern, Stuttgart: Haupt

Ulrich, Werner (2001) The Quest for Competence in Systemic Research and Practice, in: Systems Research and Behavioral Science, Vol. 18, pp. 3-28

UNESCO, ed. (2001). EOLSS-The Encyclopedia for Life Support Systems, available under: www.eolss.com/

UNESCO-UNEP (1983) Glossary of environmental educational terms, Vesprem, Hungary, quoted in: François1997: 18

Utterback, James M (1994) Mastering the Dynamics of Innovation, Boston, MA: Harvard Business School Press

Van Lee, Reggie, Fabish, Lisa, McGaw, Nancy (2005) The Value of Corporate Values, in: Strategy + Business, Issue 39, pp. 52-65

Vithessonthi, Chaiporn (2005) A Perception-based View of the Employee: a Study of Employees' Reactions to Change, Doctoral Dissertation, Nr. 3040, St. Gallen, Switzerland: University of St. Gallen

Volberda, Henk W., Lewin, Arie Y (2003) Co-evolutionary Dynamics Within and Between Firms: From Evolution to Co-evolution, in: Journal of Management Studies, Vol. 40, December, pp. 2105-2130

Von Foerster, Heinz (1984a) Observing Systems, 2nd ed., Seaside, Cal.: Intersystems Publications

Von Foerster, Heinz (1984b) Principles of Self-Organization - In a Socio-Managerial Context, in: Ulrich, Hans, Probst, Gilbert JB., eds.: Self-Organization and Management of Social Systems, Berlin etc.: Springer, pp. 2-24

Von Foerster, Heinz, et al. (1974) Cybernetics of Cybernetics or the Control of Control and the Communication of Communication, Urbana, Illinois: University of Illinois, The Biological Computer Laboratory

Von Hayek, Friedrich A: Die Theorie komplexer Phänomene. Tübingen: J.C.B. Mohr 1972

von Krogh, Georg, Ichijo, Kazuo, Nonaka, Ikujiro (2000) Enabling Knowledge Creation: how to Unlock the Mystery of Tacit Knowledge and Release the Power of Innovation, New York: Oxford University Press

von Krogh, Georg, Nonaka, Ikujiro, Nishiguchi, Toshihiro, eds. (2000) Knowledge Creation. A Source of Value, London: Macmillan

von Rosenstiel, Lutz, Molt, Walter, Rüttinger, Bruno (2005) Organisationspsychologie, 9. Auflage. Mainz: Kohlhammer

von Werder, Axel, et al. (2001) Management intentionality in long lived companies: a longitudinal study of Siemens and AEG. Berlin : Wirtschaftswissenschaftliche Dokumentation Technische Universität Berlin

Waldrop, M Mitchell (1992) Complexity: the Emerging Science at the Edge of Order and Chaos. New York, NY <etc.> : Touchstone

Warnecke, Hans-Jürgen (1992) Die fraktale Fabrik: Revolution der Unternehmenskultur, Berlin: Springer

Weber, Burkhard (1994) Unternehmungsnetzwerke aus systemtheoretischer Sicht. Zum Verhältnis von Autonomie und Abhängigkeit in Interorganisationsbeziehungen, Diskussionsbeiträge, Hochschule St. Gallen: Institut für Betriebswirtschaft, Nr. 9

Weber, Michael, Schwaninger, Markus (2002) Transforming an Agricultural Trade Organization: A System-Dynamics-based Intervention, System Dynamics Review, Vol 18, No. 3, Fall, pp. 381-401

Wheeler, David, Sillanpää, Maria (1997) The Stakeholder Corporation: A Blueprint for Maximizing Stakeholder Value, London etc.: Pitman

Wiener, Norbert (1948) Cybernetics: Control and Communication in the Animal and in the Machine. Cambridge, Mass.: MIT Press

Whyte, William Foote (1991) Making Mondragon : the growth and dynamics of the worker cooperative complex, 2nd ed.. Ithaca, NY: ILR Press

Willemsen Maarten H (1992) Ist die Schweiz ein lebensfähiges System? Kybernetische Diagnose des schweizerischen politischen Systems, Bern, Switzerland: Haupt

Wolfram, Stephen (2002) A new Kind of Science. Champaign, IL : Wolfram Media

Zander, Ed (2005) Motorola's odernizer, Interview, in: Wall Street Journal Europe, June 23, p. A5

Zhu, Zhichang (2000) WSR: A Systems Approach for Information Systems Development, in: Systems Research and Behavioral Science, Vol. 17, pp. 183-203

Index